"I am seventy-four," my mother says. "I am crippled and house-bound. I cannot go out and tell others, so you tell them for me. Tell other mothers not to second-guess the truth and not to excuse the man who may be molesting their daughters.

"Tell the truth, maybe it will help someone else."

"By sharing her personal story about abuse in its many forms, Linda has opened the door of hope, new hope, for countless abused women and girls. **I strongly urge pastors to read this book.** The church, more than ever before, needs to not only address this issue but provide counseling, help and assistance to so many and, sadly, a large number who suffer silently. Churches that would open their doors on this issue—for conferences, women's retreats, counseling sessions and more—are desperately needed. Linda ministers to this need through her speaking to these groups across the country." —**Pastor Wesley Peterson, Pastor Emeritus, Christ the King Church, Oxford, Michigan**

"A book that every woman should read. I believe that God teaches the spiritually mature women to disciple the younger women. This book is written so that everyone, no matter what their educational level, can understand and apply the lessons shared. I pray someday copies of Redeeming Our Treasures will be in the thousands of prisons and jails across America and around the world, as so many of these women have abusive pasts."
—**Garry Sims, Director, Hope Aglow Ministries**

"Although it's heart-wrenching to read your story, you've shed light on the subject of what's going on in the mind of the abuser and why the abused feel as though it's their fault."
—**Sally Snider, A/G Missionary**

"You did a wonderful job telling your story and being so vulnerable. I have not experienced anything like the abuse you have, but I learned so much from reading your book. I believe that God will use this book in a very mighty way to help women who have experienced abuse to heal and become whole again." —**Michele Gallina, A/G Missionary**

"Linda Settles has written a book that I can offer to survivors of abuse to help them come to terms with the emotional, spiritual, and psychological effects of abuse in their lives. I will definitely recommend *Redeeming Our Treasures* to members of my congregation."
—**Pastor Dale Hollin, Columbiaville, Michigan**

"*Redeeming our Treasures* is extremely direct, yet gentle enough for the reader to be able to endure its truth. I really like the way Linda brings things to the surface and then allows some reprieve for any feelings that may have been uncovered, validating them and sympathizing with them. It has stirred up many deep feelings and emotions for me, yet I don't feel threatened or extremely overwhelmed. I am amazed at the way she has captured emotion and experience and put it into words that I have never allowed myself to express or even think. This book has unburied many repressed emotions for me, and validated so many more. The validation is huge for me!" —**Patty, Oxford, Michigan**

"This book changed my life!" —**Kelliann, business owner, Lake Orion, Michigan**

"Linda, I am continually impressed at your strength and courage and wisdom! I hope this book finds its way into the office of every therapist in the world!"
—**Laura, Oxford, Michigan**

"Your book is outstanding! It helped me come to terms with what I went through and where I stand today. I found the end very comforting—it helped give me peace of mind. Many women could benefit from this book." —**Emily, Sterling Heights, Michigan**

"*Redeeming Our Treasures* is worth ten years of counseling." —**Renee Rowe, LMSW, ACSW, Oxford, Michigan**

"My husband is reading your book. I believe it will help him understand what I have been through. Thank you." —**Bridgett, Lynchburg, Virginia**

Redeeming
Our Treasures

Finding Joy in the Shadows
of an Abusive Past

Linda Settles, M.A.

Edict House Publishing Group, LLC
Lynchburg, Virginia

Redeeming Our Treasures: Finding Joy in the Shadows of an Abusive Past
©2009 by Linda Settles

Edict House Publishing Group, LLC
400 Court Street
Lynchburg, VA 24504
Phone: 434-821-4005
www.EdictHouse.com
Email: info@edicthouse.com

For more information on how to schedule Linda to share her dynamic and powerful message with your group, and to receive a speaker packet, visit www.RedeemingOurTreasures.com or e-mail her at speaker@RedeemingOurTreasures.com.

Cover and book design by Elizabeth Petersen, Mendocino Graphics
Book production by Cypress House
Cover illustrations ©iStockphoto.com/skynesher, ©iStockphoto.com/csourav, ©iStockphoto.com/LordRunar
Book illustrations: See photo permissions on Page 316–318
All scripture quotations, unless otherwise indicated, are taken from the *HOLY BIBLE, NEW INTERNATIONAL VERSION®. NIV®*. Copyright ©1973, 1978, 1984 by International Bible Society. Used by permission of Zondervan. All rights reserved.

Publisher's Cataloging-in-Publication Data
Settles, Linda.
    Redeeming our treasures : finding joy in the shadows of an abusive
past / Linda Settles. -- 1st ed. -- Lynchburg, VA : Edict House,
c2009.
    p. ; cm.
    ISBN: 978-0-9790238-3-5
    Includes index.
    1. Adult child abuse victims—Mental health. 2. Adult child sexual
abuse victims—Counseling of. 3. Inspiration—Religious aspects—
Christianity. 4. Spiritual healing. I. Title.

    RC569.5.C55 S48   2009 2008937429
    616.85/82239--dc22 0901

Printed in the USA
2 4 6 8 9 7 5 3 1

Dedication

I dedicate this book to my dear husband Mike and to our two daughters.

I dedicate it, also, to the courageous survivors who have shared their lives and
their stories with me, as well as those whose stories are yet to be told.
It is for you that I have written this book.

Acknowledgments

I would like to express my profound gratitude to so many people who have made this book possible.

First of all I would like to thank my Lord and Savior Jesus Christ for staying with me when life seemed hopeless, and showing me the way out of my despair. I would like to thank my husband, Michael, for walking the healing journey with me for more than twenty years. I am grateful also for my children, Christina and Bethany. You have taught me so much by your unconditional love. I learned what childhood looks like by observing you in yours.

I would like to thank my sister Donna for her constant love and encouragement. I appreciate also the memory work that she has done, confirming aspects of some memories that helped to put them into an accurate framework of time and space.

I want to express my appreciation as well to my mother and siblings who have affirmed my need to write this book. Thank you for your support.

I want to say thanks to Karla Wachenheim, copyeditor for Edict House

Publishing Group and my personal friend. You were the first to read the completed manuscript. I don't think you knew how much it meant to me when you called me and said, "This book is amazing," thus annulling all my fears of overwhelming my readers by the depth and scope of my past experiences.

I want to express my gratitude also to Renee Rowe, LMSW, ACSW, a counselor of deep spiritual energy and profound wisdom. Renee invested many hours in reading and evaluating the manuscript for *Redeeming Our Treasures*, and made numerous suggestions that found their way into the final book. Thank you, Renee, for your gentle wisdom.

So many others: friends, colleagues, counselors, family members, and authors of other books that have enriched my life and increased my understanding have contributed to this book, often without even knowing that they were doing so. A special thanks to other survivors and professionals who took time to read and review the book. I have listened to your suggestions and used many of them.

Finally, thank you to colleagues in the book industry who helped bring this book from a rough manuscript to a completed product: Cynthia Frank at Cypress House, Sharon Castlen, my publicist and marketing professional, and editor Dr. James Coggins.

Contents

By wisdom a house is built
and through understanding it is established;
through knowledge its rooms are filled
with rare and beautiful treasures.

—Proverbs 24:3–4

Foreword

MOST OF US are lonely. We are alone in our pain. We don't share the secrets of our life even with our best friend of the time. So we suffer in silence. We look for happiness in unfulfilling places, or we find pleasure in things that don't really lead us to what we desire—peace. We are longing to be understood; we are longing to understand. We are lost in the pain of our abuse, incest, and neglect. Some of us are so lost that we don't even know that we are lost. Some of us do all the right things trying to heal the pain, the memories, and our shame. We turn to God whether we know him or not and plead with Him to do something. As we scream to the heavens, most of us hear silence. We feel alone. We go to church; we leave lonely. We go to counseling; we are improved, but not healed. The peace that passes all understanding feels beyond our reach.

This is the place where Linda meets you. As she welcomes you into her heart, she is ever aware of yours. Linda becomes a friend as she walks with you and has the conversation that no one else in the whole world has been willing or able to have. Like a good friend, she speaks the truth gently and with love. You will begin to trust what she says as her words begin to describe and comfort the most lonely parts of your being, the place of your unattended pain.

Step by step you will be able to connect with yourself through the opening of your heart, your mind, and your spirit. As you begin to have mercy upon your unattended pain, the core of your loneliness is revealed. You have truly been lonely for love and healing. You have been longing for the questions to be answered: "Where were you, God? And where are you now?"

With Linda, you can leave the shores of isolation and cross the bridge to healing through addressing the silence of the heavens, the pain of abuse, and the hurt within you. Linda has been there; she has felt the conflict between the reality of her own abuse and the pain of not seeing God. She has felt the sting of misappropriated scriptures and the abandonment of those who were supposed to nurture and protect her. You can be enlightened and healed no matter where you are on your own personal journey. Awareness is the key to healing. Repeated awareness is necessary for the process of recovery.

The more clarity you have about the dynamics of abuse, connection with yourself, and the truth about God, the more aware you will be of your own place on the road to peace.

~Renee Rowe, LMSW, ACSW

No life is so damaged, no soul so stained, that God would disdain to die for it.

Preface

I WOULD LIKE TO introduce myself, and I would like you to know why I have written this book. I wrote it for you and for myself. It is, in a way, a journal, a remembrance, a memorial.

During the process of writing it, I've come to know myself better. I've reached deeper into the unfathomable riches of God's love, His mercy, and His grace.

And now I have opened my book for all the world to see. Not because I need the affirmation of my fellow travelers on the journey to recovery, nor because I am a masochist, lacerating old wounds by reopening the door to the past. No, I have published this book because some of you have asked me to show you the way—the way to live after the degradation of abuse.

There are others who are far more qualified than I to provide clinical information about the disorders that follow us from the citadel of suffering. They have written well. Some of their books are listed in the appendix, and I hope you'll read every one of them, as I have. Some of those authors have suffered, too. They have climbed the slippery slope of recovery and now reach out to others, such as myself, who need to understand "the problem of pain," as C. S. Lewis put it. Thank God for our teachers. They are God's gift to all of us.

What I offer you is my story, replete with healing concepts bestowed on me by my Creator through His Word, His Spirit, His anointed teachers, and my experiences. Out of the wealth of these gifts, I offer you hope—hope of a future filled with joy, satisfaction, and wonder, the future of a wounded warrior at her best.

Please do not think that I write as one who has already arrived. I do not look down from the lofty heights of complete recovery and bid you come to me. I am still on the journey. I write with the transparent heart of a ready writer, so that you can look into it and see my scars, my partially healed wounds, and my victories.

I follow the Wounded Warrior of Galilee, who carried His cross down the Via Dolorosa with grace and dignity. I want to be like Him. I am tired of following from afar. I hasten my steps. I hope you will join me in my journey. If you are already there, or if you have passed this way before me and you are miles ahead, following our Master to the place of ultimate healing, perfect peace, and profound joy, I thank God for you. You have shown us that it can be done.

Wherever you may be on your journey, I hope to hear from you somewhere along the way. My web address is on the copyright page. God bless you as you continue the process of redeeming your treasures.

~

Some have asked, "Are you going to write under your own name?" I long to use a pseudonym because I know my weakness. Though I hate to admit it, I fear the censure of those who would fail to understand or who would maliciously malign. Why would I want the world to know my darkest secrets, my deepest pain? And who in the world can be trusted—knowing my pain—to not exploit it, re-victimizing the

No life is so damaged, no soul so stained, that God would disdain to die for it.

part of me that has not yet achieved the pinnacle of peaceful coexistence with my past?

If you are inclined to read this book, you may well have suffered abuse yourself, or you may suffer still. Or perhaps you suffer vicariously, hurting for someone you love but can't understand. You read in the hope of attaining understanding and empathy. I have nothing to fear from those who read for these reasons—for you have no desire to demean or to defame.

On the other hand, writing under the a pseudonym may be a legitimate attempt to protect myself from those few readers who lack compassion. I failed to protect myself in the past. My urge to do so now is demanded by discretion and dictated by my understanding of the fallen human race of which I am a part.

When Jesus Christ walked the earth, it is said that though many followed Him, He "did not commit Himself to them—for He knew what was in man." (John 2:24–25.) That knowing led Him at times to commune alone on isolated mountains and in lonely gardens and to offer Himself, *when the time was right,* to the dregs of humanity, who would haul Him off to "the place of the skull" and hang Him on a rough-hewn tree.

The victimization of God? I don't think so. The victim yields to an abusive power greater than himself—while the Savior who died in "the place of the skull" surrendered voluntarily, sacrificing Himself to redeem a race of inferior beings from the consequences of their heritage, their weakness, and their choices. He was committed—wholly and ultimately—to His mission.

With His overawing power, He taught us (if we will be taught) the pathway to power—power over our tormentors, power over our future direction, and power to rise again after the death of our dignity.

He called us to commit to something greater than ourselves—charging us: "Whoever wants to save his life will lose it, but whoever loses his life for me will save

No life is so damaged, no soul so stained, that God would disdain to die for it.

it… I am the living bread that came down from heaven. If anyone eats of this bread, he will live forever." (Matthew 16:25, John 6:51.) To live forever, not just exist until our earthly frame dies—but live! To feast eternally, not just in the "hereafter" but now—in this life, on this earth! To feast on the bread of life freely offered by the One who gave everything *for us* and will accept nothing less than everything *from us* if we are to experience all that we are meant to experience, to realize our potential as beings who have been implanted with the seed of divinity—the life of Christ himself. What did Job say in the midst of his suffering? "I know that my Redeemer lives… and in my flesh I shall see God." (Job 19:25a, 26b.) Our hurts, habits, and hang-ups (as they say in Celebrate Recovery) get in the way of our view of God and blur his perfect image, blinding us to the wonder of His life in us.

In my story, I hope you will see not just the victim but also the victor who vaulted beyond the tears, the annihilating fear, and the depths of disgrace into immeasurable joy. I hope you will recognize that, by the grace of God, I have climbed beyond sorrow, often with bleeding hands and ravaged knees, like Luther scaling the holy mountain, to find God.

How do we move from the unfruitful existence of powerlessness, the continued death of victimization, into the resurrected life? We do it by daring to do His will even though we are weak and afraid, by risking the loss of our treasures, those things we have fought so hard to recover: our self-respect, our self-esteem, and our acceptance of our own self-worth.

You see—self, self, self. That's what the Wounded Warrior of Galilee asks us to surrender—our self. He asks us to give up our feeble grip on the pursuit of self-fulfillment by submitting to His greater plan and His greater purpose for our lives. He does not ask that we submit to the demands of selfish men and violate our self in the process. He asks that we submit our self to Him, the author and finisher of our faith. He alone has the right to ask this of us—for He alone is capable of perfecting

No life is so damaged, no soul so stained, that God would disdain to die for it.

our treasures without damaging them.

He requires that we commit ourselves, not to humanity—those who share our own proclivity for drama, gossip, and contempt—but to the One who was crucified in the company of thieves and murderers and in the scathing presence of "holy" men who disdained His touch while pointing self-righteous fingers at His bleeding side.

Writing this story has been somewhat like revisiting the grave—dying once again to my own efforts at pursuing a life without pain, my efforts to put the past behind me. Didn't the Apostle Paul say, "This one thing I do, forgetting those things which are behind…I press toward the mark…of the high calling of God in Christ Jesus." (Philippians 3:13–14, KJV.)

What the enemy of our soul would like to negate is that remembering is an integral part of forgetting. We can forget what we know—only on a subconscious level—when we allow our tortured consciousness to remember the traumatic event, to process it, and to grieve what has been lost. We can put to rest the recollection of an evil that threatens to undo us without losing the entwined goodness of our past—those precious years of innocence, no matter how few—the tender moments of childlike trust and unconditional acceptance we experienced, or thought we did, from the very one who later abused us, or the one who should have protected us but looked the other way while the abuser did his evil work.

Our challenge today is to provide a proper burial for the memories that plague us, and at the same time to release the good and precious truths that kept us alive.

When freedom comes, the God who heals, the God who restores, makes His presence known to us, in us, and through us. Our beauty shines like a bright star in a dark night. Our joy erupts into a world often unprepared for the transformation that the life of Christ evokes in those who dare to journey bravely, one faltering step at a time, into the darkness of a painful past; into buried memories that await the dawn of truth to make them known.

No life is so damaged, no soul so stained, that God would disdain to die for it.

Though often well-meaning, those who urge us to forget what we haven't resolved are in the same camp as those who urge us to love and to forgive in a context that reduces those words to something far more shallow than they were ever intended to convey.

Love, as understood by the advocates of forgetting, is more akin to pretense—give him a hug, act like you like it, repress your emotions because you are commanded to love, but love isn't shallow, nor does it pretend.

The word "forgive" can bruise when hurled with self-righteous confidence at a wounded person by the "forgetters." They toss the word around, secure in their knowledge of the holy book, and re-victimize the victim. "Love, forgive, and forget" becomes "Pretend, deny, and repress."

This is not what the great apostle had in mind. He was not advocating the kind of forgetfulness that sends the survivor on his way trying to pretend that "none of this ever happened."

We are all products of our past and the fruit we've allowed to grow out of it: fruit of bitterness, rage, and disappointment, fruit of misery, self-pity, and loneliness. Or fruit of compassion, endurance, and determination, fruit of empathy and understanding. Perhaps an entire orchard grows in our garden. Those trees we tend most will thrive.

Comfort others with the comfort you have received. This, too, is the exhortation of the Apostle Paul (2 Corinthians 1:4). But we cannot find this comfort if we do not first remember in order to truly "forget what is behind." When we hide from our past, we miss the truths that would be evident if examined by the mature mind, truths that were twisted and distorted by the abuser in his conquest of our childhood. The past must be examined so that we can understand our present self and

No life is so damaged, no soul so stained, that God would disdain to die for it.

resolve the conflict between what we remember and what we know.

I have done this—yet again—as I rewrote my story, reliving the suffering of untold indignities, regurgitating the shame of coerced seduction, revisiting the rites of passage.

Returning to these shadow-lands and mining for treasures left buried beneath the rubble, I have come away stronger, more intact, more committed to the task.

As a result of this return journey, the child part of myself—the emotional self, which was left behind, unable to clear the hurdles, unable to follow my body and intellect through the passage to maturity—has finally grown up. I can see more clearly now the realities distorted by my damaged emotions, the lies that immobilized the child within me.

I am finally ready to leap across the chasm, to pursue the abundant life promised to me by the One who modeled resurrection, the One who laid down His life to take it up again, glorified and multiplied, like the fish and the bread, to feed the multitude. Following the One who rose above the heads of His tormentors and called them to come up higher, I am ready to soar!

I dedicate this story to others who have dared to abandon the dubious security of denial and venture into the hostile world of naked truth. I pray that you may emerge on the other side of chaos and experience the redemption of hope, love, joy, and dignity.

This is the third time I have written my story. The facts have not changed, but I find that my perspective has altered immeasurably. Of those who failed me I have written with less judgment, more compassion, and greater understanding this time around. If I should wait ten more years to write, or twenty, I might write with a more godly hand and a less worldly perspective.

To protect my children, I considered using a pseudonym. They know a little of my story, caught in snatches of interrupted conversations and impromptu reactions

No life is so damaged, no soul so stained, that God would disdain to die for it.

to the platitudes of life. They will not read this book unless, God forbid, they experience someday the rupture of their own innocence, the rape of their dignity, and look to me for understanding.

It is for other mothers' children that I write—those who have suffered as I have in the citadel of sorrow that is abuse. I write for those held hostage to the false belief that they are responsible for the well-being of others whom they have no power to protect. I write for the woman or child whose divided heart commands, "Go! You have the right to protect yourself!" while simultaneously demanding that she stay and sacrifice her dignity, her dreams, and her life—one day at a time—to the monster of abuse. I write for the one who suffers the worst forms of degradation, quite possibly at the hands of someone she loves and wants to protect from the consequences of his own actions.

Come away with me. Let the sky fall in. It is not your fault. You are not to blame. Whatever happens, it's the abuser who has broken the pillars that hold up the house, and it's not your place to stand, feet braced against the foundation and arms extended above your head, exerting every ounce of energy that you have to keep the roof from collapsing on the one who is responsible for the damage. How I wish I had had the courage to drop my arms when I was thirteen—not thirty. But I did not. And that is why I must write this book. To tell you not to stay. To tell you that there is help, today. If you are being abused, it will take every ounce of strength that you have to separate yourself from the abuser and believe—truly believe—that you can walk away. It is not your fault. You are not to blame for the outcome of the abuser's sin.

My husband has walked with me through the process of recovery—and continues to journey at my side. With his hand in mine, there is no obstacle in my path that I cannot cross over, go around, or dismantle. Every memory recovered has brought with it hours, days, or weeks of emotional chaos that demanded my undivided attention, often at the expense of those who depended on me for their care. That is okay.

No life is so damaged, no soul so stained, that God would disdain to die for it.

I am a better mother to my children and a better wife to my husband today because I took the time, made the effort, to process my pain and claim my healing—one day at a time.

I will tell you my story, not just the recitation of my pain, but also the resurrection of my soul, the recovery of my treasures. And I will tell you my name. For it is time for me to put away my mantle of shame, and to gaze unafraid into the eyes of others who would share my story. Perhaps you, too, have a story to tell.

Linda Settles

~

A Word of Encouragement from Mike Settles, Linda's Husband

I HAVE READ Linda's story. I have lived a part of it with her and wouldn't have it any other way. I hope that other husbands of women who have suffered abuse will read this book. It will help you understand how to empathize with your loved one's pain, validate her goodness, and encourage her in her healing journey. *Redeeming Our Treasures* is for all who have suffered abuse in any form and for those who love them. It may be, as well, a vehicle of understanding for those who feel they have failed a loved one in some way, through denial or even collusion with the abuser. This is a book of hope for everyone who has been affected by abuse, abandonment, neglect, or betrayal.

As Linda's husband, I want you to know most of all that I admire her strength. I am so glad that she was brave enough to share her heart with me, to bare the shame

No life is so damaged, no soul so stained, that God would disdain to die for it.

and disgust that she felt because of the abuse. My wife has no need for shame. The shame of abuse is not hers to carry. I am glad that she has accepted that.

Linda and I grew to love each other long before we had matured beyond the great deal of emotional and spiritual baggage we had accumulated in our lives. We were both broken, and we knew it. We believed that our love and our faith would help us heal, and it has. We are still in the process of healing. We have grown through twenty-two years of marriage, years that have brought their share of conflict, pain, and misunderstanding—but also years that have given more than their share of joy, compassion, and insight.

There have been times when my wife has dealt with the pain, the shame, and the trauma of her past in ways that have been difficult for her—and for me. There have also been times when I have processed my own conflicts, and that has not been easy for her. Together, we have grown in our relationship with one another, with God, and with others. It has been worth the effort, every minute of it.

Linda and I know that *Redeeming Our Treasures* will reach the hearts and souls of wounded people everywhere. We want you to know that we care about you and are here for you. Please talk to us via our Web site, www.redeemingourtreasures.com, and we will stay in touch with you. Never stop searching for the truth, for the truth will set you free.

No life is so damaged, no soul so stained, that God would disdain to die for it.

SECTION 1
To Tell the Story

I Have Been There

Can I forget—now that I'm free—
The hopelessness, the destiny
Of darkness that pervades
The secrecy of home;
That hiding so efficiently
Devours the life of little ones
Who have no place to go?

Day follows day into the night
And none can estimate the plight
Of stricken faces pressed in pillows,
Knowing, yet denying,
Sorrows that the night can hold.

Cover me! Let no one see
Death devouring dignity!
The child is left alone.

Chapter One

Staying Alive

THERE IS AN old Native American proverb: *Do not judge another until you have walked a mile in his moccasins.* I have walked a mile through the mental, emotional, and spiritual death that is victimization. The choices I made along the way were no more intentional than that of a swimmer caught in a rushing river. Keeping my head above water was the all-consuming chore of my life, and I did whatever it took to survive. Most of what I did shamed me. All of it damaged me. Yet I cannot say even now what I should have done, for I was not alone in the water. My mother and my siblings suffered, too. We were immersed, all of us, in the river of my father's rage, and the years swirled past like autumn leaves while each of us did our best to survive in our own way.

Perhaps you, too, have suffered victimization in one of its many forms. Though my particular pain was sexual abuse and the physical abuse, mind games, and emotional torture that went along with it, you may find yourself in the pages of this book as well.

If you were the target of hostile, controlling, parents, it may have seemed "that's just the way they were." No matter why they behaved as they did, your tender emotions were fractured like brittle bones beneath the force of words calculated to wound. Maybe spankings came in the form of angry blows that left welts on your back or bruises on your legs. Maybe it was not your parents who abused you, but another who had power or authority over you: a teacher, a neighbor, an older sibling, your father's friend.

Abusers come through many doors, and it seems they abound in our society. According to a study I read about recently, 38 percent of all women interviewed had been sexually abused by the time they were eighteen. Like shadows in the night the predator comes at us when we are the most vulnerable and invades the sanctity of our soul.

Perhaps you count yourself lucky if you were simply "left alone," by parents who were too busy to pay attention to you; and yet you wonder why you feel inferior, invalidated, and unimportant. If this is your story, you have survived neglect—and your heart is in need of healing.

Neglect is a crime of omission—damage done by the absence of action rather than the commission of it. And yet neglect is a horrendous crime against a needy child who craves the love and attention, admiration and respect, of those he loves most, his parents and siblings. You try to fill the holes in your soul with inappropriate relationships, pornography, or some other unhealthy habit.

For too long we have closed our eyes to blot out the memory of our weakness and our pain, but now we know that blindness will not save us. Denial will not protect us. We know that it is time to come out into the light, to expose our wounding and our broken soul to another human being. We must be brave, for we know somehow that change demands more pain before the healing comes. We wonder how we can bear another sorrow. Haven't we suffered enough?

No life is so damaged, no soul so stained, that God would disdain to die for it.

Yes! Yes, we have, and that's why we must be brave. "He is no fool who gives what he can not keep to gain that which he cannot lose" (Jim Elliot, *Shadow of the Almighty,* 1958). Jim carried the gospel of Jesus Christ to a tribe of people who were well known for their senseless violence. He gave up his life on earth—that which he could not keep—in order to gain what he could never lose—the souls of men, women, and children who would come to know God through his sacrifice.

We cannot keep our secrets—they will destroy us if we try. We cannot maintain our fragile peace while hiding in the shadows of our pain. We must give it up. Take our heads out of the sand and look reality in the face. Admit our weakness, our losses, and our sorrow. Only then are we free to grow. Free to live—life beyond the grave—beyond the death of our dreams, our hope, and our dignity.

He is no fool who gives what he cannot keep—our secrets, our false dignity, and our carefully constructed pretense of "having it all together"—to gain what we can never lose: authenticity, true peace, and a life that has been transformed by the grace of God.

Let's pay the price. Let's take the challenge. Let's embrace the pain inherent in transformation and watch our lives and relationships transcend the shadows of our past abuse.

No one can hold us back! We alone possess the key to the chambers of the heart that holds our treasures. We need no one's permission to open the door. We can go there against the will of our abuser and reexamine what he did to us in the light of a new day. We will see with different eyes the child held captive "back there," and the love of God will flow into the shadowed places of a broken heart, flooding us with joy, with light, and with a peace that passes understanding. Come on, my friend, it's time to go!

No life is so damaged, no soul so stained, that God would disdain to die for it.

Chapter Two
Coming Out of the Sepulcher of Abuse

REMEMBER THE STORY of Lazarus? It is found in the book of John, chapter 11. Lazarus was the friend of Jesus. He was dead for four days before Jesus came to his tomb. Jesus called, "Lazarus, come forth!" And he came out of the grave.

Imagine the man. His entire body is wrapped with grave cloths. Binding is wound tightly about his feet. His arms and hands are bound against his sides. See him shuffling through the opening in the sepulcher—coming out into the light. By the grace of God, Lazarus was given another chance to live, a chance to enjoy the glory of another sunrise.

His tenure in this world was forever altered by two unique facts: One, he had experienced the grave. Lazarus, unlike his family and friends, had spent long and lonely hours in the arms of death. Who, not having been there, can comprehend that? Secondly, he was wrapped in the bindings of the grave, his every movement hindered by the trappings of burial.

Jesus glanced at his friend and knew immediately what must be done. *"Take off the grave clothes,"* He commanded, *"and let him go!"*

Imagine the joy of those who loved him—Lazarus, once dead is now alive again. Consider this. How quickly would you or I approach the decomposing body of a man who has just emerged from the darkness of the sepulcher? Martha, Lazarus' own sister, protested, "No, Lord, (don't roll away the stone) for by now he stinks."

Perhaps you, too, have emerged from the grave, and stand beside me, your face raised to the morning sun. You knew all along that there was light beyond the darkness, life after death, and a whole new world to be sensed, experienced, and enjoyed. Maybe you didn't know how to get there. Neither did I. But I'm here—basking in the light of each new day. Still shedding the grainy remnants of my burial every now and then, but climbing ever higher, reaching for the sun!

> *How eager are we today to grasp the soiled cloths of our brother's wounding and begin the tedious process of setting him free?*

What happened to me was tragic. Twenty-eight years in hell is a long time. Will I ever fully recover? Probably not, at least on this side of eternity. So I need to understand recovery. If recovery is a destination, some celestial plain that we strive to reach so that happiness can find us, then I am the most miserable of women, for I have no hope of attaining that destination.

But if recovery is a journey fraught with peril and battles, a quest for becoming the person my Creator designed me to be, if it is a pathway rather than a plain, then I have reason to hope. For happiness is a fleeting illusion at best, here one moment and gone the next.

Larry Crabb begins his book, *Finding God*, on a personal note:

> *I have come to this place in my life where I need to know God better or I won't make it. Life at times has a way of throwing me into such blind-*

---

ing confusion and severe pain that I lose all hope. Joy is gone. Nothing encourages me.

Can you relate to Larry's statement? I know I can. I've been there—recently. I'm not there all the time, not even most of the time, but I remember when I was, and I am in that place often enough that I will not forget, ever.

Sometimes, I want to cut it short, to say, "Enough is enough. I'm out of here," and go on to my eternal reward. But then I remember that I am, as someone has said, "a spiritual being on a journey to earth." My Creator has numbered my days, and my journey is not over until he calls my number.

What does my journey offer that compels me to go the distance? That is what this book is about. My journey will be different from yours, but the pathway to healing will be the same. And we will go the distance.

Reflections

I am a survivor of incest. Victimized by my own father, and left to his devices by my mother. And yet, I do not believe that my pain is necessarily "worse" than yours, or that the damage done to me is more insidious than what you may have suffered. There are myriad miseries offered to the human condition, and though my particular sorrow was sexual, abuse wears many faces, and those who have suffered the debilitating effects of violation from other venues have discovered that abuse has a nature of its own. It is a monster that bears down upon the defenseless child and robs him of his dignity, his worth, and his dreams. Physical and verbal abuse, emotional battering and neglect, as well as sexual abuse in any form will leave their imprint on the heart and soul of the one subjected to it. We cannot measure the effect of abuse on the wounded heart by examining the external evidence of it.

No life is so damaged, no soul so stained, that God would disdain to die for it.

In his classic work *The Wounded Heart,* Dan Allender clarifies this point:

> *Sexual abuse is damaging no matter how the victim's body is violated. At first, many will doubt the veracity of that claim; it does not immediately stand to reason that being violently raped by one's father can be compared to being lightly touched through the clothing by a gentle, grandfatherly next-door neighbor… The degree of trauma associated with abuse will be related to many factors, including the relationship with the perpetrator, the severity of the intrusion, use of violence, age of the perpetrator, and the duration of abuse. But in every case of abuse, the dignity and beauty of the soul have been violated. Therefore, damage will be present whether one has been struck by a Mack truck traveling fifty miles per hour or "merely" hit by a tricycle rolling at the same speed.*

Every form of abuse leaves its imprint upon the soul, whether the victim is a child, a battered spouse, or a vulnerable parishioner, patient, or student. Those in a position of authority or power over a person whose defenses are compromised will answer to the Divine Father who sees all, knows all, and does not forget the suffering of his children. Those who choose to abuse had best beware—your sins may be hidden behind the walls of your house, but they will be shouted from the rafters in a day to come.

If you have suffered any form of abuse, you may recognize yourself in the pages of this book. You may be angry, resentful, or depressed. You may know many of the reasons you feel the way you do, but it's possible that you do not know. Something is wrong with the picture of your life, and you haven't been able to figure out what it is. If there's a "wrinkle in your spirit" and you're tired of the chronic irritation of it, then read on. You'll find you're not alone in your travels.

No life is so damaged, no soul so stained, that God would disdain to die for it.

We live in a violent society, one that is eroticized by the media, the entertainment industry, and the diminished morals that have become acceptable to the majority of our populace. Venereal disease and spiritual compromise abound. Is it any wonder then that the children should suffer? It was the children who were offered to Baal on the pagan altars in times of old. Just because your neighbor and your neighbor's neighbor were mistreated by those who should have protected them, that doesn't make your experience of abuse or neglect any less painful. What is common in a society is no less damaging because of its prevalence. Abuse hurts. And that hurt often breeds destructive habits, negative thought patterns, and unhealthy relational styles that cycle through the victim's life, creating more brokenness and despair along the way.

It is time for the cycle to end! Victory is available, and it's never too late to end the cycle of abuse. Take the first step—admit you have an ache in our soul and open your heart and mind to discovery. You will not walk alone. Somewhere along the way, you will learn to trust your Heavenly Father. You will come to better understand Him as you walk the healing path, and you will find yourself dropping off your "baggage" along the way.

The path to an understanding heart always leads through suffering. Those who have suffered much can offer a depth of comfort to others who suffer the same pain—empathy that no one else, regardless of their training or degrees, can possibly extend to the wounded soul.

> *[God] comforts us whenever we suffer. That is why whenever other people suffer, we are able to comfort them by using the same comfort we have received from God.* —2 Corinthians 1:4

Questions for Reflection

Insights that may be helpful to someone who has processed a lot of pain, and has come to understand many of the dynamics of abuse, may be devastating to another who stumbles upon the same idea without being properly prepared to process it.

If you have done a lot of recovery work and are ready to go deeper, these questions may be helpful to you. If, however, you've just begun your recovery journey, please do not try to answer these questions without the help of a qualified counselor to walk you through them.

If you are ready, and you choose to look deeply into the shadows of an abusive past, I pray that you will walk slowly, intentionally, through the corridors of time and approach that place hand in hand with another who has passed this way before.

Getting Ready

Before you read further, you must take care to protect yourself from the flood of emotions that these questions may trigger. We will prepare in three ways:

1. Make certain that someone who is qualified to empathize and understand the dynamics of abuse is available while you read, and for some time afterward if you should need them. You might want a therapist or lay counselor to be with you during this process.

2. Create a safe place from which to view the past. Your safe place can be an imaginary setting that is peaceful and calming. Creating such a space in your mind will make it available to you even when you're physically unable to go there.

I create my own space by being alone and remembering the one place where I felt secure in the past. The Old Mill is the setting for a scene in the classic film *Gone*

No life is so damaged, no soul so stained, that God would disdain to die for it.

With The Wind. It is a beautiful place. The earthy brown and gold tones in the natural rock building, the colossal stone wheel, and the lagoons bridged by naturalized cement walkways lend the place an aged ambiance that calls to me even when I'm far away. I went there often in the early hours of the morning during a crucial time in my life. I felt safe there, secure that my father wouldn't find me. I was sheltered from prying eyes while I grieved.

Please take time to envision your own safe place. Practice going there when life seems out of control. Go there, as well, if your emotions threaten to overwhelm you as you process the trauma reintroduced by memories of your past suffering.

3. Give yourself permission to experience your emotions. To cry, to wail, to release the pain. It is through this process that we wring out the pain—some of it, at least—of the trauma we have suffered.

∼

If you have done these things and are ready to go forward, take a deep breath, get out your journal and a pen, and get ready to write whatever comes to mind as you read the following questions.

> **Behind every pain there is a message. When we learn to discern the message, we begin to discover the purpose in the pain and experience healing in the process.**

1. Does something in this chapter evoke deep feelings of sadness in you? Or perhaps anger?

2. Are you wearing the "grave-clothes" of your past—covering yourself with sin, shame, or denial? Or perhaps you live in fear, as I often do, hiding from love to avoid disappointment. Perhaps you feel unworthy of the gifts that God desires to grant you, and sabotage relationships without understanding why.

No life is so damaged, no soul so stained, that God would disdain to die for it.

3. *Can you remember when you first experienced shame?*
   Rage? Powerlessness? What happened? How old were you?

4. *Do you often feel those same feelings today?*

5. *What do you think your feelings are telling you?*

Take your time and think it through. Spend time with God even if you haven't yet learned to trust Him. It has taken many years to come to the place where you are today, and recovery will not occur overnight. Recovery is a process, and healing is a journey. I can't promise you that every day will be better than the day before, because you may go through some painful *seasons* in the pursuit of wholeness, just as I have, and as I do even now. But I can assure you, with my whole heart, that you will look back on the journey and take note of where you are and where you have been, and you'll be glad that you stayed on the healing path.

∼

> **Be not weary in well doing, for you shall reap (a good harvest) if you faint not.** —Galatians 6:9

My Prayer for Today

Oh, God, our Father, give us today strength for the battle, joy for the journey, and grace to grieve what we have lost. Enlarge our capacity for love and fill us with Your Spirit.

Amen.

No life is so damaged, no soul so stained, that God would disdain to die for it.

Chapter Three
The Valley of Shadows

F OR TWENTY-EIGHT YEARS I walked in the shadow. That dark ethereal world where the living dead walk among the tombs of buried memories and decaying dreams. The place where hope has died and human beings become enslaved to fear. Among the tombs, the wind howls, "It is your fault." I could have died; then I would bear no guilt. But I didn't die—I chose to live, but something inside me did not choose. Innocence died, and I was left to pay the price.

He is proud. He taunts me. He flaunts his victory. He is big, and I am small. In fact, I am nothing at all. I've already said that, haven't I? I am nothing at all.

I step into the light. Gazing back, I cringe. I feel my stomach tighten. I'm going to be sick. I can hardly believe that was I back there, supporting myself by clutching at the tombs of the dead. Reeling like a drunken woman long after the lights went out.

Some say I must not look back, but they are wrong. I am safe now. I no longer dwell in the shadow, but I know that the dead will haunt me until I have dared to excavate the remains of my treasures that I have buried among the tombs. I must dig them up. I must grieve their loss. Then perhaps I will be free to discover new treasures—even better than the old. Perhaps I will find that what's buried in the shadow is not my treasure after all, but illusions. I viewed my treasures with the eyes of a child. A child believes what she is told. And she forgets what she cannot bear to know.

Reflections

Blessed oblivion. Forced forgetfulness. These are gifts of God provided to innocent children who must forget in order to survive. In the words of Renee Rowe, the therapist who helped me so much along the road to recovery,

> *Memories should only be recovered if the survivor is safe and has some stability in their life. Tell your readers that they don't have to go through this alone again. Tell them to proceed gently. If they feel triggered, they need to stop and seek out a safe person. For survivors of sexual abuse… their defenses are lifesavers.*

Our defenses, like stone walls sheltering the helpless victim from his enemy, kept us alive in the crucible of our suffering, but those same defense mechanisms will imprison us if we don't dismantle them once the danger has passed.

"To everything there is a season," King Solomon said, "and a time to every purpose under the heavens." (Ecclesiastes 3:1.)

"*When I became a man,*" the Apostle Paul declares, "*I put away childish things.*" Did you ever make a move across town? If you have, you know that it takes time and dedicated effort to put away all the things that are no longer useful where you now live. Sometimes, it's difficult to part with those things that have benefited us in the past, even though they would only clutter the garage in our new home.

No life is so damaged, no soul so stained, that God would disdain to die for it.

We must look back, not as Lot's wife who gazed back on Sodom and became a pillar of salt. Perhaps she longed to return to the city she had forsaken, a city of denial, numbed emotions, and blind love. She must have looked the other way when the sins of that city became a stench so offensive to the holiness of God that He came in person to stretch out His hand against it. To Lot's wife, Sodom may have been evil, but it was, at least, familiar.

We will look back upon the "city" of our past as does a soldier who's come home from war. He has been changed by the battles he has fought, the victories won, and the wounds taken. He views the city with changed eyes. He is a man now. His muscles bulge beneath the stripes worn proudly on each sleeve. The old neighborhood bullies dare not trouble him now. They hide behind their doors as he walks freely through the streets of his hometown, his eyes searching.

He is looking for treasures that linger in the city of his youth—family and friends who care, childhood memories that may, with time, diminish the horrors of war that linger in his dreams and intrude into waking thoughts more often than he would choose.

Who can doubt the word of a good and just God who declares, *"I know the plans I have for you to give you a future and a hope."*? And yet, we doubt. Suffering makes us doubt. Shame insists that we will not have a good future because we don't deserve it.

Only by going back into the tomb and digging up our treasures, the truths that we once believed—before they were taken away from us—do we lift our face to the sky and shout, "I'm going to make it!" Such truths as: God is good. People can be trusted. Life is fun. I can make good choices. These are our treasures and we will—we must—reach out and take them back!

> *You shall know the truth and the truth shall make you free!*
>
> —John 8:32

No life is so damaged, no soul so stained, that God would disdain to die for it.

Chapter Four
Looking for a Way Out

TREMBLING, I picked up the phone. I put it down. Three times I tried. Then with shaking hands I dialed the number. A telephone counselor answered and I began to explain the reason for my call. "You see, I– well... I've never told anyone before, but my father... uh..."

Overcome by shame. Paralyzed by fear. Terrified that the anonymous person on the other end of the line would validate my own perception of my worthlessness, I hung up. I felt naked in the light of exposure. Like a soiled napkin during menses, I would be tossed in the waste bin of life to rot there. To tell another human being what I had done, to reveal what my father had done to me, was unbearable.

When the phone bill came in a few days later, I hid it before my father could see it. What if he discovered my call to a counselor? He would know that I had told. Fear was bitter in my mouth He must not find out.

It would be several months before I would find the courage to try again. Meanwhile, I explored other avenues of help, only to find them dead-end streets, only to find myself deeper in despair than ever before.

One light shone in my darkness and gave me the courage to try again. I heard a radio program about sexual abuse on a Christian station. Women came on the air talking about what had happened to them. It even had a name. For the first time in my life, I realized that I was not alone in my pain.

Shortly after listening to that program, I turned on the TV and was shocked to see a talk show on sexual abuse. Several women told their stories. I could have been one of them. They appeared with bags over their heads so that no one would know their identity. They were courageous, intelligent, and profoundly honest. If I hadn't heard their stories, my next call would have extinguished the one light that had come on in my darkness.

My father had called me to come home from work, pick him up, and take him to the real estate office where I worked with him and my mother. I had been ignoring his not so subtle signals for weeks, hoping to somehow escape the inevitable. I was weary and sick at heart.

That morning, in my desperation, I began calling local churches. I finally reached a pastor who agreed to take my call. He listened in stricken silence as I exposed my secret, in a desperate plea for help. In halting words and broken sentences, I told my story.

Speaking the words for the first time, assuming shared responsibility with the abuser, confused, terrified, and ashamed, I spoke into the silence, uninformed and unhealed, bearing the burden of the abuser's guilt and the evidence of his shame. I was desperately seeking understanding from a representative of the Lord Jesus Christ, longing to be set free from the burden I could no longer bear.

And then the religious professional on the other end of the line did exactly what I feared most. He reacted with shock and disgust. He didn't know what to say, but being a pastor he had to tell me something. So he told me to go to a bookstore

---

No life is so damaged, no soul so stained, that God would disdain to die for it.

and buy a book about sexual temptation. Something about Eve eating the apple. I thanked him and hung up.

Death called to me from the grave: "Give it up! There's no way out. You're dirty, ugly, scarred, and wasted. See what others will think about you if they find out? What kind of person would let her father use her like you have? Nobody cares what happens to you."

I would not be here to tell my story had it not been for the direct intervention of a God whom I thought didn't even care that I existed. Too many times He had ignored my cries. I knew He was real, but I was just as sure that He cared nothing for me.

I was tired, broken, and ready to quit. My fears of hell or hopes of heaven could no longer deter me from the relief suicide promised to my aching soul. The Arkansas River with all its undertows and swift currents beckoned me. For the first time, I set my foot on the path to the river, intending to fake an accident so no one would know how weak and defeated I was.

I began my walk in a light rain. Soon it became a downpour. With my eyes fixed on the sidewalk, my feet seemed to move of their own volition toward the only relief in sight. Resignation settled over me like a blanket, soothing my fears and draining my energy. Tears coursed down my cheeks unchecked.

Then I felt a hand on my shoulder. I was not startled or afraid. I slowly turned and looked into the serene eyes of a young man. "It will be all right." I don't know if he spoke the words or if they came from deep within my own soul. For a brief moment he stood there, his eyes locked on mine. I turned around and walked away from the river. I looked back and the young man was gone.

Within a few days, I placed another call to the counseling ministry that I had first called weeks before. This time my call was transferred to a counselor who dealt specifically with sexual abuse. We talked for over an hour. He assured me repeatedly, "It is not your fault. You are the victim."

No life is so damaged, no soul so stained, that God would disdain to die for it.

I asked, "How can I be the victim when I did not run away. There were feelings…"

"That," he said, "is the weapon abusers use to entrap you. When you can't leave the situation, they know your body will betray you and you will physically respond to them."

> **Just as a hammer will bruise human flesh, the sexual touch produces sexual arousal.**

This is the seduction of our body, but more than our body. For what I experienced was not merely a physical response to unwelcome touch. It was the betrayal of my self—the self that loved God and my mother, though I felt abandoned by both, the self that valued truth, the self that yearned for righteousness. That self yielded to a more powerful self, a self seduced by the things the abuser did to my body. That agonized, inferior, hateful self, the guilty, ashamed, dirty self, the self that accepted pleasure— dirty, filthy, despised pleasure, like Judas accepting thirty shekels of silver. When the moment passed, I wanted to fling the bag of coins at his feet and go out and hang myself.

The counselor was right. When we cannot leave the situation, we survive by yielding to a power greater than ourselves and find ourselves trapped by our response. A response that the abuser knows—he knows—will happen. Just as the blow of a hammer will bruise human flesh, the sexual touch produces sexual arousal. The abuser knows it, and that is why he dares to defile the young. He hopes that the child's sexual response will enslave her to his filthy passion. Her defenses are so small, her logic so limited, and her needs so powerful, that the victimized child will blame herself, not the abuser, and that is the secret power of all abuse.

The abuser's power is compounded when he is a family member. Incest. The word itself sends a shudder through me. Invert the "c" and the "s" and you have insect. Vermin. Of course, if you invert the "I" and "n" you have nicest. I still notice

---

No life is so damaged, no soul so stained, that God would disdain to die for it.

those things—after twenty-plus years. The abuser was the "nicest" to me at one time. Taking my part in family quarrels, showering me with affection. But when my innocence failed me, he became an insect, devouring me in the night.

That is how abuse works. Where our spirit is numbed with pain, and our soul is needy for love, we are vulnerable to predators who know how to exploit our pain and make us feel responsible for the outcome.

I was not caught in a single thread of deceit and manipulation. Like a spider who paralyzes his prey, wrapping her in his silken web and slowly devouring her life, my father began victimizing me when I was small and innocent—unable to understand the violence that was quietly eroding my soul.

Memory

I am three or four years old. I know because we still live in Newport, across the street from the cotton patch. We return home and are surprised by my uncle, who is only eight at the time. He and his family have come up to the capital city for a visit, and he thought it would be fun to hide in the closet. To jump out and scare us. A child's prank.

It should have been funny. But it wasn't. I was embarrassed and afraid. I wonder what he would have witnessed if he had stayed in the closet. I remember checking closets at times, and under my bed, to make sure no one was hiding there.

I called my mother when I processed this memory. "Do you know anything about it?"

She remembered it, even though more than fifty years have passed since it happened. "I remember your dad beating Eddie (who was four years old at the time) and Johnny," she tells me, "but I never understood what they had done."

～

No life is so damaged, no soul so stained, that God would disdain to die for it.

The Song of the Wounded Child

My song!
Where is my song?
I have lost it
And I cannot
Get it back.
It was here,
Lifting easily
From thoughtless lips

As it will when
We are a child.
Then he came
Into the room…
He stayed
Too long, I fear
For search though I may
I search in vain.
I cannot hear it.
It has gone.
I cannot get it back.
Where is my song?

Another sick man once told me, "You need to honor your father."

"What is there to honor?" I asked.

"There must be something. Surely in all those years there was something honorable that your father did. You must have some good memories."

I honestly wish there were something, but even the things I thought were good were corrupted by his evil desires. My most painful memories are those in which my father appeared to love me, to be nurturing and caring, for he would later reveal his fantasies to me and infuse even my good memories with the poison of his lust, his using, abusing, and lewdness. No. There are no good memories.

The reason I say this man was sick is because when his own wife began to process the abuse she experienced at five years old and sought the help of counselors, this man accused her of deliberately arousing the therapist with her memories of abuse. It is my belief that he had experienced his share of violation in his own young years, for I met his mother—a woman who, even in her old age, kept a sex toy hung on her bedpost and asked her son to purchase pornographic magazines for her reading pleasure.

Reflections

I remember when I was "special" to my father. I was the oldest girl and took a lot of responsibility for my siblings. Maybe I thought I had earned my father's attention. I don't remember when that began to change, but it was not instantaneous. Somehow, I learned to "compartmentalize" my father's behavior. I adored my father, but hated my abuser. It was impossible to tell where one began and the other left off.

Many victims experience positive feelings in the beginning stages of abuse. They feel "chosen" and grown-up. They may be treated as special. Acceptance of special treatment is one layer of abuse that often binds us to guilt. But we are no more

No life is so damaged, no soul so stained, that God would disdain to die for it.

responsible for those feelings than we are for the act of responding emotionally or sexually to the abuser.

As a wise counselor pointed out to me, victimization is not limited to children. "Even adults are victimized with threats, within marriage, or by anyone who has power over them; a doctor, a counselor." And, I would add, a pastor. "It isn't anyone's fault if they have been victimized," she said.

These words may seem like an escape hatch in your house of shame—one that you dare not go through. But remember it is the truth that sets us free. And the truth is **it was not your fault**.

I once wrote a letter to myself:

> *I am sorry for everything that you went through. I hate the abuser and I hate everyone that knew what he did and allowed him to do it. But most of all, I hate myself. I hate myself for allowing it to happen.*

Years later I wrote another:

> *I am sorry for everything you went through. I had no idea you suffered so much—for you hid it well, even from yourself. Now it is time to stop hiding. It is time to look your abuse in the face and stand up to it. YOU (abuse) are not who I am. You happened to me—but you are not a part of me. I hate you. I do not hate the people who allowed you to use them and I do not hate myself. I hate abuse and I will do everything in my power to shut you down! Not only in my life but in the lives of other people.*

Everyone who reads these words, listen to me: abuse in any form is hideous, it is painful, and it is wrong. I renounce you, abuse, in every form, and I declare that you no longer have any power over me. I forgive myself for my weakness. I choose

---

No life is so damaged, no soul so stained, that God would disdain to die for it.

to forgive the one who abused me, and perhaps, in time, my feelings will follow my choice and I'll find a way to forgive, not only from my will but from my heart. Until then, I rest in the grace of the One who will not condemn me for my humanity with all its limitations and deficiencies. *His grace is sufficient for me.*

Perhaps you, too, have a letter to write. Say it now—with pen and ink—and then lock it up so that no one but you will know what you've said. Do not share your treasures until you are ready, and then only with whom you really want to share them. This is a boundary that the abuser deprived you of—but no more. Your memories are your own, and your response to your memories is okay. It is okay to be angry with the abuser. Someone has said that depression is anger with a history. Are you depressed? Maybe it's time to process your anger and your shame and your helplessness.

The Apostle Paul said, "When I was a child I thought as a child, I spoke as a child: but when I became a man I put away childish things." (1 Corinthians 13:11.)

We can mature into responders who process our feelings and then act on them. A child is a reactor. He acts on his feelings and has little or no means to process them. That is why he believes what others tell him.

Questions for Reflection

Before we ask the following questions, we need to address an important clarification.

We are delving into memories that sometime hold the key to understanding why we react, or overreact, to situations that occur in our lives today. We are searching for understanding of why we think, feel and respond as we do. I want to caution you not to get discouraged if memories don't return to you in the same way they do for some others. I will again rely on the words of Renee Rowe, my personal encour-

No life is so damaged, no soul so stained, that God would disdain to die for it.

The Scream That No One Heard

Did you ever learn the silent scream?
It's a mechanism that I know well.
The only way one can relive
The torment inside when one cannot tell
Another living soul the hell of life.

Did you ever open wide your lips
And tensing every muscle—strain
To let the horror out that overfills your brain?
Till finally, you swoon, you fall
And realize that—after all
It is just another day—one more time
I can do this, if I must
There is no one I can trust.
So silently, I empty me of the stuff of life.

ager and therapist, to clarify this point:

The blessed reality of recovery is that we need to know the depth of our pain, not all the memories. The memories can stay wherever they need to be in order for us to function. We need some of them to access the depth. Some survivors do years of good (recovery) work with only body memories (no pictures). There are four levels of consciousness: Behavior (the pictures); Affect (the feelings); Sensations (hearing, smell, touch, body memories); and Knowledge (a conscious memory). There comes a point in time when we know what the depth is and we don't need all the memories to recover.

Questions for Those Who Are Ready to Go Deeper

1. *When I was a child I believed:*

   (Can you think of a false belief that set you up for abuse?)

   > **The Apostle said, "Now we see through a glass darkly, but then (when perfect truth has come) face to face..."**

2. *What do you see now?*

   (Have you realized some truth that opens the door to more questions and a deeper understanding of your past and how it affects you today?)

3. *Can you remember an incident that seemed to change the way you felt about yourself from that time forward?*

4. *Who was there with you?*

5. *What were you feeling?*

No life is so damaged, no soul so stained, that God would disdain to die for it.

Some Feeling Words

In the beginning, when you believed you had a choice, you may have felt:

loved	aroused	embarrassed	helpless
accepted	excited	confused	rejected
special	angry	ashamed	guilty
chosen	afraid	dirty	in pain

Are you in a safe place now? Do you have some distance from the abuser? Do you have a safe person to walk with you through the pain of remembering?

You may want to take a walk, write in your journal, or just sit quietly. I have a special room with a rocking chair and a CD player in it. When I feel sad, confused, or needy, I like to go sit in my rocking chair and turn on soft instrumental music. I like the old hymns of the church—but you might prefer total silence or a different style of music. Music has the power to soothe and calm us. We need to learn to calm ourselves, to take care of ourselves, and to rest when we need to process.

~

My Prayer for Today

Oh, Lord, when You lived on the earth, You showed us that You loved the little children. You drew them to You. Inside every one of us there is a child who longs to know You. But sometimes we are disappointed because we don't think You care about us. Wouldn't You protect us from the abuser if You loved us? Help us, Oh Lord, to understand. As we walk the healing pathway, help us to find You somewhere along the way.

Amen.

No life is so damaged, no soul so stained, that God would disdain to die for it.

Chapter Five
A Broken Spirit

I AM YOUNG, perhaps three or four years old. My father is getting me ready for bed. I am happy. Laughing. "Skin a squirrel," my father says as he tugs off my pants and prepares to get me into my pajamas. I giggle. This is a game we play often. My father pulls on my pajamas and sends me off to bed.

I adored him then. Of course I did. He was my daddy.

Memory

Now I am five years old. Eddy, my older brother, has angered me and I stick out my tongue at him. He promptly spits on it. Without thinking, I slap him. Hard. My father grabs me and demands that I apologize to my brother. Overwhelmed with righteous indignation, I do the unthinkable: I say no to my father. Even after he yanks off his belt and bends me over the bed, I persist in saying no. He begins to beat me. "Tell your brother you're sorry."

"No." I don't know what I was thinking. No one says no to my father.

Then comes the blow that, as he later boasted, "conquered" me. He picks me up and throws me onto the bed. Glaring at me through squinted eyes, my father—who never says a curse word and lives "by the holy book"—says, "Damn you."

Turning on his heel, he walks out the door; I believe, out of my life. The sense of loss—of abandonment—is unbearable. Daddy has given up on me. I will not be forgiven. Ever.

～

When my father returned several hours later, an unhealthy bond forged of fear and guilt had wrapped itself around my five-year-old heart. He bragged about how he had conquered me, saying that he thought I had beaten him when I refused to apologize, but afterward I always did as he asked. Everything was "yes, sir." He was right. He had won. It would be twenty-eight years before I dared to take back my life.

Reflections

Fear of abandonment. I struggle with it still. If I don't please you, will you leave me? If I don't give in to you, will you abandon me?

The abuser never makes a physical move on a child before he has set her up. He first makes her aware of her powerlessness, her dependence on him, her

perceived part in the abuser's depravity. He holds her hostage to something that is magnified in her immature mind to give him power over her. Sometimes, the child is impoverished; if not physically or economically impoverished, she may be starving for love, acceptance, or esteem. The abuser homes in on the child's need and

No life is so damaged, no soul so stained, that God would disdain to die for it.

then exploits it. After the child responds to his offering, she becomes enslaved to the abuser through fear, guilt, dependence, and shame.

Questions for Reflection

Please do not attempt to work through these questions without following the suggestions in previous Questions for Reflection sections.

Some of the following may trigger a flood of emotions that should be processed in the presence of a counselor. If you feel yourself dissociating or becoming overwhelmed with emotion, please stop reading, retreat to your "safe place," and call your counselor or trained support person.

> 1. *How did the abuser set you up? Once you know, you will recognize the setup and might be able to intervene on behalf of someone you love, as in the story below.*

Amy (not her real name) is a ten-year-old girl who gets up early every morning to make breakfast for her father before he goes to work. Amy's parents have a rocky relationship, and the father has a serious addiction—a sexual addiction. The child's mother knows it, but she sees no problem with allowing her daughter to assume the responsibility of "taking care of Daddy" while she sleeps in each morning. She calls it "bonding."

This is an example of a setup. The child feels special and enjoys an inappropriate bond with her father. She feels "grown-up" and needed. Even if overt sexual abuse never occurs, the child has been damaged by the inappropriate relationship she shares with her father.

Did you notice how the three people in this story are getting their needs met in inappropriate ways? The mother needs to sleep and to avoid intimacy with her

---

No life is so damaged, no soul so stained, that God would disdain to die for it.

husband. The child needs love and affirmation from her father. She has a hard life and she needs to feel special. The father needs intimacy, and his pornographic videos will no more satisfy that need for him than they did for his father, a convicted child molester. He seeks to get his needs met in an inappropriate relationship with his daughter, a relationship that masquerades as loving while setting the stage for a heinous crime against her. Even if it goes no further, the inappropriate bond formed by this relationship will affect the child for years to come.

Wake up, family! You are people of the church, but you are also incredibly selfish and foolish to pretend that all is well in your needy household.

Thank God for church leaders who have awakened from their dreams of innocence among the family of God, and come into the reality of life as it is, not as we want it to be.

In the foregoing story, the pastor's wife gathered her courage and approached the mother, warning her of the setup. More truth came to light and the father was forced to face his addiction. He went into a recovery program and began working on his problem. The setup was interrupted by the intervention of a caring woman who dared to be proactive to save the life and dignity of a child. Thank you, God, for those who care enough to take action of behalf of those who cannot do it for themselves.

So the question remains, how were you set up? What needs were met in inappropriate ways that set the hook to entrap you?

If you haven't experienced sexual abuse, and are reading this book so that you can help others, I applaud you. I encourage you to read books such as Dan Allender's *The Wounded Heart* and others listed in the back of this book so you'll be better informed and more sensitive to the wounding of those who may suffer the soul-numbing sorrow of sexual abuse.

2. Who failed to protect you?

No life is so damaged, no soul so stained, that God would disdain to die for it.

If a parent or another person in a position of authority or power over you was allowed to abuse you physically, emotionally, verbally, or sexually, then the parent(s) who failed to intervene share in the responsibility for the abuse.

Often, one parent will perpetrate the abuse while the other denies it, passively refusing to deal with the abusive behavior and its consequences.

Sometimes, the victim suffers the compounded betrayal of a perpetrator who abuses and another parent who openly colludes in the perpetrator's sin.

I have heard heart-wrenching stories from men and women long past their prime, survivors whose pain had not diminished over time, as they recalled hurtful, demeaning, hostile words and actions of parents, older siblings, and others who were allowed to abuse or diminish them.

Others have suffered the intangible heartache of neglect. Harder to recognize than overt abuse, neglect has a profound effect on the child who was ignored, marginalized, or invalidated during the tender years of youth. I say, "harder to recognize" because it is easier to acknowledge acts of commission than those of omission. Neglect is largely a crime of omission against a child, and its effect will not diminish with time. Only by actively pursuing the truth, and applying the principles of processing and forgiving, will the child damaged by neglect be set free to live unhindered by the consequences of his parents' sin.

3. *Who came to your games, took you shopping, or stayed up to chat with you after dates and parties? Who took the time to notice when you were happy— or sad—and rejoice in your gladness or put an empathetic arm around your shoulders? Who delighted in you and enjoyed you just for who you are? On a more basic level, who made sure that you had food to eat and were in bed at a decent time? Who made sure that you made it home by curfew?*

If the answer is no one, or that most of the time it was no one, you were neglect-

---

No life is so damaged, no soul so stained, that God would disdain to die for it.

ed as a child. You can grieve the sorrow of neglect and overcome its negative influence over your life. But first you must recognize the arenas of your wounding. In later chapters we will learn to grieve and let it go.

> 4. *I believe I was neglected as a child because:* _____
> (Write your answer in your journal)

~

In the prologue to *The Wounded Heart,* Dan Allender writes:

> *This is a book about damage, the damage done to the soul by sexual abuse. It is also a book about hope, but hope that loves only after the harm of abuse has been faced. If there is a central reason for this book it is found in the need to face what is true about the damage done to the soul and the damage done to others related to the past abuse.*

When we have been subjected to physical, emotional, or sexual abuse—or as so often happens, a combination of the three—or neglect, each of these forms of victimization has the power to plunge us into a lifetime of degradation and despair. The process of overcoming these things offers opportunity for the human soul to soar above complacency, to become strong and resilient, and to give honor to God who replenishes our resources so that we need never again be ashamed. When Joseph confronted the brothers who had beaten him and then sold him into slavery, he said, "You meant it for evil but God meant it for good in order to bring it about as it is today.... (Genesis 50:20.)

No life is so damaged, no soul so stained, that God would disdain to die for it.

Do we dare believe that? Can we truly accept that God means everything that happens to us for our good? I, for one, cannot believe that everything that happened in my life has been good—but I agree with Joseph that when evil occurs—God's intention is to intercept the evil and bring good out of it. Like gold that has been purified in the furnace of affliction, the survivor who dares to believe that God is at work to bring light out of darkness and good out of evil will begin to experience the goodness of God at work in her. She will seek His truth and grow strong in His grace.

In a time of great discouragement, the psalmist, David wrote, "I would have lost heart, unless I had believed that I would see the goodness of the LORD in the land of the living." (Psalm 27:13, NKJV.)

No matter what evil has befallen us, we need not despair. For God's goodness is greater than any evil, and His intention is to overcome evil with good.

~

My Prayer for Today

God, help us to recognize Your hand at work in bringing light out of darkness, order out of chaos, and good out of our past, even though there were those who meant it for evil. Thank You for giving us life and breath so that we can grow beyond the pain of the past and provide life-giving encouragement and hope to others who will see the wonders that You can do with us when we submit ourselves to You and dare to do the work of recovery.

Amen.

> *The Victorious Life is not about what happens to us, but about what happens through us!*

Reach out and touch another soul today.

No life is so damaged, no soul so stained, that God would disdain to die for it.

Darkness

Darkness has come
And covered all the room
In eerie shadows, mystic gloom.
I hide beneath the covers
Silently, I weep… silently
I keep my bruised heart
Alive
By seeking solace from the
One who doesn't hear
A little girl
Who cowers under covers
In the dark.

Chapter Six

Early Memories Recovered

IT IS COLD. And dark.

A few stray beams of light seep through the window near the bed and I know that it is morning. I look down, aware already of my shame. Yes. It is true. My panties have disappeared. They are nowhere to be found. I am lying on the edge of the bed. My mother is sleeping, snoring lightly. My father sleeps, too. But I do not sleep. And I know that I was in the middle, between the two of them, when sleep found me the night before. I know what happened in the night. I know that everything is changed somehow. A secret loss haunts me, but I must not tell. I must forget.

It is twenty-eight years later. I am in church. I stand in a crowd of worshippers, yet I am alone. Alone with my memories, wondering if they are real. And yet I know.

I call my mother. This is what I remember. Is it true? My mother tells me that it is true. That she had forgotten, too. She chose to forget what she dared not believe. It was too dangerous to remember. Love and hate, dependence and fear, these are dangerous emotions when you put them together. They make you wonder if you are

crazy. My mother wondered, and she doubted. The man who lay beside her was a Christian man, so she believed. He would not—could not—it was unthinkable. No. Best to let it be.

~

A few weeks after I wrote this chapter, I found myself in the midst of an internal conflict that refused to be quieted with anything less than the truth.

The truth, that double-edged sword that divides between bone and marrow. The instrument of death that braves the gloom to sweep through corridors of the past, raising the dust of discarded memories, presenting them once again to my consciousness as if to say, "will you let me in now? Can I come out of the cellar? Open me up to the light that streams through the window of your soul. Look at me through eyes grown wiser. Eyes unmasked. Allow Truth to do His work on me and I will cease to be your enemy. For your memories are not the source of your torment—but the revelation of it. They are speaking—they are telling your story—if only you will listen. If only you will hear."

"But I can't," we say. For the child within us cringes at the truth—realities masked in shadows of denial and distortion.

Did you ever listen to a child tell the story of a horror so intense that it overwhelmed his emotional and mental abilities? It may have been no more real than a horror flick on TV, or it may be something more devastating, such as having been in a terrible accident where he saw someone die—his young eyes beholding the blood, his ears filled with the sound of terrified screams and cries of pain.

His rendition of the event, filtered through a mind ill equipped to deal with an

No life is so damaged, no soul so stained, that God would disdain to die for it.

event so traumatic, will bear little semblance to the truth. He will make inaccurate assumptions about what happened, especially about his part in it.

Consider the "magical" thinking of children whose parents divorce. It is common knowledge that the children often perceive themselves as the cause of the marriage breakdown.

Reflections

The mental and emotional resources of a child are inadequate to deal with the immensity of violation. There is a beast in the cellar of our soul—a memory so threatening that we dare not let it out. We sense our inadequacy and slam the door shut. We become so accustomed to slamming the door that even when we have grown older and stronger, we cannot—will not—allow the door to swing open.

In the words of my therapist Renee Rowe, "No brain is prepared for trauma—at any age. Everyone, child or adult will tend to have the same responses. A rape victim will have the same inaccurate assumptions. It is the nature of trauma and its effects upon the brain."

Like a diver surfacing from the shadowy waters of the deep, or a jogger immerging from a dense fog, we gain clarity as we begin to process, as we learn to heal. We reclaim the truths that have been stolen from us and we get angry. Anger yields to sorrow. A chasm of grief opens up in our awakened soul and we mourn our losses. We embrace our pain. It's only then that we begin to see ourselves in the light of truth and we resolve to be victims no longer.

I will fight for the child. The child in me who dared not approach the beast in the cellar has matured into the strong, powerful woman I have become. A woman empowered with a strength not my own, a Power greater than any I might hope to possess, and a determination to kill the monster.

No life is so damaged, no soul so stained, that God would disdain to die for it.

I am ready now. My heart has asked once again, "What is the truth? The truth that must come out of the cellar is this:

My mother did know when my father molested me at five years old in her bed. Even though she denied it, even to herself, refusing to accept what seemed debilitating to her fragile hold on life and love, she knew. The truth is that, in the years that followed, she walked in on scenes that would have shocked her—saw evidence that could not be ignored—and turned away as if nothing had happened.

Memory

I am in my teens. My father has just finished his evil work. The evidence of his satisfaction is on his bedside table. I am still in the room, sitting on the side of his bed, staring at the floor when my mother walks in. I am paralyzed, torn between dismay—for my shame is evident—and relief. Now, it will end. The child who long ago lost her ability to say no to her father will be rescued. It won't be my fault. He can't blame me. I didn't tell. If he goes to jail, or even if he kills himself, as he has threatened to do, it is not my fault. My mother will take over now; she will end it.

My mother looks at my father, then at me, and walks out of the room. She says

she never saw the evidence on the table. I know now that denial has the ability to "make seeing eyes blind," but all I knew then was that the unthinkable had happened, and it didn't change a thing.

I found myself, only days ago, sitting in the office of a therapist, one who has helped me so many times before when I became "stuck." With her help, I walked back through two memories living in my cellar—memories that have stolen much from me, hiding behind a hurt so awful, a truth so painful, that I chose to live with it rather than expose it.

No life is so damaged, no soul so stained, that God would disdain to die for it.

In *My Utmost for His Highest*, Oswald Chambers says that it's not that difficult for most of us who are passionate in our faith to perform the will of God when we know that we'll suffer for it. But the first moment we're asked to submit to God in a matter that will bring pain to one we love—that is the test of our submission. That's the point upon which fully devoted followers of Christ may stumble. To allow our loved one to suffer because we have been faithful—this is the most difficult of our assignments.

And yet it is to this that I'm called if I would bring the beast out of the basement. For I have held my mother's hand as she cried and confessed her denial, her sorrow, and her weakness. Today I must talk with her about the beast still hiding in the cellar. Will it crush her? Will it bring new shame and dismay to a woman quickly approaching the end of her days?

I plunge into the truth before I can turn back. "The truth is," I tell her, "that you were in collusion with my father, that while he actively abused me, you knew that he did so and allowed it." The truth is that I was the offering on the altar of my father's depravity—the morsel thrown to the beast so that you could go to work and gain some small reprieve from his relentless abuse. I was the scapegoat, except that it was my father's violence and perversion that I carried away from the camp.

"Go to the park with your Daddy, honey. Go read to him. Your daddy wants to go on a ride? Well, he just shoved me around and screamed at me for the past few hours, so I will say nothing when he goes to your bed and says, 'You want to go on a ride with me?'"

Sure, every little girl wants to be dragged from her bed after hours and hours of hearing her father yell at her mother and shove her into the walls. Sure, I want to "comfort" him in the dark hours of the night, locked away in the prison of his vehicle as he roars down country roads, secure in his power over the child who performs, physically, whatever he asks. He doesn't care that mentally she is dead, decompos-

---

No life is so damaged, no soul so stained, that God would disdain to die for it.

ing emotionally and spiritually, as surely as if her heart has been ripped out and her blood has grown cold.

He will bring her home in a few hours and you will pretend to be asleep. I know you tossed and turned and worried. But that didn't keep the monster from devouring your child in the night.

I know you are sorry, and I would have spared you the pain of facing your past, but then the story would be warped and twisted, for the defilement that imprisoned my soul could not have happened if you hadn't abandoned me to the beast that broke into a little girl's soul and gained control of her mind, will, and emotions, leaving nothing but an empty shell, a robot clothed in human flesh, programmed to do his will so that those I loved would not suffer as I did.

Knowing that I was wasted, worthless, and unwanted, what could I have lived for but to shelter, protect—with my small strength—and be used for the sake of others who might have a chance in life as long as I maintained my watch?

This is the thinking of an abused child, and though the child grew up, the thinking did not change. Shame was multiplied with the years, but the paralysis that began, perhaps at birth, would not abate as the ball dropped in New York City with each New Year. It would take years of heartache and hard work to recover the memories written in this book, and more years of counseling, study, and processing to understand them.

I can say with the Apostle Paul, "I am what I am" (1 Corinthians 15:10), and therein lies the power of the Almighty in us. Jehovah God revealed his name to Moses, a man who was called to fulfill His purpose and fled to the desert. Moses asked, "Whom shall I say has sent me?" The voice of God answered from the flames, "I Am that I Am."

If we will be all that we can be—authentic in our day-to-day experience—and approach the burning bush as Moses did, expecting to be changed, then our suffering

No life is so damaged, no soul so stained, that God would disdain to die for it.

has purpose and our life is worth living.

"Tell the truth," my mother says. "Maybe it will help someone else."

I have underestimated the woman my mother has become. I have told her the truth—and she cried. Not a cry of self-pity that begs to be protected or excused, hers is a cry of remorse, an expression of repentance.

"I am seventy-four," my mother says. "I am crippled and house-bound. I cannot go out and tell others, so you tell them for me. Tell other mothers not to second-guess the truth and not to excuse the man who may be molesting their daughters.

"If anyone—anyone—has the courage to tell you that they suspect your child is being abused, don't just ask advice from friends, relatives, or church leaders. While friends and relatives looked the other way, more than one leader in my church told me that my husband would 'never do that' and assured me that if I would just 'submit' to him, he would be a better husband and father and everything would be all right. Submitting to a monster will not save your children."

Go to a counselor who has the expertise to prepare your child to acknowledge the truth, for she will lie to you. How can she tell her mother what "she" has done—for in her childish mind she is guilty, dirty, and responsible for what has been done to her. She believes she has been naughty, and she is ashamed. She cannot possibly understand that a horrendous crime has been committed against her. She has internalized the abuser's shame, and she will not be able to dismiss it until she gets the help she needs.

No life is so damaged, no soul so stained, that God would disdain to die for it.

Questions for Reflection

Before proceeding, please take appropriate measures to take care of yourself as suggested in earlier Questions for Reflection (see page 9).

1. *Perhaps you are reading this book because you are guilty of neglect, denial, or even deliberate collusion with the perpetrator of child abuse. You want—no, you desperately need—repentance of your sin, forgiveness for the harm that you have done. If so, there is hope for you. No sin is so great that our God cannot forgive it, no crime so horrendous that He will not heal the heart that is broken over the commission of it. If this is you, keep reading. Allow the truth to penetrate the layers of lies and rationalization that have blinded you to the agony you have sown into innocent lives. Talk to a trained professional or lay counselor, and begin the healing process. As long as there is life, there is hope of healing and reconciliation with God, even if the person you have harmed does not find it in her heart to forgive you. What are you going to do, today, to begin the healing process?*

2. *If you have suffered abuse or neglect, how do you feel when you read question 1? If you feel anger, resentment, or even rage, that's okay. It is where you are, and God understands your reaction. I have been where you are today—and I understand, too.*

God doesn't condemn us for our emotions or for our reaction against the horrors, the injustice, and the agony sown into our lives by the perpetrator(s) of our pain. But he loves us too much to allow us to wallow in it. He'll teach us, if we seek Him, how to rise above our emotions and respond out of our spirit, a spirit restored to wholeness by the one who will not let us go—ever. What do you need the Holy

---

No life is so damaged, no soul so stained, that God would disdain to die for it.

Spirit of God to do for you today? Tell Him about it. Write it in your journal or call a friend.

> **Every burden is easier borne when the load is shared with a friend.**

∽

My Prayer for Today

Oh, God, we thank You that You are with us as we do the hard work of recovery. You have promised never to leave us or forsake us. Help us to believe, today, that even when we experience emotions that feel out of control or "bad," You love us still and You do not leave us alone in our pain. Help us to accept all of our emotions as a part of the process of recovery and know that we are not "bad" because of them. Help us trust You and trust the process, knowing that even this is working together for our good.

Amen.

> **And we know that God causes all things to work together for good to those who love God, to those who are called according to His purpose.** —Romans 8:28

No life is so damaged, no soul so stained, that God would disdain to die for it.

Denial Is Not a Choice

but a built-in response to traumatic events.
Denial puts the brain to sleep so that insanity
does not overthrow reason on all acounts,
isolating inconceivable atrocities into manageable
pockets of the brain where they remain comatose
until awakened. Sadly, some souls slumber until death
overtakes them.

Chapter Seven

What About Mother?

MOTHER WAS RAISED in poverty. Her father was a gentle man, tall, quiet, and soft-spoken. I don't believe he was very happy, especially not when he was at home. When he was not working, he spent his time in the woods, hunting small game. Mother told me he was not around much when she was growing up.

Grandma wasn't around either. She went to work in her own mother's grocery store when Mother was twelve years old, leaving my mother to care for her six younger siblings. Had it not been for uncles and aunts who stepped in to take her to the movies on Friday nights, Mother would have had no life at all except for that of an adultified child, forced into running a chaotic house full of younger siblings. Abandonment and poverty were Mother's experience and, later, her two greatest fears—fears that would be used to secure her silence.

I believe Mother did the best she could, but at eighteen years of age she opted out of it all by marrying a man seven years her senior, an angry controller who took over where her mother had left off. A year and half later, my brother Eddie was born.

Eleven months later, I was on the scene. Children followed in quick succession until there were seven of us kids for my mother to care for—seven kids to be used as leverage by the manipulator who fathered us all.

The small commodities my father's wages provided must have seemed like great wealth to my economically deprived mother. Though the early years of marriage were financially rough, they were more than Mother had expected. A home, though small and unkempt—sporting several broken windows and an overgrown lawn—was still her own. It didn't take much to make Mother happy. She had developed the survival mechanism of focusing on the bright spots in the canvas of her life, and screening out the ugly blotches, a practice that enabled her to deny the physical, emotional, and sexual abuse my father perpetrated upon her children.

The modeling provided by Mother's own mother might have added to her confusion about the nature of sexual abuse and the responsibility of the parent to proactively protect the child. Known sex offenders were affectionately tolerated in mother's family—and responsibility for taking care of herself was placed solely on the shoulders of the child.

Grandma allowed an uncle, a known sexual offender, to sleep in the bed with my adolescent mother and her sister, telling her that she should get up immediately if Uncle D "did anything." Of course he "did something," and my mother got out of the bed—telling her mother about it the next day. Uncle D said that he was "testing her virtue." Uncle D's access to Grandma's home and her children were unaffected by his criminal behavior. Mother had "done the right thing," and that was all that mattered—a convenient philosophy, as it relieves the parent of all responsibility to take care of her child, and allows the mother to continue her relationship with the abuser. After all, it was not his fault.

Maybe your mother told you as well that sexual touching is wrong—that good little girls don't allow it. However, knowing that sexual violation is wrong will not

No life is so damaged, no soul so stained, that God would disdain to die for it.

protect a child from it. Her knowledge of the "wrongness" is innate. That knowledge is the double-edged sword that cuts deeply into her soul. "I have done wrong. I have been bad. I am ashamed." The responsibility for protecting the child—with all the guilt and shame if she somehow fails to do so—has been transferred to the child.

How can a child, with her fragile ego, lesser strength, and limited ability to communicate, tell anyone what "she" has done? She has no way to measure the damage that has been done to her body, mind, and soul, and blames herself for her inability to repel the abuser. She is easily intimidated by threats and by her own fears of embarrassment or disgrace. When trusted friends or family members perpetuate abuse, she may be silenced, as well, by the perceived need to protect someone she loves. She may fear emotional or physical abandonment or even rejection by the person who has won her love and confidence.

Her trust is easily violated and her small strength easily conquered. To tell your child that she must protect herself from sexual predators—that she must expose the sexual advances of the abuser while simultaneously giving him access to her, denying the symptoms of his victimizing nature, and depriving her of the love and nurturing that she so desperately needs—is like placing a thirsty child at the edge of a contaminated spring and commanding her not to drink. She will not see the toxins in the crystal-clear water that offers to quench the thirst in her aching soul. The part of her brain that discerns evil intent, especially in those whom she loves and trusts, is not yet mature. She doesn't know that her innocent response to the abuser's offering will lead to sexual victimization. By the time the predator makes an overt move on her, the traumatized child believes the lie that she has invited, or at least accepted, the victimization that robs her of her soul.

Especially in the case of incest.

Unfortunately, the child's acceptance of false responsibility is often validated by those she loves most, other family members. The mother of an incested child may view her daughter as a rival, especially as the child grows older, and project her own contempt and condemnation onto her. The mother's anger, jealousy, and contempt reinforce the perpetrator's position that the child is his accomplice in the crime he continues to commit.

It is common knowledge in recovery circles that children in dysfunctional families take on predictable roles. Some become the family mascot, learning to laugh everything off while they shrivel up and die inside. Others become the "black sheep," getting attention and mining for familial love by bouncing from one misbehavior to another, often resorting to addictions in order to survive. I was the "caregiver," the child who took on the role of an adult caring for my younger siblings, doing my best to protect them, nurture them, and provide for them. They were my life. I don't think they knew that—at least most of them didn't. But I would die for them. I did, in fact, give up my life one day at a time in a futile attempt to protect them from my father's violence, and relieve the monotony, the oppression, and the despair of the home in which we lived.

Paternal Incest

When a child has been victimized by her father or stepfather, it is unlikely that she will find her way out of victimization until the leverage that the perpetrator used to annihilate her defenses has been removed. She has been traumatized. She has lost her voice, her power, and her sense of self. The perpetrator views her as an extension of him—existing only to meet his "needs." All too often, the mother is a colluder to his crime—reinforcing his position. Sadly, the victim of incest may feel utterly worthless—her value depleted by the insidious attack on her person.

The family dynamics that accommodate the "setup" of the incested child often renders her powerless to change her circumstance as long as she is needed to maintain the family dynamics. When the family structure changes in ways that provide

No life is so damaged, no soul so stained, that God would disdain to die for it.

safety for her and others whom she may be trying to protect, she may be able to escape the horrors of incest. Some victims may escape upon graduation from high school or some other personal rite of passage; unfortunately, many do not. The victim of incest who has been sexually abused by the perpetrator and abandoned by the colluder may become stuck in the tragic dynamics of incest for many years after becoming an adult. Her body may have matured, but her ability to reason, process, and make decisions may be frozen in an earlier stage—terrorized by the abuse of one parent, and her worthlessness validated by the abandonment of the other.

About My Mother

My mother employed the defense mechanism of denial to avoid taking responsibility for protecting me. While understanding her history has helped me to forgive her, I have also come to understand the nature of denial. I will quote my favorite mentor, my therapist Renee Rowe:

Denial isn't a choice. Denial is an unconscious dissociation from the truth when our system is overwhelmed with the reality of our circumstances and our feelings. Denial can be positive—a break from our feelings. If it weren't for denial many more would go crazy.

I saw my mother hanging on to her sanity by a thread. Few women could have suffered all that she did and remained sane. Another word from Renee: "We have to fight to be conscious in order to heal." My mother lived most of her life in a semiconscious state, drifting from one painful episode to another, without the slightest idea of how to escape the tyranny of the man who would certainly have killed us before he would have let us go.

Just as I could not face the truth of my father's depravity in its entirety until I was safely out of his reach, neither could my mother. With safety and stability came the strength and courage to "fight to be conscious in order to heal."

No life is so damaged, no soul so stained, that God would disdain to die for it.

I have sat across from many women in counseling sessions and heard their stories. Some of them were victimized by their fathers or stepfathers while their mothers watched. How does one recover from a betrayal so insidious? Is there healing for such a wound as this? Is there a fountain somewhere, a fountain that flows with pure, sweet forgiveness for the mother who has committed such heinous crimes?

"There is a fountain filled with blood drawn from Immanuel's veins," the old hymn sings, "and sinners plunged beneath that flood lose all their guilty stains." Lose all their guilty stains! My mother sought my forgiveness, and the fountain flowed. Her stains have been purged by the righteous blood of our Redeemer. He has forgiven her. And I, as my heart is unburdened of its sorrows and my memories laid to rest—not in the cellar of unconscious remembrance but in the light of God's love—I sit in my Father's lap and lay my head on His chest, allowing cleansing tears to flow. They mingle with the blood that floods the fallen soul, and together give life to the weary woman who has carried, long enough, a burden too heavy, a defilement too deep, a sorrow that can no longer be stifled.

Reflections

Some memories stay submerged forever, and others surface when it is safe for them to do so. They peek out from behind bundles of built-up defenses, and dare us to believe that they are true. How do we know? We often wonder: is this a memory or a fabrication of my imagination? Sadly, even those memories that we are certain of may be less than fully accurate.

I am fortunate that my mother and some other family members have been able to confirm some of the memories I have recovered. Other memories I have to trust. I believe any memory that carries with it a tremendous emotional load tells me something important. Things may not be exactly the way I remember them, but the way

No life is so damaged, no soul so stained, that God would disdain to die for it.

I react to the memory, and the other memories triggered by its recovery, will tell my story, if I allow it. The way I react to the memory will bring the monsters out of the dark where they may be dispelled in the light of a new day.

Questions for Reflection

Are you ready to go deeper? Do you have the support of a professional counselor or a trained layperson to help you in the process? Have you practiced going to your safe place? If not, please skip to the next chapter.

1. *What are the memories that you doubt?*

2. *What kind of emotional load do they carry?*

3. *Do the characters in the memory act in ways that are consistent with their behavior at other times?*

More good advice from a wise counselor: Do not confront without the counsel of someone who can guide you in such a way that you will not be re-victimized. Rarely do perpetrators or family members who were in collusion with them tell the truth. The effort to have them confirm your memories will most likely result in re-victimization.

The solution? Most people have to claim their own truth without any external confirmation.

> ### *If you do not stand firm in your faith … you will not stand at all.* —Isaiah 7:9

No life is so damaged, no soul so stained, that God would disdain to die for it.

～

My Prayer for Today

Oh, Lord, I pray for wisdom for my readers. Wisdom to discern the memories that surface as they read this book, and afterward as they process what they have read. Let them do no harm to themselves or others, but open their hearts to the truth—for it is the truth that will set them free. Lead every hurting heart to the healing balm found in the Word of God and the words of a wise counselor.

Amen.

No life is so damaged, no soul so stained, that God would disdain to die for it.

Chapter Eight
When Did It Start?

THE RECOVERY OF the memory of abuse at five years old was a breakthrough for me, for I had done a good job of forgetting. I had totally wiped the event from my memory, but I had often wondered when did the abuse start?

Until one day in 1985, when the first memory of early abuse surfaced, I believed that my father first molested me when I was thirteen. My earliest memory of it was then. But something clued me in that it began much earlier. I thought, Why wasn't I shocked, or at least surprised, the first time I remembered my father violating me at about thirteen years old?

The recovery of the memory filled in that blank. I had forgotten, but I still *knew* what he had done. We may forget—but we cannot *un-know* something. *Knowing* is like learning to read: Once we know how, we can't *un-know* it. Look at a sign along the highway and try *not* to read it. Impossible. Your will may say, "don't read that sign," but your mind will do so anyway, for you know the meaning of the symbols that spell out the words.

To Be Somebody

Is there no hope for one like me?
I have not been taught to set the table
Properly...

Or which way to pass the food
Which fork to use—and why
Anyway are there two?

Thank you, I have learned,
And please,
But I must know more than these
If I am to be somebody.

Somebody who fits right in
Who laughs and jokes and then
Knows when to get quiet
At just the right time.

Somebody who stands around
In a circle of friends
And doesn't stand out
Like a broken thumb.

Maybe if I get a manners book
And read it thoroughly
I can learn enough
To be somebody.

When we *know* something that traumatizes us, even though we can't quite remember it, it continues to traumatize us until we can bring it to the surface and resolve it. Because of what I knew, I always felt I was different from other children. I was like a chipped plate at a flea market, confined to the vendor's shelf, stuck there forever because no one wants a chipped plate.

~

The memories began to come back more frequently. I remembered nightmares I dreamed when I was in the second grade. Strange men were coming to take me away. I clung to the wooden gate in my front yard, but they were too strong for me. I called for my mother, but she didn't hear. I could see her through the kitchen window. She was smiling and singing while she washed dishes. When I asked my mother if she knew about the dreams, she said I used to cry out in the night and she would come to comfort me, but she thought I had simply had a bad dream.

Child's Play

Two little girls beneath a tree
Played with dolls, as children will.
"I'll be the mother," one child said,
"And you can be the dad."

Suddenly, the other leaped
Panic-stricken to her feet.
She ran, while the other
Stood and gazed
All the way home.
Though she's only
Lived awhile,
She cannot be
A little child.

No life is so damaged, no soul so stained, that God would disdain to die for it.

Chapter Nine

My Choice

SOMETHING ELSE HAPPENED when I was in the third grade. I stopped eating. I began dropping weight, so my mother took me to the doctor. He put me on half-and-half milk, but I couldn't drink it, so he hospitalized me. The doctor put me through numerous tests, but could find nothing wrong with me. He kept me there for a couple of weeks. In the absence of my father, who never came to the hospital during that time, I resumed eating and was sent home. There was no diagnosis. The tests Dr. Gray administered could not diagnose what ailed me at age eight. Many years later, I related the memory of my hospital stay to a counselor. She smiled and said, "You chose to live."

Chapter Ten
Eddie's Choice

WHILE DRIVING HOME from counseling, I found myself deeply confused. What was it that nagged at me? Something that hovered just beneath the conscious level of my mind was breaking my heart—but I couldn't remember what it was. I prayed, "Oh God, please reveal to me what I'm experiencing. What's causing so much grief in my spirit? What happened that I can't bear to remember? Please, Lord, help me!"

The words came gently, quietly: "Eddie chose to die." A dam broke somewhere inside me. I sobbed out all the grief I had held inside for over thirty years. My heart ached for my brother. I had not remembered his suffering, until now.

Memory

Eddie was eleven months older than I. He was my protector and my friend. There were a lot of bullies in our neighborhood. They once locked my younger brother in an old shed. We looked for him for hours. They chased Eddie and me many times, and Eddie always knew where to hide.

Everyone loved Eddie. He was a sweetheart. All the teachers wanted to take him home with them. One, Mrs. Butts, actually did take him home, for a day. She told my mother that he was the sweetest boy in her class. I was a little jealous—no one ever said that about me. I didn't think I had a lot of personality. I kept to myself most of the time.

My father chose to take my brother and me to Newport to take care of a rental house that he owned. Something happened on that trip that made Eddie sad. Really sad.

My father said that Eddie, on his own initiative, found a way to unlock a screen door by making a hole in the screen. For this, my father beat my brother so violently that Eddie went out into the backyard and vomited. My great-aunt witnessed the incident and told my mother. I don't remember the beating, but I do remember the shame and grief on my brother's face. Now I wonder, was it because of something that happened to him that day, or was it because of something that he stumbled upon behind that locked door? Did my father threaten him? I don't know.

About two weeks later, Eddie went to school and told his beloved teacher that he didn't want to wait until parent–teacher night to display his artwork and projects. He requested permission to take them home to his mother. Eddie seldom asked for anything. His teacher later told my mother, "It's almost as if Eddie knew he was going to die."

On a Wednesday evening, my mother sent Eddie to the store. Mother was terribly ill with the flu and needed something to settle her stomach. We had moved to a better neighborhood, and it seemed safe to send Eddie to the nearby grocery. He was precocious and could be counted on to be careful.

Shortly after Eddie left, I heard the screech of tires half a block down the street. A neighbor who lived on the corner rushed over to tell my mother that Eddie had been hit by a car. I ran out the door, but Mother forced me back into the house to

No life is so damaged, no soul so stained, that God would disdain to die for it.

stay with the younger children. So I waited.

The ambulance carried my brother away. He was in a coma for three days. He never came home. He had walked directly into the path of an oncoming car.

It rained the day of the funeral. I stood alone. When they lowered my brother into the grave, I turned to leave along with the rest of the mourners. My pastor's wife came and wrapped her coat around my shoulders. I had lost my dearest friend and my only protector.

Yet he was not lost. I knew Eddie was in heaven. A part of me envied him. Part of me felt abandoned. Only now can I understand why one moment I prayed, vehemently, for my brother to live, and in the next moment I prayed that God would take him. I felt confused by my own prayers. Now I know that my most loving prayer was the one I prayed when I gave him up. Eddie could no longer be my personal protector. He couldn't shelter me from the torment that lay ahead. And he couldn't live with the pain of our reality. He chose to go home.

I do not believe that Eddie intended to end his life when he stepped in front of that car. I believe he simply decided he didn't want to live in this world anymore, and he believed his heavenly Father would somehow take him out of it. I believe his thoughts were far away from the busy street he was crossing on that dusky summer evening and he simply didn't care to look for the traffic that bore down on him. His heart was set on a better place.

In a way, I believe Eddie's life ended two weeks earlier when he unlocked a door, believing he was helping his father, and endured a pain worse than the beating that followed. While I chose to bury the truth, Eddie chose to leave a life that held such violence, betrayal, and despair.

No life is so damaged, no soul so stained, that God would disdain to die for it.

Reflections

This chapter makes me sad. Eddie was not only my brother but my friend. I still grieve his loss. What have you lost? Friendships? A marriage? A childhood? What are you feeling right now?

Even now, I don't know what Eddie saw on that terrible day two weeks before he died. I know I was present, and I know that something about it nags at me when I let myself go there in memory. But I choose to let it go. I don't dwell on what I may never recover, but on the fact that Eddie is free of it—and I'm being made whole in spite of it.

What do you need to let go of?

∼

My Prayer for Today

Oh, God of the fatherless and widows, God of the abandoned and broken, You see the broken people that seek after You in the quiet places of their hearts. Come and heal our broken lives as You alone have power to do. Your Word tells us that You carried our sin and our sorrows. Help us to believe that. Help us to give them up and walk away from the hurts of the past, the hang-ups of the present, and the hindrances to our future. We will walk in the way of peace and trust You to shine Your light upon our path.

Amen.

No life is so damaged, no soul so stained, that God would disdain to die for it.

Chapter Eleven
Abuse Intensifies

S OON AFTER EDDIE'S DEATH, my father began to abuse me more openly, but in subtle ways that I didn't understand. He and all of us children would often stay up late at night and watch TV while my mother slept. She needed her sleep, for he would make certain she left for work the next morning.

I was uncomfortable with something about how close to me my father lay on the couch, but I couldn't explain why I felt that way. I had no memory of earlier abuse, and thought that something was wrong with me for feeling that way. I was drawn by what I perceived as my father's affection for me, but somehow repulsed by something else that I felt but couldn't define. He would later reveal to me the fantasies that consumed him at that time—and, of course, it was my fault.

It would be many years later before I would hear the words "It wasn't your fault" spoken by a counselor and finally be freed from the false sense of responsibility that my father transferred to me.

Reflections

When a child is neglected, abandoned, deprived, or otherwise mistreated, he is a prime target for abuse. But we don't like to admit that we have been any of the above. I have had women tell me, "My parents were never around, but we did all right. It's just that this one neighbor…" Another said, "My mother had eight children and had to work to help my father make a living. I wasn't neglected, there just wasn't much time left to go around." She didn't understand why she welcomed the sexual advances of a relative, because she didn't recognize her vulnerability.

Questions for Reflection

Please approach this section carefully. Do not process these questions alone. Read on only if you are ready to go deeper.

1. *What made you vulnerable to the predators in your life?*

2. *Whom do you try to defend when someone suggests that you were not properly cared for?*

True forgiveness isn't found in pretending that the offense never occurred, but in fully embracing the extent of the wrong and deciding instead to "let the offender off the hook with you and on the hook with God." (Neil T. Anderson, co-author of *Christ-Centered Therapy*) God will do a better job than you ever could of bringing that person to justice.

～

No life is so damaged, no soul so stained, that God would disdain to die for it.

My Prayer for Today

Heavenly Father, I ask that You help my friends to face the truth about those they love who may have let them down. Help them not to judge them harshly nor to deny their responsibility, but to respond with truth and grace to revealed wrongs, even those wrongs that were not intended to harm. Grant them wisdom, and do what needs to be done to bring healing and health to their wounded souls.

Amen.

No life is so damaged, no soul so stained, that God would disdain to die for it.

Chapter Twelve
If I Should Tell

If you tell, Daddy will go to jail.

I DO NOT KNOW how old I was when I heard those words. But I know that I chose to forget them. I know that I couldn't tell. What child could send her own daddy to jail?

It was during a worship service over twenty years later that the words returned to haunt me. Once again, I stood naked before my Lord—stripped of my defenses—safe at last, and offering everything to Him as I stood in His presence and lifted my voice in praise. Like my first memory of early abuse, it slipped out of its watery burial place, in the sea of forgetfulness, in the sea of my denial to be more accurate, and hit with the force of a ton of bricks dropped on my head.

Another memory from early childhood! A memory that was so emotionally loaded that it made my knees weak. I walked around in a shock-induced fog for days, and then I accepted the fact that I had endured much more than I could remember, at an earlier age than I wanted to admit.

It is interesting how abusers often come from a family of them. If I count the abusers in my extended family, there are at least three. How do I know? Their exploits were common knowledge. Unfortunately, in my family, the children, and especially the teenage girls, were more often vilified than the abusers. I cringed when I heard the gossip about what "they" had done.

One of them, Uncle X (not his real name, of course), set me up, believing incorrectly that because I was needy and neglected, I would allow him to do what my father was doing to me. I think there must be some informal "abuser club," because so many of them seem to find the same victims. Thank God I managed to escape my uncle's trap. I haven't seen him for over twenty years, and I hope I never will.

My experience, and perhaps yours as well, is that while the dysfunctional family may often breed abusers, it also produces gossips. One member abuses, the others gossip. All a part of the trap that is set for the victim; for while the abuser incapacitates the victim's will, the gossip sets the price too high for the victim to take it back. The process would certainly demand exposure, and exposure would intensify shame.

I remember when Lennie (not his real name) was arrested. He had been caught in the act of molesting his teenage daughter in a public place. Lennie and his daughter became the subject of family gossip. There were some who shook their heads in disbelief, but I don't remember any compassion for the child whose life had been destroyed.

"He couldn't have done it if she didn't want it," my grandmother said. Everyone, it seemed, agreed. I knew that I would fare no better if my secret were exposed.

Years later, when I returned to visit my mother's family, my suspicions were confirmed. By that time, the news was out that my father had molested me during most of my life. My mother's sister had come to pick me up at the airport. The drive turned into a question-and-answer session, concluding with my aunt's observation,

No life is so damaged, no soul so stained, that God would disdain to die for it.

"Yeah, Mother always said there was something going on between you and your daddy." When I didn't reply she added, "Mama's pretty smart about those things, you know."

Oh, yes. I do know. She made enough sly comments about it when I was a young teenager to make sure I knew that I ought to be ashamed, but I don't think she was very smart. A smart person, grandmother or not, would have planted both feet in the hindquarters of a perverted individual who dared molest a child, and given him reason to regret his despicable behavior.

If you knew, or even suspected, that I was suffering the humiliation of sexual abuse by my father, why—why—didn't you intervene? Why would you let him get away with it? My wounded heart whispered to me that it was because I was unlovely, unwanted, and unworthy. The truth is that other sexual predators had been tolerated in the family long before my father came along, and those who suspected him of incest were emotionally conditioned to deny it, excuse it, or hold the child equally responsible for it.

What an evil scheme by the one who comes to steal, kill, and destroy the lives of those too young to fight back. It's not the family that schemes to do this, it's the enemy of the family, the enemy of all of our souls who plots to kill. He merely uses the weaknesses of human beings who yield to his manipulation to get the job done.

It's crucial to our recovery that we not fix our hatred on the sinners—our abusers, the family members who enabled them, or others who failed to intervene—but on the one who drives all the evil in this world, Satan, our true enemy, for hatred will destroy the soul that harbors it.

My father proved that no one cared what he was doing to me. He made a practice of violating me in the presence of others. We had one housekeeper who walked in and out of the room while he openly molested me. I thought surely she would tell my mother. She finally quit her job, but if she said anything, I never heard about it.

No life is so damaged, no soul so stained, that God would disdain to die for it.

What did I just say? I blew right past that memory in three sentences. My father molested me in the presence of our housekeeper. She quit her job, but nothing was ever done about it. And that's it? Stop! I need to pause, take a deep breath, and ask what my memory is telling me. I cannot do this alone. It's too heavy, too dangerous. I seek out my therapist and we do some work on posttraumatic stress.

If you have experienced abuse, I can assure you that post-traumatic stress disorder (PTSD) has come to live in your house. It will destroy you and wreak havoc on your relationships if you allow it to hide in the shadows, doing its destructive work. But it does not have to hide. Every particle of our past has the potential to destroy, or to bring glory to the God who has delivered us from the hands of the violent man.

Don't tell me that the man was not violent—if you were abused, the abuser was violent. Abuse is a violent act of destruction, rupturing our peace, damaging our soul. Silent seduction of the soul is just as insidious as the rape of a young girl's body. Either way, recovery will require that the victim learn to recognize the symptoms of posttraumatic stress disorder and deal with it in a way that restores health and peace to her distressed soul.

I went back to the memory I've just described. I invited another person into the recovery process. And together we revisited the scene of the crime.

Memory

I close my eyes and quiet my spirit. I am in a safe place now. I've learned how to go there when the pain becomes intense.

I hope you have created your safe place, too. One that exists in your mind, where no one can take it from you or invade its safety. It's the place you can go when you are under assault, when memories taunt you—and when you must forcibly expel them from the shadows in which they hide.

No life is so damaged, no soul so stained, that God would disdain to die for it.

If I Should Tell

I know it well! The sense of scarlet
Springing up inside of me,
Consuming all pretense
Of dignity.

I can imagine. Oh the shame...
Of shocked faces—wagging tongues
"I knew it all along," they'd say.
"Look what they have done."

Shriveled up, like iron-scorched lace
Inside this body—behind this face
Is another person, longing to escape.
But I don't know how.

If I should tell...
I can see it now.

No life is so damaged, no soul so stained, that God would disdain to die for it.

In my mind I go to Old Mill and wander there. I visualize the scenery, the buildings, the feel of the grass, the fragrance of the foliage, the scent of flowers, the rustling of wind through autumn leaves, the morning dew on the grass. I imagine myself sitting on a ledge that circles the tall stone building alone in the early morning solitude. This is my safe place.

Now I am ready. I settle back in my chair and close my eyes. It's quiet here. I have invited the Holy Spirit, my Counselor sent by God, to walk with me through this process. Here I go, back into the past. I can feel my heart beat faster. I breathe deeply. God help me. I am sitting on my father's bed. He hears the housekeeper coming. There's no need for me to relate the details of abuse—if you've been there, you know what happens next. But I am not the child on the bed, not now. I'm an adult observer. I'm watching the eyes, the window of the soul. I see the housekeeper. A black woman, robust, strong, she's in her late twenties or early thirties. Her hair is pulled back from her face. She takes in the scene in my father's bedroom. Her eyes register surprise. She shakes her head, as if to say, "this is not happening. It can't be." She leaves the room. A few minutes later she comes back.

I glance at my father's face now. A face consumed with lust, depraved. A twisted smile. His face looks pasty, pale. He is watching the housekeeper. This time she looks disgusted. A little sad. And determined. Abruptly, she leaves the room.

∼

Suddenly, I know what I've missed. I remembered the scene, but I missed the *story* because I fled from it so quickly that I didn't read between the lines. Until now. Now, having relived the scene, I know the story, and something deep down inside me, beneath the layers of turmoil and trauma, has changed. I have discovered two things:

No life is so damaged, no soul so stained, that God would disdain to die for it.

One, I believe my father was using me in much the same way that the sex addict will sometimes look at pornography with the object of his lust in order to arouse her. He shared me—his little piece of porn—with the housekeeper, hoping to arouse her.

Two, I had an ally in the housekeeper. Though she quit her job a few days later, I believe she tried, in some way, to make a difference. She alone, of those who knew or even suspected the abuse, directed her accusing gaze at my father. I was exonerated. She did not turn her loathing on me. He made me feel like feces under his feet. She gave me dignity—if only for a moment.

I know that we shouldn't allow one person of any race to influence us regarding all others of that race, but I've always been drawn to black people with a sort of affinity that I didn't understand. I realize now that I'm predisposed to liking others who share an essential characteristic with the woman who rejected my father without incorporating me into his lewd obscenity.

Why does the dissection of this memory give me such peace? Because it tells me that I was not alone as I believed. Someone, even though I do not know her name, cared about me. She knew my secret and she did not shame me.

When I entered my therapist's office, carrying the burden of this memory unresolved, I was overwhelmed. When I left, I was at peace. When I entered, she asked me what I felt like when I thought of the memory. I said I felt like I was a pile of dog poo.

"Shit," she said. "You feel like shit."

How we hate the crass words that best describe our agony. She was right. I felt like shit. Dirty, smelly, a blight on the landscape.

When our session was finished, she asked what I felt like. I felt vindicated. Relieved. I felt sorry for the child forced to submit to her abuser, like a child porn star in an X-rated movie. I felt strong, protective. I would protect the child. And the child was—and is—a part of me. I felt like a brave, strong, woman who had just slain her dragon.

No life is so damaged, no soul so stained, that God would disdain to die for it.

Long Forgotten

I had accompanied my father and several other relatives on a trip to Illinois where one of his cousins had been involved in a tragic accident. I remember my father pressuring me to share his hotel room. I was terrified. I remember walking across a busy street, trying desperately to catch up with my aunt and her daughters. I kept hanging around them, hoping to avoid my father, to get out of spending the night alone with him. I hated the way he looked at me, the way he touched me. My aunt must have realized that I didn't want to stay with my father, for she told him that I was staying in her room.

The next day, he made me pay for it. He openly violated me on an elevator—in the presence of his male cousin. The cousin stayed on good terms with my father as if nothing had happened, saying nothing about what my father had done until years later, when it was too late to make a difference.

> *The wicked freely strut about when what is vile is honored among men.* —Psalm 12:8

Reflections

Those who suspect that a child is being abused have the responsibility of reporting it. I know of a grandmother whose six-year-old granddaughter told her in explicit detail what her mother's boyfriend was doing to her. The grandmother called social services and reported it.

Social services contacted the mother. The mother responded by not only telling her child to deny the charges, but by actually convincing her that it didn't happen. The child denied that anything had happened to her. The saddest part of this story is that the grandmother was denied access to the child because of her intervention. The boyfriend eventually left the situation, but the child learned a harsh lesson: it's not safe to tell.

No life is so damaged, no soul so stained, that God would disdain to die for it.

I've often wondered if the story might have turned out differently had the grandmother known how to prepare the child for the pressure she was sure to face when the truth was revealed. What if she'd said, "Honey, you're so brave to tell me about that."? If she had knelt down on the child's level, looked her in the eyes, and said, "I want you to know that it wasn't your fault, and no matter what anybody tells you, you did the right thing to tell me. I want you to promise me something... promise me that you'll keep telling the truth no matter what happens, okay?" It might not have changed anything, but at least the child would have been prepared for what happened next. And maybe, just maybe, she would have had the courage to tell the truth.

One day Jesus Christ was teaching in Galilee. He called a little child to him, set him in the midst of them, and said:

> *Whoever causes one of these little ones who believe in me to stumble, it would be better for him to have a heavy millstone hung around his neck and to be drowned in the depth of the sea... woe to that man through whom the stumbling block comes!* —Matthew 18:6–7

The disciples of Jesus must have been greatly impacted by these words, because not only Matthew, but Mark and Luke recorded these words in their epistles. Woe to the one who causes a little child to stumble!

Questions for Reflection

Caution: Please do not address these questions alone. Approach them only with the guidance of a counselor who can help you process them.

1. If you were abused, what made you afraid to tell?

2. Maybe you did tell, and someone invalidated your truth. That person, if he or

---

No life is so damaged, no soul so stained, that God would disdain to die for it.

she has not repented, stands on dangerous ground. God is seriously angry with those who cause a child to stumble.

3. Because of what you have been through, do you think you would you recognize the signs of victimization in a child? What would you do about it?

Chapter Thirteen
Plunder of a Young Girl's Soul

THE PROCESS OF BECOMING "Daddy's girl" was subtle at first. I was always the helper, always the nurturer. I actually enjoyed reading to my father. When he asked me to teach him to read and spell better, I agreed willingly. I loved to teach. I was flattered: I must be really smart to actually teach my father. I was unprepared for the awkward discomfort at the table. Something I couldn't define about the way he looked at me, the way he touched me, stirred up familiar, though forgotten, feelings. I began to spend a lot of time in the bathroom. "I've got to go to the bathroom," usually meant a reprieve of at least ten or fifteen minutes. I kept books hidden in the closet and I immersed myself in them. I resorted to another practice as well. Fantasy. I had the beginning spark of a novelist, even then.

Behind the closet door, beneath the piles of dirty laundry, was an escape hatch. I pulled the soiled clothing aside and lifted the hatch.

And then, my hero at the time, Captain Kirk, the awesome commander of *Star Trek*, would enter the room. I was his secret right-hand girl. We sat together on the side of the tub, planning remarkable strategies to save the world.

Other heroes came along: Little Joe Cartwright from *Bonanza*, and the beautiful, bald Kojak. Oh, my, that eight-by-eight room became my sanctuary where a life filled with excitement, affection, and respect came to life in ten-minute increments.

Now please don't hold this against me, but I even learned to imitate the sound of flatulence from behind the closed door, as proof that I really needed to spend that much time in the bathroom. I could sometimes stretch my break out to fifteen minutes or more by employing this diversionary tactic. It was embarrassing to my father when company happened to show up while I was in the midst of my game, but I may have secretly delighted in his embarrassment.

That is how it came about that I began to read to my father. It was part of his education. Eventually, he began to spend more time in bed, and that was where he wanted me to read to him. After an argument between him and my mother, my father would often retreat to his bed, and my mother would urge me to go lie down with him and read to him.

How could I let my mother know that I dreaded going, that something terrible waited for me there? I seemed to be the sacrificial peace offering.

I dared not offend the only person who seemed to care that I existed—my father, my abuser. Before long, however, there was no question about what I saw in his eyes, because it transferred to his hands. At first, I employed the defense mechanism of denial, ignoring the signals his touch was sending to my brain. But eventually, revulsion and excitement began to inhabit the same heart, sickening me while simultaneously seducing me.

After a while, I had to admit that the touch felt good, even though I hated myself for accepting it. I vacillated between two equally strong feelings—hatred and desire. I hated the guilt, the shame, the sickness that I felt every time my father touched me, but I could not deny the pleasure of my physical response to it, either.

No life is so damaged, no soul so stained, that God would disdain to die for it.

Like a piece of meat torn between two wolves, I was broken, bleeding, and helpless to determine which beast would win.

I did the laundry. I cleaned the house. I got sick and prayed to die, all to no avail. I no longer enjoyed reading to my father, in fact I hated it, and I hated myself because I knew that after a while I would respond to his touch and become a participant in the act that shamed and sickened me. Thinking I was a willing participant, I didn't realize that the will had been jerked out of me and that it was his will that I was submitting to. I desperately wanted to understand what was happening to me, but was too ashamed to ask for help.

The only one I asked was the abuser. Once, when he was pouting and acting miserable because I would not come and "read" to him, I remember going into his room with a basket of folded laundry on my hip and asking, "Would Uncle Basil do this to Janet (my one-year-older cousin)?" I wasn't being confrontational; I really wanted to know. Was it just me going through this, or was this a terrible but common part of growing up?

My father responded with wounded anger. "How could you ask that—like it would be the same thing?"

How was it different? More confused than ever, I wandered off, acutely aware of my father's anger as he retreated into offended silence. I didn't know what to call it back then, but I experienced my father's withdrawal as emotional abandonment. I learned to fear that feeling—that dark, oppressive loneliness, that sad, angry silence—more than I hated the guilt and the shame.

I read a story once of the history of piracy. The pirates would light a beacon to attract the attention of a solitary ship lost at sea. Those aboard the ship assumed that help was near when they saw the light, and hurried toward it, only to be captured and plundered.

I knew I was being plundered, but a child alone in the storm on a leaky ship will

No life is so damaged, no soul so stained, that God would disdain to die for it.

go toward the only light she sees, for any kind of love is better than no love at all. She will not know, until the storm is past, that what was offered to her was not love, not even in some twisted, perverted form, but lust, deprivation, and manipulation. She will not know that the feigned affection of the abuser is but a prelude to jealousy and violence, and that when the trap is sprung, there will be no way out.

A Loss of Freedom

I was in the seventh grade when I lost my last tentative grip on autonomy. Like a tree shredder that sucks the careless worker into its steel jaws, the next trap my father set devoured me. The child that I was ceased to exist, the self was sucked out of me.

My school gave us a half day off. Knowing my mother wouldn't be home, and dreading going home when my father might be there alone, I chose to spend the extra time with Laura, another girl from my class. I believe I experienced my first taste of freedom that day. My father timed me everywhere I went, and watched the clock to make sure I had no time for myself. He couldn't time me now, for he didn't know that school was out early! I had three hours to do anything I wanted—a rare opportunity.

What can two seventh-grade girls do in three hours without wheels or money? We walked down to the new Holiday Inn on the corner and rode the elevators up and down. We robbed the ice bin and felt really naughty. And then I went home.

My father was waiting for me. I could tell by his icy glare that I was in trouble. "Where were you?" How had he found out that we'd gotten out early? I told him the truth. He said he didn't believe me. "If you were at the hotel," he said, "you must have been looking for a man to sleep with."

I never saw it coming. Accused of looking for sex? At thirteen? I went to church

---

No life is so damaged, no soul so stained, that God would disdain to die for it.

every Wednesday night and twice on Sunday. I was a good girl. I never went out—anywhere. I had never done anything to earn my father's distrust. But of course it wasn't about trust. It was about manipulation.

It got late. I was tired. My father wouldn't let me go to bed. Every time I started to nod off, he would yell at me. I was used to him yelling and throwing things, but it was usually at my mother.

I longed for the morning so I could escape out the door to school. Again I was disappointed. The other children left for school, my mother went off to work, and I was left alone with my father. Day after agonizing day. I'm not sure how long it took for him to get what he wanted, but he wanted a confession. It didn't matter if it was true or not. So I made something up. Laura and I went to her house and her brother was there. He had just come home from prison and…

My father asked for details. Of course I couldn't give him any. I had no idea how one went about having sex. My father didn't care. He had what he wanted. I was overcome with shame and despair.

My father put his head in his hands and sobbed loudly. When my mother came home, he told her of my "confession."

She said something like, "Oh, Linda, how could you?" and walked out of the room. I felt like a rag doll on a trash heap—dirty and worn-out.

I remember sitting at the kitchen table, scrunched as small as I could make myself. I didn't know what to do. My father, my abuser and, ironically, my only supporter, had abandoned me. Hate poured out of his eyes, hate, disappointment, and betrayal. Like a jealous lover, he seemed sick of me.

I hated myself, too. I knew I was making mistakes, doing everything wrong. I was done with it. The only way out was suicide. I wasn't sure if I had the courage to see it through, but I began my letter….

I could hear my parents talking about me in the next room. My mother was

No life is so damaged, no soul so stained, that God would disdain to die for it.

agreeing to take me to the doctor to see if I had really been sexually penetrated. Hope flared in my heart. They could tell that? I'd be exonerated! I crumpled the note and threw it away. I got ready to go. The doctor would give me an okay! I could prove my innocence. All would be forgiven.

Then my father told me that he believed me. I breathed a deep sigh of relief. This would soon be over.

Later that evening we got a call that my father's mother was in the hospital. My mother wanted to go and be with her. I could only beg her with my eyes not to leave me. She didn't get the message. That night, my father would not allow me to go to my bed; he made me go to his. He closed the door to my siblings' bedrooms, warning them to stay in their rooms. I don't know what reason he gave them, if any at all, but I kept watching the shadows in the hallway, certain that one of my siblings would walk into the room and witness my humiliation.

The next morning, I went to school with my eyes fixed on the ground. It would be a long time before I would dare to look anyone in the eyes again. I was nauseated and weak. I longed to end my life. I began to fantasize about suicide. I made desperate plans to escape. Every day as I walked to school, I thought of how I could just keep on walking. Anywhere would be better than home. But I couldn't bear to leave my siblings. What would happen to them if I weren't there? Which of my sisters would take my place? I couldn't take them with me and I couldn't bear to leave them behind.

Reflections

I was forced to fabricate a lie. I was not a liar and was ashamed of my deceit. I did it to survive. By the time my father made his move on me, openly molesting me, I was already feeling dirty and spiritually compromised. When my mother left to spend the night at the hospital, I had no energy left to fight. I was mentally, emotionally

No life is so damaged, no soul so stained, that God would disdain to die for it.

Somewhere

If I could leave
Where would I go?
Somewhere quiet.
Somewhere I know
There is such a place.

Somewhere a laugh
Is not a joke
At my expense.
Somewhere a smile
Is more than
A cheap reward
For giving in.

The touch of tender
Hands, somewhere,
Can be trusted.
Somewhere there are
Eyes that shine
With love, not lust.
Somewhere, I can rest

And not awake
At night
To the sound of
Angry voices and
Hurt cries.

Somewhere, there is
Someone who will
Love me as I am
The real me
That even I
Myself have
Never found.

If I can just
Keep dreaming
And believe
In such a place
Perhaps, someday
I will find a way
To go there.

and physically exhausted. This is the set-up my father used to destroy the last of my defenses. What about you? What was the setup the abuser used to entrap you for that first overt move to violate you?

I know that sexual abuse is not always physical. In *The Wounded Heart*, Dan Allender explores the types of sexual abuse. He says that mental and emotional sexual abuse, which cannot be physically proven, can be just as debilitating as physical sexual abuse. If that is your experience, what happened and how did it affect you?

A few years ago I counseled with a twelve-year-old girl whose family attended our church. She was about to start menses and was hormonally out of control. She wasn't promiscuous, and had never been abused. She came from a stable, loving family. Yet every day she got an uncontrollable urge to masturbate. She agonized over what she was doing, feeling guilty and ashamed.

Within a few months, she started her first period. The urges diminished. She no longer needed the release masturbation had offered to her overwhelmed emotions, and gladly moved on without it.

Imagine if that child had been raised in an abusive home. What would have happened if someone in the home, a father, a brother, a friend, or an uncle who had frequent access to the girl at that vulnerable time in her life, had been an abuser? Her life story might have been forever altered. Thank God that didn't happen, and she is a well-adjusted teen today, one who wears a covenant ring to express her commitment to sexual purity.

Sadly, more than one of every four women has a different story to tell, for they will have suffered sexual abuse before the age of eighteen. Boys are violated, too. By some estimates, one in every six boys will suffer sexual abuse. Add to this number the one in seven women who will be physically raped, and it is obvious that sexual crime is pandemic in our society.

The dynamics of rape and sexual abuse are, obviously, different, but every

No life is so damaged, no soul so stained, that God would disdain to die for it.

sexual crime infiltrates the heart of the child where it does its insidious work causing defilement, distress, and shame. The rapist takes what he wants by using physical
violence. The abuser uses violence as well, emotionally battering the child's soul into
submission. Sexual crimes of both natures project the shame onto the victim, like
hot tar that bonds to the flesh, burning, wounding, scarring. Extracting projected
shame from the victim's wounds is vital to recovery.

According to the prophet Isaiah, Jesus went to the cross bearing our shame and
carrying our sorrow (Isaiah 53). Intentionally, deliberately, He did that for us, and we
have no right to continue to carry what He died to purchase. Let Him take it. He
alone can bear it, for we are not strong enough. It will crush us, but He knows what
to do and has the power to do it. He has taken captivity captive and let the con-
demned go free!

～

My Prayer for Today

Oh, God, You see our wounds, and I know that You long to heal them. Processing
our pain is like applying antiseptic to an open wound: it stings and it cleanses. We
submit ourselves to You—not an easy thing to do when we've experienced the
betrayal of our soul in the past. As much as we are able, we trust You with our heart.

Amen.

No life is so damaged, no soul so stained, that God would disdain to die for it.

I am going to kill the old man," my father said, throwing the guns in the trunk of his car. And then he was gone. Leaving me to pace the floor while the other children slept.

Chapter Fourteen
They Will Pay

WHEN I REFUSED to acknowledge my father's unspoken demands, he manipulated me by mistreating my mother and siblings, treating them more harshly and more violently day by day until I gave in. He never said that he'd leave them alone if I submitted, he just got over being angry when he got his way. It was like turning a switch off and on. If he could use me to relieve his sexual tension, he became conciliatory and even made an effort to treat everyone better. If he couldn't—we'd better all look out!

Memory

My father had pushed my mother around and yelled at her all night, every night, for a long time. I could hear things breaking and my mother crying out as if in fear or pain.

She left, telling us it was just for a while, until she could figure out what to do. She went to her mother's house. I didn't get along with my grandmother, but I loved

Grandpa. He treated me with respect. He let me know, in his own wordless way, that he loved me.

My father commanded my mother to come home. She wasn't ready. He went to his closet and took out his guns. I don't know how many, but it looked like far more than he needed to do what he said he planned.

"I'm going to go kill the old man."

My stomach retched, reacting as much to the sick rage in my father's watery blue eyes, as to his words. My grandfather. He's going to kill my grandfather. Why? Because Grandpa had allowed my mother to come home.

After he drove away, I walked the floor, biting my nails, squeezing my sides, bruising my flesh, imagining my grandparents dead, my mother shot, bleeding, maybe dying. While the younger children slept, oblivious to the drama taking place on my grandparents' farm, I paced. I worried. I prayed.

Finally, he came back in the door. "I didn't kill the old man," he said. "I just couldn't do it." As if he were the most tenderhearted man on earth for showing such great compassion, he put his head in his hands, shedding crocodile tears. "He says your mother is coming home," my father said, and I felt relief wash over me. Weak and tired, I went off to bed, hoping it would be soon.

Reflections

I don't know how old I was, but the message was clear. Anyone who dares leave this house against my father's will not only risks her own life, but the life of anyone who supports her.

It was only when I reprocessed this memory many years later that I realized why my father had taken so many guns. The drama of loading seven or eight rifles into the trunk of his car, all the while raging about what he was going to do to

No life is so damaged, no soul so stained, that God would disdain to die for it.

someone I loved, was an effective lesson for one small girl who might have somehow worked up the courage to flee.

Questions for Reflection

Please do not attempt to answer these questions without the support of a counselor.

1. *How did the abuser manipulate you? Did he intimidate you with his rage and violence toward others? Did he treat you as special, and manipulate your need for love, acceptance, and esteem, or did he frighten you if you didn't comply? Maybe he did both, reward you for compliance and punish you for not obeying.*

   a. *How did he reward compliance?*

   b. *How did he punish resistance?*

2. *Were other people involved in his strategy? Whom did he use against you?*

3. *Is there anyone who would have helped you had they known? Why didn't you tell them?*

4. *What would you say to a child in the position you were in?*
   Say it to the child within. You may want to write it in your journal. Don't worry if you can only write one or two words. It's a start.

～

No life is so damaged, no soul so stained, that God would disdain to die for it.

My Prayer for Today

Heavenly Father, I know that my reader is suffering as she looks back into the sepulcher of abuse and examines the 'truths' that she believed as a child. Help her to recognize the lies that made her vulnerable, the lies that kept her confined to a world of pain. Keep her safe as she walks the healing pathway and let her know that you walk beside her.

Amen.

The Raising of Lazarus, *by Karl Isakson*

The dead man came out (of the sepulcher), his hands and feet wrapped… and Jesus said to them, "Take off the grave clothes and let him go."—John 11:44

No life is so damaged, no soul so stained, that God would disdain to die for it.

Chapter Fifteen
Where was God?

As GOD BEGAN to gently touch the fabric of my life, loosening the silken threads that bound my broken heart, memories began to emerge. They came at unexpected times when I wasn't consciously thinking about the past. As I remembered, I began to understand how I had become entrapped, why I'd responded as I had. It would take many months of remembering, processing, and understanding before I would ask the question that had lingered, just beneath the surface of my consciousness, most of my life. The question I didn't dare ask, for the answer might crush my already bruised heart, was "Where were you, Lord? If you loved me, why did you allow me to suffer so?"

Reflections

The eleventh chapter of the book of John, particularly the story of Jesus restoring life to Lazarus, has special meaning for me.

There was a time, several years before I had the courage to flee the sepulcher, that I heard Jesus calling me in a unique and wonderful way. Though I failed to heed his call, I knew that I had heard him, and in time I began to believe that there was hope after all.

Why Did You Not Come Sooner?

You called him forth—Lazarus!
He came at the sound of your voice.
He loved you so—you roused him
From the grave.

And yet, you could have come
Sooner.
Before he suffered all the pain,
Before he died and others grieved his loss.
You could have come—but you
Chose to stay.

Three days he lay in that dark tomb.
He knew you could have called him
Sooner.
He knew he didn't have to die, for you
Had the touch of life.

"Where were you, Lord?" his sister cried
And just like me—he died—
Not knowing you would come.

A thousand times I thought you'd come
Unwrap the grave cloths from my feet
You'd shout, "Roll back that stone!"
You'd come for me.

A thousand times—my hopes have died
And I, with Lazarus' sister, cried,
"Why did you not come?"

No life is so damaged, no soul so stained, that God would disdain to die for it.

I was in my twenties, maybe twenty-five, perhaps older. Time has a way of distorting itself when we live in a traumatic fog. Every night when I retired to my room, I sat in my rocking chair and opened my Bible. After a while I noticed that every time I opened the Bible it parted at the same place: John, chapter 11. Something about that seemed strange to me, so I began reading different Bibles. Still, they opened almost invariably to John chapter 11. I began asking, "God, what are you trying to tell me?" I wasn't afraid, but I was progressively aware of some kind of supernatural involvement taking place in the comparative peace and quiet of my late-night refuge.

One Sunday I went to church as usual, the only difference being that my father, who usually insisted on sitting with me like the doting parent he pretended to be, stayed home sick. So I was free to listen to the message without the familiar discomfort of sitting in church beside the man with whom I was engaged in a shameful, debilitating dance of death.

The pastor came to the pulpit and said, "Open your Bible to John Chapter Eleven." My heart began to beat faster. It pounded so hard that I thought it must be visible. My mouth went dry and I opened my Bible. There it was: John, chapter 11.

The message took twenty or thirty minutes, but I can sum it up in a few sentences. Jesus called Lazarus out of the sepulcher—the grave. He came forth alive—but still bound.

"What," the pastor asked, "is binding you today? What keeps you from serving God with joy and freedom, unhindered by the trappings of the grave?"

"Come to the altar," he invited, "and leave your grave cloths here. You can be free!"

I was one of the first people out of my seat. I practically ran to the altar. God was calling. I knew he was calling me.

I would like to say that I left my grave cloths at the altar that day. I would like to tell you that I walked away from there a free woman, unhindered by my past and my

---

No life is so damaged, no soul so stained, that God would disdain to die for it.

pain. But that would be a lie, for I didn't walk away free. But I walked away believing that someday, somehow, I might be. And I believe that was the message my Heavenly Father was speaking to me. That was the hope that he prepared my ravaged heart to receive.

I know the plans that I have for you, the Lord God spoke through the prophet Jeremiah, *plans to give you a future and a hope*. I know, too, and today I'm living out the hope that You gave me back then. I'm so glad that You knew, You planned, and You gave, for that is why I'm alive today.

More Reflections

"Where were you, God?"

Have you dared to ask? Maybe you've asked the question a thousand times. If God is a loving God, and He is all-powerful, why did He allow this terrible thing to happen to me?

You are alive today. And you are in recovery. You have come out of the sepulcher of sexual abuse. Or maybe you haven't. Maybe you're still there and are looking for the way out. Keep searching, keep reading, keep processing, and the light of God's love will penetrate the cold, dark, tomb of abuse. The stone will be rolled away, and you will come forth, just as Lazarus did. Maybe you'll be "wrapped hand and foot with grave cloths" as Lazarus was when Jesus called him out of the grave. But Lazarus did not stay bound by the trappings of his death—and neither will you.

Jesus said He came so that we might have life and have it more abundantly. Abundant life! Unrestrained, unbounded, unfettered, unwrapped! Let's start unwrapping the grave cloths. The process starts with the question, Where were You, God? Mary, the sister of Lazarus, must have asked this question, for she fell at the feet of Jesus and said, "Lord, if you had been here, my brother would not have died." Mary questioned, but she questioned on her knees, and Jesus wept. He groaned in

No life is so damaged, no soul so stained, that God would disdain to die for it.

His spirit (John 11:33) and was troubled. Why do we think He doesn't care? Because we don't know Him. We're ignorant of His passionate love for us. But we need Him, and if we're going to rely on Him in the future, we need to know where He was in the past. Perhaps by daring to look back—into the shadows of the tomb—we'll see that He was there all along.

Let's look at our life and ask Him to show us where He was.

In My Life, God Was There...

In people who cared and somehow tried to intervene and help me. Mrs. Brown, my junior high school counselor was one of these. She did her best to draw the truth out of me. Who was there for you?

In circumstances: When I would have taken my life or been destructive in some other way, something happened that changed my mind. Was it just coincidence, or did my Creator plan the diversion that saved me? List any possibilities of your own.

In my own actions: I'm amazed when I think of what could have happened. I could have lost my mind and never got it back. I could have taken my own life. I could have killed my abuser. I could have—you name it.

He was calling. We didn't hear. The hurricane of pain that swirled around us kept us from hearing His voice. He would have led us out of the grave if we had been able to hear. It's not our fault that we didn't hear him. Neither is it His.

After one terribly painful episode when I had tried with everything within me to be strong at any cost, someone I loved was suffering over something my father had done to punish me for my resistance. I cried out to God, "I put myself out on a limb for You—and You let me down!" And I heard Him say to me, "I put myself on

---

No life is so damaged, no soul so stained, that God would disdain to die for it.

You Came For Me

How did you know
If you were not there
That Lazarus had died?
Could it be that you
Were present
Kneeling at his side?

Yet, countless souls
Around the world
Fled helpless jars
Of clay that day.
How could you
Be with all, yet stay
In Galilee?

Could it be
That you did come
To seeking hearts
Around the Globe,
Unseen, to hold
Them while they died?

For it is not
Your mission here
To see that none
Would die.
You came
To offer new
For old.
For rusted vessels
You brought gold.

You came
To overcome the grave
Yet, we must
Enter just the same
Until we hear your call.

Then—rise we shall
At your command
And you yourself
Will loose the bands
That bind us
To the grave.

the cross for you ...." I know that God the Father agonized over the abuse I endured. I know because of something Jesus said: "Whatever has been done to the least of those who love me—has been done to me." (Matthew 25:40.)

God was in me when my father abused me. He did not leave me or forsake me. God have mercy on the man who violated a child whose faith was in the Lord.

"Where were you, God?"

"I was in you." God.

∼

My Prayer for Today

Thank you, God, that You didn't leave me, even though I couldn't see you, feel you, or hear you. I know that You were there, for I am alive today and in recovery. Please help me to see You in my past. Help me to see You in the interventions that kept me alive, in the diversions that kept me sane, in the small joys that gave me hope, and in the victories that have been mine. Thank You for the victories that are in process inside me.

Amen.

> *He places detour signs across the road that leads to hell,*
> *and calls until his voice is heard by he who*
> *knows it well.*

No life is so damaged, no soul so stained, that God would disdain to die for it.

Chapter Sixteen
Where Was the Church?

Twenty-plus years have passed since I walked away from the sepulcher of abuse. Our society has gone from denial of the existence of sexual abuse—especially in the Church—to acceptance that it is a problem, even among believers.

I once heard a pastor say, "It is said that the only crime in which the victim bears the shame is sexual abuse!" This should not be so, especially in the household of faith. It is time for the fellowship of believers to embrace the survivor as a victor rather than a victim.

Survivors do not want to be pitied, they do not want to be marginalized, and they dread being shunned. The church of Jesus Christ will not be able to help the survivors among us heal until we learn to handle their pain.

Recently I heard of a licensed counselor who set up her practice in a secluded place, while letting her church family know that they could come and receive counsel for sexual abuse without anyone knowing. It is as if she was saying, "Keep the secret in the closet. I will validate your shame." I know she meant well, but no wonder we're afraid to go to the church and confess our victimization. The church will pull the drapes and leave us in our darkness.

But not every church! Many churches, today, open their doors to hurting people from every walk of life. They offer Celebrate Recovery and other step programs that are designed to set people free. Participants get together, usually once a week, and sing and clap their hands. They share their stories around the Word of God and affirm each other. The church is waking up to the wounded among us.

There have always been some in the church who loved us unconditionally. I knew a few of those people, and they probably kept me alive. It was through them that the light shone through the cracks and gave me hope that someday my darkness would end.

One of those people was Floy Avants, an old-time preacher who loved me enough to be my "Missionette mom" and pray for me. I talked to her a few years ago, and she told me, "Remember the potholder you made for me when you were in Missionettes? I've kept it in my kitchen ever since, and every time I pass it, I pray for you." You prayed me through it all, Sister Floy. For over forty years you've stood in the shadows and prayed for a child who became a woman who loves God and wants to pass it on. Thank you.

And then there were Brother George and Sister Dorothy. They loved me. They may not have understood my situation, and they didn't intervene, but they reached out to me with the hands of Christ. They made me feel like maybe I was worth something after all.

I once called the church I had grown up in and asked a question that had nagged at me for a long time. I asked someone who'd been there all along, "Did you and other leaders in the church know that I was being abused?" She said that they suspected it, but didn't know what to do. She summarized the church's response to the problem in the next sentence: "We were afraid that if we said anything, your

No life is so damaged, no soul so stained, that God would disdain to die for it.

Step in the Water

"Step in the water," they all said,
"And God will take you
By the hand and lead you to the
Promised land."
What water? Where is the water?
Already—don't you see
It is over my head!
Where do I go to step?

The promised land? Oh, how I
Want to go!
But it is not for me.
I am over my head already
And sick in my soul.

It is for the pretty ones—the sweet
For little girls with braids and curls
Whose mother's pray them
Into sleep.
It is for the deacon's little boy..
For none like me.
It is a ploy to soothe me
While I drown…

No life is so damaged, no soul so stained, that God would disdain to die for it.

father might kill you and your mother or even the whole family."

How did they know about his violence? Maybe my mother told someone about the guns. Maybe she told them about how he'd threatened to kill her parents. Maybe she told them he sometimes held the gun to her head all night while he railed at her. I don't know, but I understand the fear that kept the church silent, for it was the same fear that kept me cowering in the dark.

Questions for Reflection

Please prepare yourself as suggested in previous chapters before you attempt to answer these questions.

1. *Did you attend church during the time that you were being abused? Do you think anyone there knew? Did you dare to tell anyone?*

2. *Did you have a hero to pray for you during that time—someone like Floy Avants or Brother George and Sister Dorothy, who would have helped if they had known how?*

3. *Who was it, and why do you think they didn't intervene in your situation?*

4. *What do you think would happen if you told your pastor or another spiritual leader today?*

5. *Does your church have a counseling team that's equipped to deal specifically with sexual abuse?*

I'm going to say something that I know is controversial. Trained lay counselors and professional Christian counselors are a safer haven for the soul of the sexually battered person than Christian friends and spiritual leaders who haven't studied the

No life is so damaged, no soul so stained, that God would disdain to die for it.

dynamics of the devastating effects of sexual abuse. What you need is understanding and empathy. You need calm, non-reactive counsel from someone who has "heard it all before." What you do not need is to bare your soul, to finally confess your history, to someone who'll be shocked by your pain. And you especially do not need to show your wounds to someone who'll validate your shame. The shame belongs to the abuser, and recovery demands that shame—like misdirected mail—be returned to the sender.

～

My Prayer for Today

Oh, God, give wisdom to my friend who reads this book in her search for understanding. Don't let her be re-victimized by well-meaning friends and leaders who don't understand the wounding of her soul. Lead her to wise counsel and give her courage to share the secrets of her heart in a safe place.

Amen.

No life is so damaged, no soul so stained, that God would disdain to die for it.

Chapter Seventeen
Little Mother

WHEN I WAS THIRTEEN, my youngest sibling, Teddy, was born. Our neighbors called me "little mother," for I was often seen taking long walks with the children, the baby in a stroller and the older ones running, climbing, and playing. We explored all the creeks and railroad tunnels near our home. I tucked Teddy into bed each night with a kiss and a prayer, until my father demanded that I stop "babying" him.

Among my five younger siblings there was ample cause for discipline, had my father been inclined to deliver it. Discipline, however, is not a term you would apply to his parenting style. Punishment, maybe. Abuse, definitely. As children, we really didn't know the difference. What I did know was that if I kept my father happy, his belt was more likely to stay where it belonged, and other, more violent means of correcting my wayward siblings were less likely to occur.

Should I have abandoned my siblings? I know that most people would say that going to the proper authorities about my father's abusive behavior would not have been abandonment. And they would be right. But I couldn't get past the "what ifs." What if I tell and no one believes me? What if I'm taken out of the house and put in a foster home, leaving my siblings behind? I knew what was in store for my sisters. Dear God, I couldn't let that happen.

Perhaps my father would have been removed from the home, but I didn't believe it. Ironically, my greatest fear was that even if I was believed, my father would submit to some form of counseling or correction, and then have the freedom to return home. An unbearable possibility.

I dreaded the "look." You may know the look as well. The eyes narrow as if in pain, the face is drawn downward in deep depression, and a potent mixture of rage, hurt, and disappointment spills out of watery eyes—eyes fixed on yours. It's your fault. But it would be worth it to take the blame, if only you didn't have to just stand there, squirming like a specimen in a glass. If you didn't have to worry about how he was going to make you pay. You could start over, maybe, find a way to make life work.

But that, of course, is out of the question. He is there. Or he'll be back. Staring at you with that look in his eyes. You feel weak, helpless, lost. You feel like a monster, a vile, wicked thing, to be the cause of his pain. But mostly, you just feel alone. Abandoned, like a discarded toy left out in the rain. Shut out, alienated, desperate.

Tell Her to Jump

When I was a young teen, my mother left again. This time I thought she was gone for good. I don't blame her. Her life was at risk and her sanity was under assault. A weaker woman would have lost her mind.

She called once. I answered the phone. She was at the bridge that spanned the Arkansas River.

"Tell your father that I am at the bridge. I am going to jump."

No life is so damaged, no soul so stained, that God would disdain to die for it.

I told him. "Tell her to jump," he said.

Thoughts of suicide raged in my head. I was at my father's mercy—and he had none. I knew what my fate would be if my mother wasn't there. Her presence in the home served to limit his atrocities. With her gone, he would have his way and I'd be lost. I wouldn't survive. I knew it.

When my mother called again, I begged her to come home, and she did. Not because it was safe for her to do so, not because she wanted to, but because she heard the desperation in my voice.

~

My father made me keep a journal. It was divided into ten categories, each labeled with one of my mother's perceived sins. She ignored him, she gossiped about him to her relatives, she stole his glory at work, she put him down, she refused to obey…. I don't remember all the "sins," but I know those were some of them.

He took me to the park and made me walk around with him for miles, for hours. Sometimes he held my hand. I wanted to puke. But I smiled through my nausea and carried on the charade, faithfully writing down all the "sins" of the day that my mother had committed.

After such a hard day, of course he needed consolation. Certainly, he deserved to take a midnight ride. He would provoke an argument with my mother, and the only way to defuse it was for me to go with him on his little ride. Mother told herself that I wanted to go. I think she even asked me a couple of times. I'm sure I gave her the only answer that I could—*of course I want to go. I'm dirt. I'm trash. I'm his plaything. Wouldn't any daughter want to go? What a silly question.*

I went to the bathroom and stood in front of the mirror. I curled my fists into a ball and beat my head until I was dizzy. I practiced my silent scream. I prayed to die.

No life is so damaged, no soul so stained, that God would disdain to die for it.

My Mother's Wrongs

Shattered dishes, broken plates
Thrown away—oh, what a waste!
But it was not your fault, I know
She made you mad—you're mad
And so...

You pushed her and the table fell
You said she was too fat, and—well
She made you mad—it was her fault.
I knew no better—I was taught....

Then you came, with furrowed brow,
To my hiding place, "We must go now...
You told me all that you'd endured
That day. I knew there was no cure.
You filled my head throughout the night,
Until it broke—oh what a sight—
With all the things my mother said
And all she did to make you mad.

Before you bring me home at dawn,
I'll hear it all—on, on, and on...
Pressing me beneath the sadness
Of my mother's wrongs
And your madness.

And then I put a smile on my face and marched out the door. He would bring me home in the early hours of morning, while it was still dark, so no one would see that my plaster smile was broken. No hope, no way out, no one cares, not even God.

∿

My Prayer for Today

Heavenly Father, I thank You for this truth—that You never *punish* your children, instead You *discipline* those You love. Some of us may have punished our own body for its betrayal of our soul by cutting, starving, or otherwise wounding our selves. Please forgive us for this wrong, and help us learn to love ourselves so that we can love others. Only then will we be free to live by the golden rule: "Love your neighbor as yourself."

Amen.

No life is so damaged, no soul so stained, that God would disdain to die for it.

Chapter Eighteen
Do I Stay—or Run Away?

L ATE ONE EVENING, I was walking home from church. I was going to spend the night at Grandma Bertha's house. I walked with my eyes on the ground. I wore my shame like a garment—a filthy rag. I was sure my guilt was obvious to everyone. Like Hester in *The Scarlet Letter* who wore an "A" on her breast, I was sure incest, though I didn't yet know the word, was inscribed across my forehead for all to see.

As I tried for the thousandth time to figure out what to do about it, tears flowed down my cheeks. A car pulled alongside, and the door swung open. A middle-aged man asked, "Is something wrong?"

Was that compassion in his voice, or did he want to hurt me? He commanded, "Get in." I shook my head, all the while wondering if I dared to do as he said. Run away. Escape. Where would he take me? Could it be any worse than home? Then I remembered my siblings. I could not abandon them. I would go home.

Grandma Bertha was my favorite person, and her house was my only refuge from the misery of home. Unfortunately, she figured out that my father was molesting me. This was unfortunate because Grandma tried to stop it, and the only thing it stopped was my being allowed to visit her. I grieved when my siblings went to see Grandma and I couldn't go. I missed her so much. I worried about her because she had emphysema and suffered a lot.

Grandma died when I was fifteen years old. That was the last time I cried. Something happened soon after her funeral that drove me deeper into the abyss of despair.

My Grandma weighed less than a hundred pounds, but I believe my father was afraid of her, for he did things after her death that he had never dared to do while she was alive. I gave up on life and accepted my position as a chink in the dam of my father's perversion, believing that I alone held back the violence and lust that threatened to consume all of us—my life had no other value. My only dream, and it was a faint one, was that I would someday escape and go to Africa as a spinster missionary. I knew that love and marriage were out of the question for me. I was damaged merchandise, used goods.

As I considered my options, every choice seemed dark and dangerous, the consequences unknown. I had no idea how to help myself. I felt like the experimental dog in Martin Seligman's discovery of what he called "learned helplessness."

What Can I Do?

I could run way	I've heard that there	They'd hurt	Perhaps, he'll let
But where	Are predators	A little girl	Me be,
Would I go?	On the street	Like me	If I do everything
Would I survive?	At every turn…	So I must stay.	Perfectly…
		Perhaps the look	And not get in
		I thought I saw	His way.
		On Father's face	
		Wasn't there at all.	

No life is so damaged, no soul so stained, that God would disdain to die for it.

Dr. Seligman and his colleague confined a dog to a hammock where, upon hearing a tone, the dog received a mild shock. The idea was for the dog, on hearing the tone, to make an effort to escape. Eventually, the dog learned there was no escape—the shock was inevitable.

Next, they placed the conditioned dog in a shuttle box that was divided into two compartments by a low fence. They sounded the tone, expecting the dog to jump over the fence, an easy feat for a normal dog. To their surprise, the dog did not jump. He lay down on the floor at the sound of the tone, pathetically awaiting the coming shock. Having learned in the box that there was no way of escape, he had lost hope and had learned helplessness as a way of life.

Like Dr. Seligman's dog, I understood that there was no way out. Before I was old enough to reason through the lies and deceit, I was totally and absolutely convinced that the price of my freedom was too high, that I alone was responsible for the unspeakable sorrows my siblings and my mother would experience if I weren't there to intervene.

Every day in the crucible of suffering, my helplessness was reinforced. Eventually, when I was older and could have jumped the fence, I no longer knew how.

Reflections

Before I would find the way out of the box, I would spend more than ten thousand days—precious days—living the lie that I could not jump out of the box. I can't say that I wasted those days, for if I would undo them, I must undo all the good that my suffering produced.

Yes, there was some good. I must find some good in it—otherwise the loss is too great to bear, and the pain too severe to survive.

Where do I find good in days such as those that crossed the landscape of my life

No life is so damaged, no soul so stained, that God would disdain to die for it.

from the age of five until thirty-three, sunrises bathed in tears, and sunsets darkened by remorse? God help me. He must, or I will die.

More than two decades have passed since I took the leap into freedom. Still, I'm intensely aware of the fact that I've spent a greater portion of my life in Hell than beyond it. And even the years that have passed since I fled my father's tyranny have not been easy. Most of them have been good, but never easy. A saying I've heard often at Celebrate Recovery is "God is good—but life is hard." True. Life is hard, but it's also wonderful! It is a gift, a blessing, an opportunity. Life is like a rose handed to me from the nail-scarred hand of my Savior who watches and waits for me to lift it to my face—to feel the velvet of perfect petals, to breathe in the fragrance of blossoms sprung from the soil of a better land.

Once I take it from him, and place it in my human vase, it begins to wilt—as all things do on this planet, but I know whence it came, and for that reason, I cherish it. The petals fall, and I would grieve, but I know that the fragrance in my rose remains. It's a part of the essence of the flower, and dried petals make potpourri that will outlast my lifetime. Whatever the state of my rose, it is a gift of love, and I must nourish it, enjoy it, and share it if I would honor the One who gave it to me with loving hands.

Where do I find value in the ten thousand days of my captivity, days saturated with tears and soaked in shame? I find it in many places—and you can, too, if you will search for it.

Let me show you some of the places where I've found it and you can gather your treasures there, too. You will find other areas, places I haven't been, laden with precious gems, and you, too, may share them with others who must find value in days that have passed across the landscape of their lives while they huddled in a box, confined by their fears, their shame, and their pain.

No life is so damaged, no soul so stained, that God would disdain to die for it.

Treasures from the Citadel of Suffering

1. Appreciation of natural beauty. I've always been aware of beautiful sunsets, crystal-clear nights, warm breezes, and growing things—flowers, trees, and fields of grass. I have seized delight in the fragrance of the night, at times, even as I rode along with a maniac whose words and actions would have destroyed me had I not displaced them by taking deep, cleansing breaths of the fresh night air rolling through the open window of a speeding vehicle. The feel of cool rain in a hot climate, the sound of a faraway train on its nightly journey—these things touched something deep inside me and reminded me that life existed beyond the grave and that I was still alive enough to see, hear, touch, and feel them. These things kept hope alive.

2. Horrors avoided by those I loved. My siblings, especially my sisters, have their scars, too. But they are not the same as mine, or as many. I know that my presence in the home saved them a tremendous load of pain, pain that they, like my brother Eddie, may have decided to escape at any cost. I can't judge, even now, what I should have done, or how I should have done it, to remove myself from the man who mutilated my soul, but I can see that because I stayed, some good was done for those I loved most. That means something to me. It's something I would not undo, and so, even today, I must find value in it.

> *Seeing therefore that we are surrounded by so great a cloud of witnesses, let us lay aside every weight and the sin which does so easily beset us, and run with patience the race that is set before us, looking to Jesus, the author and finisher of our faith.*
>
> —Hebrews 12:1

3. My knowledge of suffering gives me intense appreciation for the absence of it. Like one who languished long in prison, I walk the streets with an acute awareness of my freedom. I can go where I like and not be followed. I stare into the heavens and know that the same heavens that look back at

---

No life is so damaged, no soul so stained, that God would disdain to die for it.

me watched and waited for me to jump out of the box and walk freely beneath the summer sun, as I do today.

Jesus. The one who gave me the fragrance of life. The one who conceived me in his imagination before I became a living soul, and the one who is committed to the process of finishing my faith, completing the work of wonder in me that will one day deliver me to his celestial door where I will be welcomed, along with others who have been faithful. Faithful, not because we are so good at doing the right thing, but because He who has begun a good work in us is faithful to complete it.

∽

Go with me on a walk into the past. Maybe it's your past. It's definitely mine. Remember: we aren't going to stay there. We'll visit for a few minutes and learn from what we see.

A teen girl walks along a lonely road. It's getting late, and the bushes on either side of the road have taken on sinister shapes. The wind has grown cold. It whips the branches on the trees and whines through the eaves of abandoned buildings along the way. The girl's shirt is wet with tears, yet she plods on, lost in her thoughts.

Someone walks with her. Concern wrinkles His forehead—a forehead marked by the scars of His own suffering. He reaches out a nail-scarred hand as if to touch the girl, but she draws back afraid to accept the gentle touch of loving hands, for she has learned from other hands that touch cannot be trusted.

You can see the radiant form of the One who walks with her, but you wonder if the teen knows that He is there. She must, because she is talking now.

"Why?" she asks. "Why? Why? Why?" Like a scratched CD, she is stuck on the

No life is so damaged, no soul so stained, that God would disdain to die for it.

> **Being confident of this, that He who began a good work in you will carry it on to completion....**
>
> —Philippians 1:6

word, as if she cannot get past it.

"Listen to me, and I will tell you why," says the Radiant One, but she must not hear, for she continues asking as if He were not speaking.

She grows quiet—aware of the hole in her soul where her will has been plucked out.

"Surrender your will to me," the Radiant One is saying.

"But I have surrendered my will to another," she says, her voice filled with fear.

"That is not your fault," He tells her, "and I will deal with him, but I cannot help you until you surrender your will to me."

"How do I get it back?" she asks.

"Stop asking 'what if' and start doing what I tell you to do and I will guide you out of this dark place."

"But I must ask. What if he makes good on his threats? What if he hurts those I love? What if my shame is exposed to the world? What if I am left alone? What if…"

The Voice is silent now, and the girl believes she is alone. Eyes on the road before her, she walks on, toward the abyss waiting at the end. He will speak again. And someday, she will listen.

We, who know her, must help her. We must support her fragile strength without condemning her for her weakness. We must believe, with the Apostle Paul, that He who has begun a good work in her will carry it on to completion. We must accept her in her brokenness and validate her journey—tell her to keep walking—until she is able to believe for herself. There are a few people who did that for me, and without them I doubt that I would be here to write my story.

No life is so damaged, no soul so stained, that God would disdain to die for it.

Questions for Reflection

I invite you to prepare your heart for the questions in this section by taking a quiet time to still your thoughts. Have you learned to enter your safe place when you need to? Is your "safe person" available to be with you as you process the questions. If so, then let's proceed.

1. Where were you, Lord?

He was there, walking with us, talking to us, but we couldn't see him through our tears, we couldn't hear him through our pain.

2. Where is he now and what is he saying to you?

He will not violate your will. Would you really want him to?

3. What does it take to get our will back when we have been, or are being, violated, mistreated, or sexually abused? What does it take to free ourselves from the violent man?

Some suggestions…

> Courage to trust safe helpers;
> Safety for those who will suffer if I leave;
> Determination to do what is right regardless of the consequences;
> Knowledge of our worth;
> Understanding of the nature of abuse;
> Someone to care;
> Somewhere to go.

> *Strengthen the feeble hands, steady the knees that give way; say to those with fearful hearts: Be strong, do not fear; your God will come… to save you.*
>
> —Isaiah 35:3–4

No life is so damaged, no soul so stained, that God would disdain to die for it.

I learned at an early age that no one on earth could be trusted. I can tell you that it's safe to trust social services or some other organization; but I don't have the authority to tell you that. People are flawed. Helpers are flawed. And organizations are certainly flawed. I can tell you to trust God. He will give you peace and lead you to trustworthy helpers who will secure those you love and extend a hand to help you.

There is a resource section in the back of this book. I only wish these resources had been available to me over twenty years ago. They weren't, and I'm not sure that I would have had the courage to avail myself of them. I hope I would have, but it's too late now. I can't recover the lost years.

What I can do is make the best of the years that are left to me and if I can help others along the way then it will have been worth it.

⌒

My Prayer for Today

Oh, Lord, I ask that You give my friend the courage to stop asking "what if" and start saying, "I will—I will do what is right. I will take care of myself. I will seek godly counsel. I will get to know the truth for the truth will set me free."

Amen.

No life is so damaged, no soul so stained, that God would disdain to die for it.

Why, O Lord, do you stand afar off?
Why do you hide yourself in times of trouble?
In his arrogance the wicked man hunts down the weak
Who are caught in the schemes he devises.
He boasts of the cravings of his heart…
He lies in wait like a lion in cover;
He lies in wait to catch the helpless.
He catches the helpless and carries them off in his net.
His victims are crushed, they collapse
They fall under his strength.
He says to himself, "God has forgotten,
He covers his face and never sees.

—Psalm 10

~

I had a dream when I was fifteen. It's vivid in my memory today. I was in love with a young man. I rode behind him on his motorcycle, wearing a black jacket that matched his. The wind was in my face, my arms locked around his waist. Then my father showed up. Rage colored his face. Disdain poured from his eyes. He grabbed me and yanked me off the motorcycle. My beloved just kept on going, seemingly unaware that I had just been apprehended by my father. Even as I dreamed, I tasted fear. I could call him back, but my father would kill him. I watched him go and grieved my loss. The death of my dreams.

It Is Easy

Let it go! They say…
"For bitterness will bring decay
And rot the bones that give
You life.

It is easy to be said
"I let it go!" but in my head
A thousand memories bang away
At what is left of me…
And will not let me go.

Further Reflections

What were your dreams—the ones you cherished?

What were your nightmares? Perhaps there was one or more that replayed often. What were they about?

Sometimes our dreams can tell us what we desire, or what we fear, though sometimes they're garbled and are more relative to the overabundance of pizza we ate the night before than to any deep, dark secret of the heart.

Emotionally loaded dreams, dreams that leave me sweating in the night and dreading the day to come, are often memories disguised as dreams, triggering whole episodes that I've buried in my unconscious mind. Often, my mother or some other relative will remember and confirm at least some part of the event. I recognize that such experiences aren't always completely reliable in their accuracy; however, I've learned to trust the emotional catharsis they provide. I can deal with the offense and the offender in the privacy of my own heart, where I can forgive without the need to convince, and set my own boundaries to protect me from re-victimization. I know

No life is so damaged, no soul so stained, that God would disdain to die for it.

that those who have offended me—and their offenses—are no longer my responsibility, but my Heavenly Father's.

⌒

Another Prayer for Today

Oh, Heavenly Father, help us to let down our defenses so that memories can surface that would help us to know the truth about our past, inasmuch as it affects our present and our future. Show us evidence of Your involvement in our life in the past, and help us to surrender to You in our present and our future.

Amen.

No life is so damaged, no soul so stained, that God would disdain to die for it.

The spider spins his web
The innocent treads softly
Unaware
That death awaits

Chapter Nineteen
Another Trap

THE MOST INSIDIOUS TRAP that my father laid for me happened while I was still a young teenager. Even now, my stomach aches when I think about it.

My bedroom, which I shared with my two sisters, adjoined his bedroom, which he shared with my mother. He started coming to me when he was going to have sex with her, telling me to listen. He said that he was pretending that it was me in his bed.

Pillows over my head, knees drawn up to my chest, I tried not to hear the sounds coming from the other side of the wall. Sick. Sick. Sick. My stomach retched. It was as if I was being strangled by shame. Hearing my mother's response to my father, and knowing that he was defiling me in the process by his evil fantasies, I wanted to die. I prayed to die. Oh, God, make my heart stop beating. God, please let me get cancer or have a heart attack or something.

My father always took me to the park the next day, where he took me on long, agonizing walks and exploited his fantasies from the night before. He told me in excruciating detail what he had done to my mother, but "we can pretend it was

you. I want you to listen when we do it again and pretend that you're the one...."
My insides curled into a tight little ball, and I hung my head, staring at the asphalt. I
walked along, digging my nails into my palms, but my father never seemed to notice.

Finally, feeling that I couldn't bear another one of my fathers fantasies, that
I couldn't live through one more night of hearing the sounds in my mother's bedroom—knowing that I would hear all about it later, knowing that in my father's sick
mind it was me in there—I made the biggest mistake of my life.

I begged my father not to have sex with my mother. He assumed that I was jealous. I played along. Anything—anything was better than going through one more
night of… that.

Once again he had just what he wanted. Once more his sticky web of deceit
wrapped itself around my unsuspecting heart. He had planned and plotted for this.
There was a sick gleam in his weak blue eyes when he looked at me. Only later would
I understand that if he ceased to have sexual relations with my mother, he'd expect to
make his fantasies come true with me. As far as he was concerned, I had asked for it.

He began pressuring me to run away with him. "We could go to a big city like
Chicago and get an apartment." Oh, God! His words filled me with pure, unadulter-
ated terror, the kind that makes your heart pound right out of your chest and your
breath come in short gasps, the kind that makes the room spin beneath your feet and
your knees weak. No! No! Please, God, don't let him take me away.

Then would come a tiny flame of hope. He wouldn't be able to take his ven-
geance on my mother and siblings if I left with him. I was pretty sure he would be
breaking the law. He probably couldn't come back. Maybe I could escape. I saw
myself running down dark corridors in the night, between tall buildings. I sensed his
nearness, his desperate determination to kill me if he couldn't keep me. Dear God.
This was the stuff my nightmares would consist of for years to come. I'm running in
slow motion. He's gaining. I'm doomed.

No life is so damaged, no soul so stained, that God would disdain to die for it.

I dare not go. I'll never get out alive. I'll be my father's slave. I keep quiet. It's too dangerous to tell him I don't want to go. Please don't make me go. I believe I said in a weak voice, "I would miss the kids." I'm not sure, but I know that he decided it was a lost cause and eventually left off badgering me about it.

By the time I was fifteen years old I spent most of my waking hours contemplating suicide. I made elaborate plans for how I could do it and make it look like an accident. I didn't want anyone to know that my life was such a mess.

Have you ever wondered if there is a correlation between the increasing incidence of abuse and the fact that suicide is the number-one killer of young people? Also, I wonder about the stupid things that kids do sometimes, such as the sixteen-year-old boy who robbed a bank near my home. He rode his bike up to the bank in broad daylight and demanded money from a teller. Within minutes the bank was surrounded by police officers, and the boy was apprehended. Why did an apparently smart kid, making good grades in school, shock everyone by attempting to rob a bank? He said he wanted to buy a car. Wouldn't his parents wonder where the money came from?

I wonder if he was actually attempting to escape from something he couldn't control by committing a crime that would force him out of his family home. I know that I often considered going into a liquor store with an empty gun and attempting to "rob" it so that I'd be taken out of my environment and not have to face the possibility of being forced to return to it.

No matter what happened to the ones I left behind, it wouldn't be my fault, would it, if I was incarcerated against my will? If I made a mistake, robbed a store? That was surely an easier guilt to bear than bearing the responsibility for the defilement of my sisters by my perverted parent, or the death of my mother or other family members because I willingly abandoned them to their fate. It would be easier if my departure was out of my control.

No life is so damaged, no soul so stained, that God would disdain to die for it.

I considered worse, for I was afraid that if I didn't do something really terrible—if my gun was empty—I might be slapped on the wrist and sent home, and then my nightmare would be worse. I'd be returned to my home to face an indignant father who'd have one more thing to use against me. My latest crime.

~

Reflections

What were your fantasies? Did you imagine irrational escape plans, plans that would have forced others to free you from your environment?

~

My Prayer for Today

God, our Father who looks upon the heart, please help us to understand why we did the things that made us feel unworthy of love. Help us to view the addictions, sins, and even the crimes that we may have committed, through your eyes of mercy. For You are merciful to the brokenhearted and quick to forgive our transgressions. Lord, be merciful to me, a sinner, and give me Your peace.

Amen.

No life is so damaged, no soul so stained, that God would disdain to die for it.

Chapter Twenty
The End of the Road

I WAS STILL in my fifteenth year when my father began making trips to a nearby city to shuttle his uncle to the hospital for medical treatments. He made it clear to me that I was expected to accompany him. I tried to find excuses to stay home. He responded with stony silence and an angry glare. He found opportunities to rage at my mother and siblings. Harsh, hateful words were spoken, and physical violence seemed imminent. Long-anticipated privileges were denied to my siblings. Everything I did was wrong. Finally I "decided" to go, insisting that of course I had wanted to go all along.

Week after week I accompanied my father. He always left late in the evening for the two hour trip, which left me at his mercy when, after depositing his uncle at his house, he turned onto a dark dirt road out in the middle of nowhere and kept me there until he was ready to go home.

I Want to Go

Don't you want to go with me?
We'll have fun! I'll buy you things
And no one else will know.

No! Please, Dad, I want to stay
With Mother. I want to play
Here—at home.

Come! Go with me—or I'll be sad
You let me down! You made me mad.
Go away, you little brat! Go play!

I'm sorry, Dad. I'll go with you.
Just please—don't walk away from me.
I'll do anything you please.
Of course I want to go

My despair knew no bounds after my father started taking me on these trips. I had absolutely no hope for the future. My father made it clear to me that I was damaged merchandise—used goods. He told me stories about women like me, always with tragic endings. I was worse than a promiscuous woman, for I was my father's property.

My father's opinion about "used women" was subtly confirmed by the Church, but never so overtly as in the message delivered by Pastor L. when he compared women who lost their virginity prior to marriage to "bargain basement goods." "What man," Pastor L. asked, "wants to settle for used goods?" He went on to tell the story of his wonderful courtship with his wife, both of them products of pastoral homes. Oh, the wonders of marital bliss when you do it like they did!

No life is so damaged, no soul so stained, that God would disdain to die for it.

If I sound cynical, I'm sorry. I know the purpose of the pastor's sermon was to stem the tide of sexual promiscuity that was flooding the church due to the "sexual revolution," but apparently the pastor never considered that some of us may have been less fortunate than himself and his bride. And to be consigned to the basement by a pastor was like being sent there by God himself. Boom! The gavel fell. Boom! You have been judged. Boom! Your father is right—you're no good.

I could have ended it. I had the opportunity, and believe me, I considered it. One of the few positive things my father did with my brothers and me was to take us hunting. I was a good marksman, maybe as good as my brothers. We used to push our .22 casings into the bark of trees and then shoot them out. I rarely missed.

I took to the woods dressed as a boy, with my long hair twisted into a camo cap. I loved to wander through the woods alone, savoring the rare opportunity of solitude. I would sit beneath a tree and watch the white clouds drift through the sky. I sometimes found a clear spring and sat motionless with my bare feet in the chilly water, listening to the sound of it trickling over stones, the gentle breeze rustling the leaves of the tall oak trees, and the chirping and chattering of woods animals. During those moments, I could almost hope for a better day.

Then my father would find me. I could read his sick desire on his face. He would command me to hunt with him. As I walked along beside him, my thoughts in chaos, I remember the battle that raged inside me. I'll kill him. I held a loaded gun in my hands. I could make it look like an accident. Immediately an opposite thought replaced that one. I can't kill him. He's my father. I love him. No! I hate him! I'll go to jail—or insane. Oh, God.

One day, almost as if he had read my thoughts, my father played a trick on me.

No life is so damaged, no soul so stained, that God would disdain to die for it.

He had fallen down a shallow ravine and cut his ear. As he came back into camp, blood trickling down his face, he told my brother, "Linda shot me." I saw the disbelief in my brother's eyes, the reproach. I knew I could never take our father's life. I drew an invisible line between my abuser and my father. I hated my abuser, but loved my father. I knew I would lose my mind if I harmed him.

When I graduated from high school, I hoped college would be an avenue of escape. I began to hint to my father, tentatively suggesting studies that I'd like to pursue. I should have known better. A few weeks prior to graduation, my father told me, "If you go away to college, I'll have to take the kids out of school. They can work to help me support the family."

I went through the line and accepted my diploma with a heart of lead. All hope was gone. I could not abandon my siblings. I couldn't bear to see their lives destroyed. I obtained my real estate license and went to work in my father's business.

It would be thirteen years before I made my way to freedom. In those thirteen years my father paid me nothing for my labor. He said that providing me with a home and food was more than I was worth.

Memory

I am in my early twenties. It's hot in Arkansas midsummer. There isn't much a poor family can do for recreation, but the Good Lord is merciful, offering the glories of Nature to the poor along with the rich, and Greers Ferry Lake was nearby.

When my father was in a good mood, he would sometimes take us there. We even camped a few times, spending the night in sleeping bags beneath the stars, without benefit of a tent. We never knew we needed one. Sometimes, my father's cousin, brother to the one who had watched as my father molested me in early adolescence, brought his family along as well.

No life is so damaged, no soul so stained, that God would disdain to die for it.

Usually, I was relatively safe on those trips. There were too many strangers around for my father to try anything. But this time was different. I had strayed from the "pack" and he caught me. I saw him coming through the water. I was literally over my head, but I started swimming back. He got to me before I could get close enough for anyone to know what he was doing. He relieved his sexual tension against my bare back, there in the lake and then swam back as if nothing had happened.

Sick. Sick. Sick. I never want to go back to Greers Ferry Lake. No matter how hot it is. I never again asked for a trip to the lake. The lake, that beautiful, cool, clean, place of refreshment had become a thing of ugliness, sickness, to me.

I came out of the water and sat on the shore alone. No matter how crowded the lake might be, I would still be alone.

Meanwhile, my siblings were growing up. One after the other they left home. Finally, only Donna, my youngest sister, was left. When she announced her engagement to be married, my mother announced to my father that when the wedding was over, she was going to divorce him.

Memory

No one is home except my father, my mother, and me. The boys have all moved away, and Rose is in college. Donna has announced her engagement and will soon be married. My father has become increasingly violent over the past few months.

Change always evokes that in him. He isn't certain he'll be able to control everything that's going to happen.

My parents are in the family room, on the lower level of the split-level house that we call home. Their voices are loud, angry. My father has brought the gun out several times lately. I think he may have held it to my mother's head the night before. Time becomes somewhat blurred when you think your father may blow your moth-

---

No life is so damaged, no soul so stained, that God would disdain to die for it.

er's head off any minute—and you know that you have to stop it. You know what it will take. You hate her for taunting him. You hate him for… everything. And so you smile and say, "Come on, Dad. She's not worth it. Let's go for a ride." And you hate yourself.

But today, there would be no "intervention." Today, it's decided that as soon as the wedding is over, my mother will file for a divorce. He warns her, "You can leave, but you won't get anything from me, you #@*!"

There were other words that I don't remember, but I'll never forget my mother pointing her finger in my father's face and saying, "And what have you and Linda been doing all these years?"

Oh, God! There it was. My shame would be marched into court and put on display for all the world to see. She knew! Oh, God, she knew all along! And she'll use it now to make my father give her a fair share in court. I wanted to die, but that was nothing new, because I'd wanted that for the past twenty years. Dirty, filthy, used. I knew what I was.

I went through my sister's wedding in a state of shock—again, nothing new. That had been my place of residency for the past twenty years. I posed for pictures, went through the motions, and wondered how in the world I'd survive.

I feared so many things. I was afraid I would lose my mind. On some deep intuitive level I knew that I'd been anesthetized by the powerful defense mechanisms I had constructed, numbed to the reality of my wounding, and I was afraid—no, terrified—that when the anesthesia wore off, I'd be in so much pain that my brain would explode, leaving me mentally incapacitated, dependent on the mental health facility down the road, the Arkansas State Hospital.

And then, the divine presence of God within me, the Holy Spirit that would not leave me even though I thought he didn't care, began to give me hope. With my mother living across town and Donna out of the house, maybe—just maybe—I

No life is so damaged, no soul so stained, that God would disdain to die for it.

could find a way out. I began to hope that I just might make it. Freedom called, and I dared to believe there was a chance that I might have a life after all.

My father thought otherwise. He seemed to believe that I was completely under his power now that we occupied the house alone. Idiot!

I no longer hate my father, who is now in his final resting place. One that I'm relatively certain is very uncomfortable. I hate what he did to me and to my loved ones, and I may need to live a little longer, submit one more time—or many more times—to the surgeon of my soul before the hostility that lurks still in memories such as these is ready to be laid to rest.

Donna lived a few blocks away. Sensing that freedom was near at hand for me, my father used the only leverage he had left. He reminded me constantly that Donna lived nearby, and, though he never directly threatened her, he claimed to believe that her husband, Dale, had instigated my rebellion and would be held responsible if I left.

"I'll kill the little wimp," he threatened. "Do you really think he can protect you?"

I never said he could. The one who could—and would—was bigger than my father and totally unintimidated by his bluster.

Finally! Four months after my parent's divorce was final, Dale got a transfer to Michigan. Yes! I took Donna to the airport to follow her husband, and watched the plane ascend the clouds of deepest blue, knowing that I would soon follow.

Reflections

Now, my mother grieves over her lack of understanding about the nature of sexual abuse. She has expressed her sorrow over her denial in the early years and her censure when I was older. She had failed to see the links in the chains that bound me to my father, and didn't know that she held the key that would have released me if she'd only known how. Some say she was the silent partner in my father's crimes. I believe

No life is so damaged, no soul so stained, that God would disdain to die for it.

this is true. I remember too much to convince myself otherwise. I remember the anger, the jealousy, and the withdrawn love. I remember the arguments and obvious signs of my father's lust for his eldest daughter, signs that sickened and shamed me while apparently escaping my mother's attention. But that's not all that I remember.

I remember a woman who cried almost daily and covered her face with her pillow to blot out the taunting voice of the man who derided her for her weight, her failures, and her fears. A woman who went to her pastor and told him her darkest fears, only to be reprimanded for believing such an evil thing about her husband, a man of the Church. He could not be capable of such despicable behavior.

I remember a woman who suffered silently as my father forced me to read Proverbs 30 in her presence, night after night, while I lay in his bed, feeling as much a monster as he was, as I watched my mother cry. When he finally allowed me to go to my bed, I would lie in the darkness of my own despair, wishing I could die.

My mother has suffered enough for her part in the drama of our lives. I love her, respect her and am unbelievably proud of the woman she has become in the aftermath of the violence done to her own soul as well as the souls of her children by the man who ruled over her with threats and violence.

No life is so damaged, no soul so stained, that God would disdain to die for it.

Chapter Twenty-one
Rescue from the Violent Man

I BEGAN TO SEND OUT RÉSUMÉS to organizations far from my hometown. I enlisted the help of the secretary across the hall from my office. She became my only friend as I prepared to escape, confidentially screening my mail and phone calls.

I confided in our accountant that I was secretly planning to leave, and turned all my father's financial records over to her. I told my mother that I was fleeing. She was elated. I begged her not to flaunt her joy to my father. I wanted her to survive.

I was convinced that once my father realized I had left, he would take his own life. I knew that he was incapable of functioning on his own. He had always used me and my mother to cover up his dysfunction. Now his true condition would be exposed. He lay in bed until around 2:00 p.m. every day, finally coming to the office to make an appearance of working. How could he survive on his own? He pretended to run a business, but he couldn't even answer the phone or balance his own check-book. He would certainly lose his business. For the first time, my father's crimes against me would be exposed to others. I felt as if I were pulling the trigger of the gun that would end his life.

I had watched my father, many years before, when he mixed alcohol with dozens of pills, attempting, he said, "to end it all." I had been alone with him in the car many times when he aimed his vehicle at a telephone pole and accelerated—only to swerve at the last moment. I think, at that time, I would have been glad to die, but I didn't want to die with him. Now he would die alone.

A Place to Grieve

So be it. I found a place to grieve. Every morning, before going to the office, I went to the Old Mill. I walked alone among the tall oaks and creeping vines. I sat on a stone behind the old rock structure and cried out silently, Why did you have to do it? You are my father. No, you are my abuser.

I pictured my father lying in a pool of his own blood, a gunshot wound in his temple. Oh, God. What can I do?

There, in the early hours of the morning, day by day, I released to God the man who should have been my daddy. I surrendered all hope of ever having an earthly father, and accepted God as my father, God who is a father to the fatherless. I realized that while I had loved God, in the person of Jesus Christ, I had never accepted God—my Father. In that place of consecration, I traded an unworthy earthly father for One who would never abuse me or violate my will. I accepted the future with all of its unknowns, as I sought strength to put the past behind me at any cost.

As my father began to sense the change in me, he became even more violent.

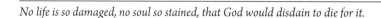

No life is so damaged, no soul so stained, that God would disdain to die for it.

When he tried to force me to submit to him, he no longer had my mother and siblings to use against me, so he used his gun. He began leaving it out and picking it up frequently. He held it on me and raged against me, trying to make me admit that I was leaving. Had I acknowledged it, he would have killed me.

Even so, I defied death as I confronted my father with the truth of what he had done to me. I reminded him of how I used to get up to go to the bathroom when I was a young teenager, forced to lie beside him on the bed, supposedly reading to him, while he violated me. I hadn't dared, then, to tell him that I was going to the bathroom to throw up. Now I told him how sick he made me. I revealed to him that I'd barely resisted taking his life while hunting in the woods at fifteen.

These confrontations began releasing my soul from my father's control even as they intensified his rage and violence. Death approached nearer each day as I struggled to put my father's affairs in order and gain the courage to leave.

I knew I was crippled by the life I'd endured for over twenty-eight years. Though I longed to be free, I was terrified that I'd crumble when I was on my own. I feared losing my mind. I knew that once I left, the secret would be out. I wasn't sure I could bear the shame of it. Would my siblings despise me? Would they think it was my fault?

It would be months—no, years—before I could face the true extent of the damage done to me over those twenty-eight years. With safety came memories that pieced together the story of my victimization—a story that I knew only partially in barely remembered pieces. The memories made me hate my father. I would like to say that forgiveness made me pity him, but the truth is that pity was responsible for keeping me there in the sepulcher for all those years—pity for him, pity for my siblings, as I imagined the violence he would do to them if I left, and pity for my mother. I had no pity for myself. I had no feelings that I can remember for myself. I was a hollow shell wandering in toxic shock, waiting for the next blow to fall.

No life is so damaged, no soul so stained, that God would disdain to die for it.

I can't say that I've forgiven my father, not completely. If I should say that I have, you wouldn't believe me, for the resentment that lingers in me is evident between the lines. But I have forgiven much, and I'm working on the rest. And the good news—the wonderful news—is that God has not abandoned me in the process. He accepts what I have to offer, and patiently waits until I can do better. I hope my readers will do the same.

No life is so damaged, no soul so stained, that God would disdain to die for it.

Chapter Twenty-two
The Fishermen Left Their Nets

I WENT TO THE OFFICE alone. I didn't work on real estate, I didn't manage property; I did hardly anything but make the few calls necessary to keep trouble at bay while I researched.

What did the Bible have to say about what I should do? Did I really have the freedom to leave, to just walk out and never look back? How could I? I had been groomed, since childhood, to believe that I was my father's keeper, the finger that plugged the hole in the dike of his fury. Could I really abandon my post?

I found my answer in Matthew, chapter 4. James and John, sons of Zebedee, were in a boat with their father, preparing their nets. Jesus called them and immediately they left their father and followed him. They left their father. I could leave too.

Maybe—just maybe—I had a choice after all.

Jesus said to another man, "Follow me."
But the man replied, "Lord, first let me go and bury my father."

Jesus said to him, "Let the dead bury their own dead, but you go and proclaim the kingdom of God." (Luke 9:59–60)

Let the dead bury their own dead.

I remember when my father's cousins came to town. It was before Grandma Bertha died, so I was not yet fifteen. They were spinster women who lived with their father. They worked so he didn't have to. I never questioned why he didn't work. I just couldn't imagine him going to work every day.

I had an affinity with the cousins. I didn't like Uncle J. He was too much like my father. There was that… cadaverous look in his eyes, like he wasn't all there. Something about him was a little bit dead.

Somehow I got the idea that the cousins were heroines, doing the right thing, taking care of father. I don't know if anyone said that I, too, was expected to play that role, but I understood it just the same.

Then one day his daughter told me a story. She was twenty-seven the last time her father molested her. Her gentle face crinkled in sad remembrance.

The first time he molested her was shortly after her mother died. She was a little girl then. And he didn't stop until she told him, at twenty-seven, that she would live with him and take care of him until he died, but she would no longer allow him to molest her.

He sat on the porch, she said, and rocked. Then he went into the fields. He said that he was going to kill himself. But he didn't. He never touched her again. And she never left him. Twenty years later, she told me her story.

"Go," she said. "Don't let that happen to you. Get out."

Yes. I will go. I have to prepare myself first. I have to know that whatever happens I'm going to make it.

No life is so damaged, no soul so stained, that God would disdain to die for it.

It was late, every night, when I turned off my light, often as late as 2:00 a.m. I spent the night praying and searching for answers. My Bible was the only sure resource I had. People might help me, or hurt me, but the Word of God was sure.

On one of my nightly quests, I discovered Psalm 27. I underlined it and read it over and over. One day, I left the Bible opened on my bed when I left the house. My father went into my room, probably looking for something that would prove his suspicions that I was leaving, and found my open Bible. Yes. There it was. My freedom statement, all underlined and highlighted.

The Lord is my light and my salvation; whom shall I fear? The Lord is the strength of my life; of whom shall I be afraid?

When the wicked came against me to eat up my flesh, my enemies and foes, they stumbled and fell.

Though an army may encamp against me, my heart shall not fear; though war may rise against me, in this I will be confident.

One thing have I desired of the Lord; that will I seek, that I may dwell in the house of the Lord all the days of my life, to behold the beauty of the Lord and to inquire in His temple.

For in the time of trouble, He shall hide me in His pavilion; in the secret place of His tabernacle *He shall hide me; He shall set me high upon a rock.*

And now my head shall be lifted up above my enemies all around me. Therefore, I will offer sacrifices of joy in His tabernacle. I will sing, yes, I will sing praises to the Lord.

Hear, O Lord, when I cry with my voice! Have mercy also upon me and

---

No life is so damaged, no soul so stained, that God would disdain to die for it.

answer me. When You said, "Seek my face," my heart said to You, "Your face, Lord, I will seek."

Do not hide Your face from me; do not turn Your servant away in anger. You have been my help. Do not leave me or forsake me, O God of my salvation!

When my father and my mother forsake me, then the Lord will take care of me.

I would have lost heart, unless I had believed that I would see the goodness of the Lord in the land of the living.

Wait on the Lord; be of good courage and He shall strengthen your heart; wait, I say, on the Lord! —Psalm 27 (NKJV)

~

I'm waiting, Lord, and I believe. My mother and my father have forsaken me always, but you will take care of me. That's all that I need to know.

When my father saw my Bible with the scriptures highlighted and underlined, he knew that I was being set free—free to escape, free to flee. Free to live!

He preferred that I stay and submit to him, but if he couldn't have that, he wanted me dead. The problem was he couldn't be sure I was leaving. The day he went into my room, snooping for evidence, and found my Bible, he met me at the door in a rage when I returned home. He grabbed me by the hair and slung me around the house, throwing me into walls and doors, demanding, "So, your father and your mother have forsaken you, huh? You think you're going to find a place to hide from

No life is so damaged, no soul so stained, that God would disdain to die for it.

me? I'll kill you." He picked up his gun, took it off safety, cocked it, and bumped it repeatedly against my chest while holding me by my hair. He raged on and on about what he would do to me.

Death came ever nearer to my door. My father said he was going to the bathroom. I thought I can run! I'll hide behind my neighbor's house until dark. Then I can escape.

As if he read my mind, he said, "If you run, I will find you. Do you really think you can get away from me?" Sadly, I believed him—and his words, and my fears, returned often in nightmares in the years to come.

The next day, he came to the office earlier than usual. Why I didn't leave before he got there is a mystery to me. I suppose fear of the unknown is sometimes greater than a familiar fear, even if the threat is infinitely more dangerous.

He railed at me all day, telling me that he was going to kill me when he got me home. He kept daring me to try to escape. My heart felt like it was going to implode. I wasn't sure I would survive the night. Pain shot through my chest and I doubled over. "Take me to the hospital."

Suspicious that I would escape if he took me there, he drove me to the emergency room and stuck with me—like a burr on my heel—even when they took me back to the curtained area. I thought, Maybe I can go to the bathroom and slip out somehow. But I feared he would find me. I wouldn't have enough time to get away.

By the time they released me, his rage had abated and he was in a "conciliatory" mood. I knew that if I defied him, I wouldn't live to see another day. I also knew that this would be the last time he would ever touch me, or see me, or hear my voice. I hated my abuser—and I had no father.

The next morning, four months after my sister had left the state, I called her at work and told her that I was going to leave. I asked her not to blame me if my father took his own life.

No life is so damaged, no soul so stained, that God would disdain to die for it.

She asked where I was going, and I said I didn't know. She wanted me to come to Michigan, to be with her and Dale. I said no. I was afraid my father would come for me. I would not endanger my sister.

Then she asked me, "Did he ever… touch you, I mean, sexually? Because he molested me."

Oh, God! My entire life had been wasted. I thought I'd been protecting my sister, but I had failed—failed to accomplish the only good thing I thought I'd achieved during my entire life, taking care of my siblings. To think of my little sister enduring his depravity was unthinkable. It was unbearable.

No! Suddenly, I was furious. The plunder of my treasures had been for nothing! I had stood with my finger in the dike of my father's perversion for twenty-eight years, endured the destruction of my dignity, the death of my dreams, and the horrors of his humiliations, and all for nothing! Nothing!

"My entire life," I answered. "He has done it for as long as I can remember. Dear God! I'll kill him. If I have to look at him, I'll kill him."

"Come here," my sister begged me. "Come to Michigan so I can help you with this. Please don't go off somewhere that I can't find you. We won't let him know you're here."

Like a child, willing to be led, I did as my sister asked. But first I called the pastor of the church I had attended since early childhood and asked if I could meet with him. I wanted his wife to be present, and she was. I was doing it! I was really breaking free. There was no turning back now. I'm sure my face was dead white and my knees trembling as I waited for my pastor to pick me up from the office and take me to his house where his wife waited to welcome me with open arms. They knew something terrible was about to be revealed, but they weren't prepared for the horrendous story that poured out of me in their living room. They got me on the next flight to Michigan where I could go and be with my sister, Donna, and her husband Dale.

No life is so damaged, no soul so stained, that God would disdain to die for it.

Even then, I was terrified. I kept looking back as I waited to board the aircraft, though it was only a few minutes, expecting my father to explode through the door, gun in hand, and end my life before I could get on the plane.

And then it was done. I was in my seat, fastening the seat belt. The plane lifted off, and the thought occurred to me, if I die now, I'll die free! Everyone will know that I was on my way out. I will not be ashamed. I felt as if Mount Everest had just been lifted from my shoulders.

Mary's song of jubilation echoed, like a sweet refrain, through my mind: "My soul glorifies the Lord and my spirit rejoices in God my Savior." (Luke 1:46–47.)

Reflections

Why is it so hard to break free of the abuser's control? Why do we suffer a river of sorrow, and even risk our life, without exposing the abuser? Maybe because we are still asking "what if" instead of "now what?" Maybe you were convinced, as I was, that you were solely responsible for the punishment, possibly even the violence, that others would suffer if you refused to accommodate your abuser.

If there is an abuser in the house, it is unlikely that you are entirely protecting others from his depravity. You may find someday, as I did, that your power to protect is puny. It would have been wiser to trust those who have authority to intervene, and refuse to hold yourself accountable for the outcome.

No life is so damaged, no soul so stained, that God would disdain to die for it.

Chapter Twenty-three
Healing Is a Choice

NOW FOR THE CHORE of removing the grave cloths, those trappings of sexual abuse that victims carry with them from the grave—the low self-esteem, ruptured dignity, and posttraumatic stress. The anxiety, vulnerability, and distrust that I acquired in the sepulcher had to be disposed of, and that is another story, one that I'll share with you in Section 2 of this book as soon as you're ready to go there. Are you ready? Then come and walk with me along the healing path.

Reflections

If you have been abused, you've no doubt processed a lot of pain as you turned the pages of this book. I pray for you that you've been encouraged, even in your suffering, as you exercised your faith and courageously made it this far. If you've been reading this book because someone you know has experienced sexual abuse, I hope it has helped you to understand that person. I believe Section 2 will help you to walk the healing path with that person.

SECTION 2
Come Walk with Me Along the Healing Path

~

I N NO PART of my life did ambivalence reign more supremely than in my walk with God. I've loved him for as long as I can remember, and wanted to belong to him, but I could not relate to God the Father. He seemed cold, stern, and harsh to my unenlightened imagination. He reminded me of my father.

So I loved His Son. Jesus was touchable, reachable. I believe my beloved Pastor George Murry (always the associate pastor, but never the senior, and therefore always present when senior pastors would come and go) taught me that. He showed me the path to loving Christ. He modeled the humility, compassion, and steadfastness of our Lord.

When he taught us to "practice the Presence of Christ," I listened, and I learned to do it. When I walked the sweltering asphalt pathways through MacArthur Park at the side of a maniac who raved about his fantasies, I hardly heard him, for I was listening to the One who spoke into my heart from the other side. I imagined Him, Jesus Christ, holding my hand. While I couldn't escape the tyranny of my father's torment, I survived it by practicing the Presence of Christ.

Today, I love to walk. Sometimes I take Chief, my beautiful German shepherd, and sometimes I walk with a friend. Always, I'm aware that the Wounded Warrior of Galilee walks with me. Now I welcome the smile and the warm embrace of my Father, the One who sent his Son to walk those lonely miles with me and rescue his child from the hands of the violent man.

No life is so damaged, no soul so stained, that God would disdain to die for it.

Chapter Twenty-four
The Man of My Dreams

I N 1986 I married the man of my dreams. I had literally dreamed about Mike when I was fifteen. Remember the nightmare of the motorcycle rider whom I loved and lost? I can't really be certain the image is the same, but this is what happened: Mike and I met as lay counselors at a rehabilitation center. Though I had never experienced substance abuse, I was drawn to work with those who had because I could relate to the pain and problems that drove them to addiction. It didn't take Mike and me long to get together. We were meant for each other.

One fall day, Mike took me for a ride on his motorcycle. We were wearing matching jackets. We passed a car dealership and I caught our reflection in the glass of the showroom. I gasped. The scene was right out of the dream I had had at fifteen. It was the only time I ever remembered dreaming of being in love. And I was in love. Within a year Mike and I were engaged, and nine months later we were married.

It took awhile for Mike to convince me that he would not turn his back on me someday. It has been twenty-two years since we said our vows, and I must admit that

I am still more vulnerable to insecurity than I should be. I married a faithful man, one who loves me with every beat of his heart. And still those old tapes play in my head every once in a while, and my father's voice says, "No man is going to want a 'used' woman. Someday, he'll leave you."

Invalidation, abandonment—I define the feeling by writing the words. Invalidation says, "You will never be good enough. You're not worth much." Abandonment says, "You will be alone again. He'll ride off into the sunset and you'll be left alone on the road to grieve."

But these are lies. I am worth something. I'm worth a lot! I'm worth something to God and I'm worth something to those who love me for who I am and what I've contributed to their lives. And I will not be abandoned—not by my husband and not by God. To believe otherwise is to position myself for failure.

～

The change was remarkable. A river, which had been an emblem of death to me, inviting me to end my suffering beneath its swift currents, now symbolized beauty and contentment because the dark memories of the past had been layered over with beautiful memories of Mike and me walking along the banks of the Detroit River, hand in hand, planning our future together.

A park was no longer a place of forced companionship where my emotions were traumatized and my dignity ruptured. It had become a place of joy where I strolled down mulched paths with the one who loves me, the one who handed me a rose and promised me his heart.

Perhaps you, too, have felt worthless. Maybe your love story hasn't had a happy ending. It's not too late. No matter how many failed relationships you may have gone through, love has not forsaken you. Maybe you feel you'll never love again. Perhaps

No life is so damaged, no soul so stained, that God would disdain to die for it.

A Wedding Poem

I never knew that loving someone
Could mean so much
As loving you has come to mean
To me.
The thought of you never
Completely leaves my mind.
Even when I am busy
And the day is long
I am missing you.
Every where I go
Everything I do
It seems there is something

That makes me think of you.
When I look at the blue sky
And see fluffy white clouds
I remember the summer day we spent
At the lake on our first date,
When you began to look
For animals in the clouds
Along with me.
When I look at the river
I think of the times we parked there
And were content just to be together.

A park, a flower, a lake
And a country road
All make me think of you
And the wonderful times
We have shared together.

If life were to end today
And all the dreams, hopes and desires
That have become so much
A part of me since I met you
Should never come to pass...
I would have experienced already
Enough joy, enough love, enough tenderness
That I would not feel I had missed out
On the truly beautiful things in life.
You are the most precious gift
That God has given to me
And your love is an extension
Of His love that I can see
And touch and feel.

Through all the years to come
In all the seasons of our life
With all the changes and challenges
The years are sure to bring
I will always want you close to me
And I will always love you, Michael
Just the way you are.

you're in a marriage that's conflicted and feels empty. You can't change the other person, but you can change yourself. If you can admit that you still have some baggage that needs to be dropped off, some grave cloths that need to be discarded, and some truths that need to be discovered, then you're well on your way to a better tomorrow.

No life is so damaged, no soul so stained, that God would disdain to die for it.

Chapter Twenty-five
The Nightmares Begin

A few weeks after the wedding, the nightmares began. I had experienced a few bad dreams, but nothing could have prepared me for what lay ahead. These were not merely nightmares, they were real-life experiences lived out in dreams.

I was safe now. My husband was there to hold me, and my Lord was there to heal me. I was ready to confront the realities of my past, one nightmare at a time.

I had found the courage, a few months before the wedding, to ask God the question I feared most to ask. I didn't just ask it, I screamed it at Him. I flung it at Him like a child flings a toy at an unrelenting parent who has frustrated him; perhaps, as a bride throws her engagement ring at the man who abandoned her at the altar. For this is what I felt during most of my thirty-three years—abandoned by God.

"Where were you, Lord? All the times I begged for help, for an escape, all the times I cried out to you and you didn't answer. Did you not hear, or did you not care? Were you too busy with others who were more important, to care about me? You saw me. You knew. You delivered others. Why not me? Where were you?"

The answer came quietly, piercing my unbelief and my pain. "I was in you."

Oh, God, my Savior, now I know:
Whatever they have done to the least of those who love You
they have done it unto You. —Matthew 25:40

You didn't intervene, but You didn't abandon me, either. You experienced my pain with me, in me, for me. My heart broke. The tears flowed. For the first time in eighteen years, I was able to cry. A geyser welled up inside of me, and living water poured down my face. I grieved, but no longer for myself. I grieved for the One who had never left me, whose light had always shone in my darkness. I grieved for Him, and He forgave my unbelief. Now I understood that there had always been a pinprick of light shining through the vast darkness of the sepulcher of depravity that had entombed my soul. He was that light—my only hope.

No life is so damaged, no soul so stained, that God would disdain to die for it.

A Pinprick of Light

A pinprick of light at the end...
It flickers, but never goes out
Completely.
Relentlessly, it stays
Coming no nearer this dark place.

Why will you not go away?
I shall never possess you!
My appointment in life...
I shall not forget it,
Is to wear this dark shroud.
No one will come near.
There is no light allowed... here.

So why do you stay? At the end
Of this dark death...
You remain relentlessly present
I cannot forget that light exists
Somewhere.
Waiting... at the end.

No life is so damaged, no soul so stained, that God would disdain to die for it.

Chapter Twenty-six
Poetry of the Night

THE BED WAS WET with sweat, but I was cold, shivering. I began shaking so hard that it rocked the bed. My body grew rigid, my muscles contracting. A therapist called it post-traumatic stress. It happened often during the first few years of my marriage. Every nightmare yielded memories that filled in the blanks about the past—erupting like ash out of a volcano, littering my life with debris.

Mike kept assuring me, "It's all right. We'll get through this." Darkness came down on me like a thick blanket. I found it hard to breathe. We waited while Mike quietly prayed.

"You know what you have to do…." Sometimes all I could choke out was, "I can't…." Minutes passed, maybe hours. Finally, as in the birthing of a child, the labor pains passed and I prayed, "Lord, please help me to forgive my father for this." That word, "forgive." is powerful. For as soon as I willed to forgive, as soon as I prayed for the power to forgive, it was as if the darkness lifted and peace flowed into our room. I relaxed in my husband's arms, drained, but at peace, and we both fell back asleep.

The following day, Mike went off to work with a cheerful smile, as always, but he called me later in the day to make sure I was okay. He knew I often felt dirty and ashamed after an episode in the night. He would always tell me, "You are the most wonderful woman in the world."

Still, I struggled with depression. Sadness lingered for days. Sometimes I knew that other memories were being triggered by the ones I had recovered. I stayed close to God and took all my sorrow to him.

No life is so damaged, no soul so stained, that God would disdain to die for it.

Poetry of the Night

I do not know what today will bring
My heart is sad and I don't know why.
I know the pain of remembering
What I would forget. Last night I cried.
And dreamed of things that cut me deep.
Too painful to remember—too hard to keep
In a human heart. I must let them go!
But how? Oh, God, I do not know!
Something hounds me in my sleep
That makes my waking sad.

Some distant memory of the past
That brings me down, makes me feel bad.
I run to You—my only hope.
You have kept me safe thus far. I know.
You brought me from the pit of hell
To the place of hope where I now dwell.
To you I run, Oh God of love!
You know the stuff this heart is made of.
Mend me, please and make me whole…
Must I remember all to know
That you were there in that dark night?
That you kept me till the morning light?
And when I "lay me down to sleep"
You, Oh God, my soul did keep.

Dark Waters

Dark waters closing over me.
I reach to grasp what I cannot see
Hold on! Hold on! My faint heart cries
I must hold on, or else I'll die

Hold on to what? The shifting sands
Of temporal things? Of circumstance?
To the winds of change that howl and chide
To the raging sea that is my life?

Nothing that these hands can grasp
Can keep me in this awful blast.
I reel and stumble—almost fall
Do you see me, Lord? Do you hear my call?
Oh, help me, God! Lord of my life!
Push back this darkness by your great light.

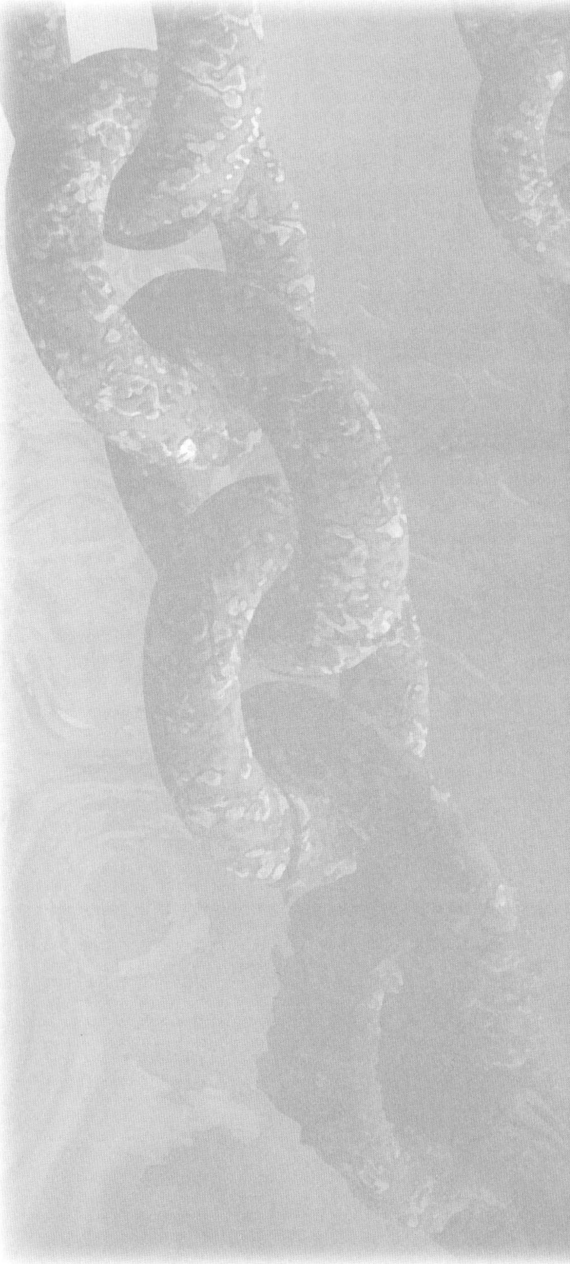

You Alone

You are the anchor
Of my soul.
You alone can take control
Of this breaking heart.

Look down upon
This child, Oh God,
For the lofty heights
Where your Spirit dwells

Touch this poor creature
Give me strength
For my hands are weak
And my courage fails.

I must draw life
And strength from You
Or I will perish like
The morning dew
That lies upon the waking grass
For a moment—then is gone

No more is seen
Or long remembered
As the day wears on.

Chapter Twenty-seven
Unfettered Love

SOMETHING ELSE HAPPENED, not instantly, but day by day as I began to experience the unconditional love of the man I had married. I became aware that I could give only a part of myself to him. I was holding back—something. I was not sure what it was.

~

I had spent my entire life stifling love. In my father's house, love was too dangerous to even consider. When a young man noticed me, I instantly looked away. When one persistent would-be suitor called me at my home, I hung up on him, but not before the room begin to spin. I almost fainted from fear. My father was downstairs. What if he had been in the room? Dear God, I couldn't let that happen again.

~

It was as if all the hopes, dreams, and desires that develop naturally in youth had been frozen in my soul, not destroyed, but placed on hold. Slowly, the warmth of Mike's love penetrated the icy depths of my wounded heart, and the real person inside of me began to emerge.

We will never forget the moment, a few months into our engagement, when I returned Mike's kiss. As he took me back to my apartment, I remember touching my hand to my mouth over and over, as if I had somehow been changed in that magical moment. Mike, in typical male fashion, was quiet, except for the words, "Wow, and we have to wait three months?"

~

There were still battles ahead, but the victory was assured. It was from this perspective that I began to open my heart and confront the truths that lay hidden deep within.

No life is so damaged, no soul so stained, that God would disdain to die for it.

Nightmares

Chapter Twenty-eight
Reality Confronted

MIKE ALWAYS KNEW when I had a nightmare. He awakened me when he heard me cry out in my sleep. When he questioned me, and I would respond that I'd had an "Arkansas dream," which meant a dream from my past, he would pull me into his arms and hold me while a flood of traumatic emotions washed over me. Sometimes I felt like I was drowning. Mike was my lifeline until the tempest was past. He kept assuring me, "It's all right."

Always present, at those times, was a dark oppression in the room, a familiar oppression, one I had lived with most of my life. I could feel it pressing down on me, robbing me of my strength. It was as if I was back in my father's house, feeling worthless, dirty, and confused. With the oppression was a terror that was almost tangible. I trembled so violently that the bed shook, and Mike squeezed me tighter as if to shelter me from a terrible storm.

What did you dream? Mike knew I had to talk about it, to get it out. It was usually a while before I could speak. Then, slowly, with tremendous effort, I would relate the nightmare with all its terror, its confusion, and its shame. I could see Mike's jaw tighten in anger at the man who had put me through so much pain.

Sometimes I whispered, "I hate him!" My stomach retched and my lungs ached. I was soaked in sweat. I squeezed my eyes shut and tried to blot out the memory of the man who called himself my father "I hate him! I hate him!" Saying the words couldn't expunge the fury in my soul. I cringed at the sickness of it. I felt as if a cockroach had crawled over me in the night.

And I was desperately afraid of cockroaches. The home I grew up in was swarming with them. I remember being afraid to get up at night to go to the bathroom, knowing I would feel them crunch beneath my feet. It was with renewed horror and revulsion that I remembered the time my father forced me to lie on the floor in an empty rental dwelling, a floor crawling with the vermin, while he molested me. Such was the nature of the dreams that came often in the night, dreams that brought back memories that I longed to leave forever in the past.

Finally, one nightmare at a time, I came to the place of forgiveness. Only by forgiving could I be free of the awful despair of remembering. Mike assured me that I did not have to feel forgiveness, that I had only to be willing to forgive my father, and God, in his time, would do the rest.

Finally, I would pray, "God, I am willing. Please help me to forgive my father." One nightmare at a time, one memory after the other, I released the pain, the fear, and the defilement to the only one who could heal my broken heart. I chose to forgive, not ambiguously, not sentimentally, for even today the thought of my father's eyes, his touch, his voice, has the power to disgust me. But incident by incident as I remember, I forgive him for what he did to me. For this, too, I forgive.

No life is so damaged, no soul so stained, that God would disdain to die for it.

Chapter Twenty-nine

The Castle Maze

R ECOVERY, FOR ME, is a never-ending story. But my story is not a tragedy. There have been some tragic parts, but I'm living in the present and loving it. Since the day I walked out of the sepulcher, life has been good. Not perfect, but good.

My recovery experience is like passing through a maze of rooms in a castle. Each room I enter has much work to be done in it. As God gives me the wisdom and strength to conquer one room, he moves me on to another—each one more spacious and splendid than the one before, each having its unique challenges and changes to be accomplished.

As I emerged from a tiny cramped cubicle, cluttered with all the refuse of a life ravaged by abuse, I began to welcome each passage, knowing that each one brought greater freedom and deeper healing.

In one room, I had resolved the question of where—where God was when I was abused. In another room, I asked, "Why?" Why did God not deliver me—somehow—from my torment? If He's all powerful, and if He loves me, why did He allow me to suffer all those years?

Safe?

I'm standing in a worship service beside my husband. The congregation is singing *There is None Like You*. I love the song. It comforts me every time we sing it. Suddenly, I am overwhelmed. What are they singing? "Suffering children are safe in Your arms—there is none like You." It sounded so sweet, so safe.

But it's not true! I wanted to shout the words, but instead I just walked out of the service. When my husband asked me later why I had left, I said simply, "It is not true. Suffering children are not safe in his arms."

I wanted to believe the words of the song, but my experience proved otherwise. I couldn't reconcile the two. Then one day, I closed my eyes and saw this picture:

There is a raging fire in a building. Flames lick the rafters, and the heat is unbearable. A thick rope dangles from a beam high above the inferno. A small child clings to a knot tied in the rope.

"Let go the rope," a man calls. He braves the flames to stand directly beneath the rope. "Let go, son, and I will catch you!"

The terror on the child's face is heartbreaking. He wants to let go—but still he holds tightly to the only security he knows. As the flames surge higher, the rope begins to fray and the father's voice becomes urgent. "Please, son, let go of the rope! I will catch you." The flames lick at the father's clothing, the heat blisters his face. Still he stands with his hands outstretched, pleading for his son to release the rope and drop into his arms.

Letting Go

The child is me, and the Father is God. I couldn't let go the rope because

---

No life is so damaged, no soul so stained, that God would disdain to die for it.

another father had convinced me that it was not safe to drop into Father's arms.

Suffering children are safe in His arms. But I resisted going there because I had learned that father's arms could not be trusted. But my heavenly Father is patient, and He will wait for me to drop into His arms. Here I come, Father! Hold out Your arms!

No life is so damaged, no soul so stained, that God would disdain to die for it.

The cords of death entangled me;
The torrents of destruction overwhelmed me.
The cords of the grave coiled around me.
The snares of death confronted me.
In my distress I called upon the Lord.
I cried out to my God for help.
From his temple he heard my voice;
My cry came before him, into his ears.

He heard me! And then...

The earth trembled and quaked
And the foundations of the mountains shook;
They trembled because He was angry.
Smoke rose from his nostrils,
Consuming fire came from his mouth,
He parted the heavens and came down;
Dark clouds were under his feet.
He mounted the cherubim and flew;
He soared on the wings of the wind.
He made darkness his covering, his canopy around him—
The dark rain clouds of the sky.
Out of the brightness of his presence clouds advanced,
With hailstones and bolts of lightening...

I let go the rope... and then...

He reached down from on high and took hold of me;
He drew me out of many waters.
He rescued me from my foes who were too strong for me.
They confronted me in the day of my disaster,
But the Lord was my support.
He brought me into a spacious place;
He rescued me because he delighted in me.

—Psalm 18

He delighted in me! And he delights in you. Let go of the rope, for the words of the song are true. Suffering children are safe in His arms.

Chapter Thirty
Breaking Up the Old Foundations

I ASK, "Lord, why is it that I sometimes feel so close to You, and at other times so far away, when all the time my heart is seeking You—crying out for Your favor, longing for Your love?"

You answer, "Your relationship with me is hindered by dis-ease that you have carried with you from the sepulcher. You must be willing to surrender all your diseased ways of thinking, relating, and processing as you draw close to me. For the darkness cannot cohabit with the light." I understand. The old foundations of my life must be broken up. A spiritual house cannot stand if it is built on a faulty foundation.

While it is true that feelings are neither right nor wrong, it's also true that our feelings affect the way we behave and how we relate to others. We're confused when our feelings are unhealthy, but we often feel powerless to change them.

Sometimes, we allow our feelings to control us. That's because our feelings arise from the old foundation that was laid in the sepulcher—concepts underlying our conscious thoughts that we accepted during the early days of our suffering in the agonizing confusion of abuse. They corrupt our understanding of life itself, an understanding that, unfortunately for those of us who suffered abuse, preceded our intellectual processing and robbed us of the tools that would have saved us.

Our foundation was laid when we were in a developmental stage of emotional processing. If information was couched in tears, authority, and/or intense feelings, it was accepted without question by the child that we were. For some of us, logic was influenced by subtle suggestions implanted by our abuser and by illogical but convincing ideas that derailed God's truth and caused us to believe a lie—in fact, many lies. As a result, our basic understanding of life was constructed upon a faulty foundation.

These faulty foundational constructs were laid in our earliest years by those entrusted with our upbringing. What we understand today about ourselves, about God, and about others, either conforms to—or challenges—those constructs. They are the basis for our worldview, the foundation upon which our life has been built.

A child has little defense against false constructs. He learns not only what to think, but more important, how to think in the context of family interaction. Let's look at an example of how this occurs.

A child goes to church and returns home upset because another child did not return his greeting. The child tells his mother. Perhaps she responds, "Maybe he just didn't notice you, or he was preoccupied. Let's see what happens next week." The child has just learned that the actions of other people are about themselves—not a statement of his worth.

On the other hand, perhaps his mother responds with anger: "He ignored you? Why wouldn't he like you? You haven't done anything to him, have you?" In this case, the child learns to look for what he may have done to cause negative consequences in his relationship with others, and thus begins the process of self-rejection.

When this child becomes an adult, he will continue his faulty processing of

No life is so damaged, no soul so stained, that God would disdain to die for it.

information, though he may not recall how he learned it, and his incorrect conclusions will lead to feelings of inferiority, resentment, and rejection.

I know of a man who left his church after several years of active membership because of the one time that his pastor failed to respond to his greeting. I was told by one of this man's relatives that most of his family behaves the same way. The seeds of rejection were sown early and became part of the faulty foundation that this man built his reason upon. His constructs were faulty, leading to distorted perceptions, illogical reasoning, hurt feelings, and ultimately wrong choices.

Renewed Foundations

How do we exchange faulty foundational constructs for healthier ones? Some say that we can't, that we will forever be controlled by the misinformation we internalized during our formative years. I contend that, though our initial conclusions may follow the perceptions established during our childhood, we can redefine our worldview, our foundational constructs, by internalizing the truth. The Psalmist said, "I have hidden your word in my heart that I might not sin against You." (Psalm 119:11.)

As our mind is transformed by the truth, through reading and meditating on the Word of God, and by the interaction of the Holy Spirit of God in our life, we can be freed from the fetters of false beliefs that would undermine our joy and damage our future. God proclaims, *"I know the plans I have for you. Plans to prosper you and not to harm you."* (Jeremiah 29:11.)

But others have sabotaged Your plan, God! They have given me faulty tools with which to build my life. You charged my parents with the responsibility to train me up in the way I should go, so that when I am old I will not depart from it. (Proverbs 22:6.) But I must depart from the way my parents trained me! How do I change the foundation of my life?

No life is so damaged, no soul so stained, that God would disdain to die for it.

The Word of God is sure. *"I have plans for you… plans to give you a future and a hope."* (Jeremiah 29:11)

When, Lord? When does my past end and the future You planned for me begin? It begins once I dare to hope, once I employ courage and determination to exhume my treasures.

But how do I do it? How do I go about detecting the false underpinnings of my spiritual house? How do I change the paths my thoughts travel when I'm processing information today?

The Psalmist said, "When the foundations are being destroyed, what can the righteous do?" (Psalm 11:3.) The wise man wrote in Proverbs: "When the storm has swept by, the wicked are gone but the righteous stand firm forever." (Proverbs 10:25.)

The storm is coming. We must submit our will and our understanding to God. Know that the tempests sent by his hand come to break up the faulty foundation—the false beliefs that we have built our thoughts upon. If we submit to the storm and seek God in it, we will always find Him there. He destroys the old foundation, the faulty foundation that will not support the righteous life, and builds in its place a firm foundation, one that will not be shaken.

Does God understand our childish ways? Did he set us up for failure by creating a faulty system where children would be shaped by forces beyond their control or comprehension, entrusting flawed people with the minds and hearts of innocent children?

Yes. He understands. But he did not set us up for failure. When we are weak, then He is strong in us. It is never too late to avail ourselves of His redemptive plan. The Apostle Peter gives us a blueprint for rebuilding our spiritual house. "Therefore rid yourselves of all malice, all deceit, hypocrisy, envy, and slander of every kind. Like newborn babies crave pure spiritual milk so that by it you may grow up in your salvation, now that you have tasted that the Lord is good." (1 Peter 2:1–3.)

No life is so damaged, no soul so stained, that God would disdain to die for it.

You couldn't help the way you started—but you can certainly choose the way you finish. Run the good race. Fight the good fight. Go back to the starting line if you must, but don't keep treading the same old paths that lead to destruction.

Peter concludes, "As you come to Him, the Living Stone, rejected by men but chosen by God and precious to Him, you also, like living stones are being built into a spiritual house." (1 Peter 2:4–5.)

No life is so damaged, no soul so stained, that God would disdain to die for it.

Chapter Thirty-one
Facing Our Fears Today

THE SEPULCHER OF ABUSE is behind you. Its dark presence recedes into the background. You have walked among the graves long enough and you are now stepping into the light! But your steps are slow, your feet feel heavy. You're tired and often afraid. You fear rejection, fear that you aren't good enough. You still feel like "damaged goods." How do you peel back the rotten cloths that bound you in the grave? How do you loose the bands that rob you of vitality?

I lived most of my life in bondage to fear. I went to bed with it at night and awoke with it in the morning. Like every emotion, fear has both a dark and a light side, and it's sometimes hard to distinguish the difference.

Obviously, if we are in a burning building, we had better be afraid. It's fear that keeps us alive in such situations. The fight-or-flight response is a God-given mechanism to keep us safe. Healthy fear motivates us to solve problems, while unhealthy fear torments us with impossible solutions, leaving us paralyzed, unable to cope with the situation.

Scriptures tell us that "Perfect love drives out fear." (1 John 4:18.) and that "God has not given us a spirit of fear, but of love, of power, and of a sound mind." (2 Timothy 1:7, NKJV.) It is by facing our fears that we conquer them.

Chapter Thirty-two
What Do You Fear?

THERE ARE MANY types of fear. I've experienced most of them! Perhaps you have as well. Our fears may include: fear of being rejected, fear of not being good enough, fear of losing love, fear of being displaced, fear of being disrespected, fear of being misunderstood, fear of making wrong choices, fear of losing creditability, fear of the dark, fear of certain people, fear of being harmed, fear of losing a loved one through death, fear of being controlled, fear of misusing my own power over those for whom I am responsible, fear of embarrassment, fear of the future, fear of the past, fear of being criticized, fear of being inadequate, fear of—the list could go on and on.

> **To whatever degree I fail to trust God, that is the measurement of my fear.**

The Apostle Paul said, *"Everything that does not come from faith is sin."* (Romans 14:23.) Some describe sin as "missing the mark." When we are controlled by our fears, we certainly miss the mark of the "high calling of God." So what are we to do about it?

If we do what we can, God will do the rest.

We Can Control Our Imagination

When we realize that our imagination is out of control—that it's taking us where it wants to go, we must catch ourselves the very minute we begin to fantasize, and stop it! Maybe the story unfolding in our mind would have a good ending, one that would make us feel better. More likely, it will carry us to the place of our fears and leave us there, frustrated, discouraged, and powerless. We sometimes "die a thousand deaths" while we are living— just because of an out of control imagination.

We Can Consider Our Options and Make a Decision Based on Biblical Principles

If we are unsure of what those principles are—or how we should apply them— we need to talk to a counselor. The wise King Solomon said, "In the multitude of counselors there is safety." (Proverbs 11:14.) Secrecy is a tool forged by Satan to keep the confused soul in bondage. A wise counselor is God's gift to wounded people. Why should we trust our distorted sense of reality until we have progressed out of the pit of despair and come into health? Often progress is hard to come by until our faulty ways of thinking have been exposed. We should not be ashamed to seek help from someone who has been trained to help us discern the truth. A wise counselor will not tell us what to do, but will teach us to evaluate our reality and make healthy decisions for ourselves.

We Can Learn to Trust

This takes time. It seems to me that most of us take one of two extremes. Either we trust no one, or we tell the world. In the first instance, we keep our problems entirely to ourselves. In the second instance, we tend to indiscriminately voice our pain, bringing offense and misunderstanding upon ourselves—often inviting re-victimization even as we seek understanding and affirmation.

No life is so damaged, no soul so stained, that God would disdain to die for it.

Sometimes we feel that we must be certain that we'll still be accepted and loved once our past is known. We speak at inappropriate times or to uninvolved people— allowing their responses to shape our own identity. We harm ourselves this way. We bind ourselves to our past and destroy relationships. To once again quote the wise King Solomon: "Like a gold ring in a pig's snout is a beautiful woman who shows no discretion." (Proverbs 11:22.) Ugh! Discretion is an ornament of beauty to a woman— and we can learn to wear it with confidence. "In quietness and confidence shall be your strength." (Isaiah 30:15, NKJV.)

Learn to discern safe people and those who are not. Do not entrust you treasures, the secrets of your heart, to those who can't be trusted to cherish them— and you.

We Can Communicate

When you feel you are misunderstood, ask a question. Don't be afraid to clarify what you're saying or to ask others to do the same. Do not second-guess what others mean by what they say to—or about—you. You can read all kinds of things into it and get it all wrong. Rejection breeds rejection—if you reject yourself you'll cause others to reject you as well. Don't use innuendo or sarcasm against others, and don't accept it from them. Ask, "What do you mean?" and listen to the answer. Let's say what we mean and be sure we understand what others are saying to us.

We Can Refuse to Ruminate

Often we keep chewing over the past like a cow chewing the same grass over and over. This is rumination. A cow has four compartments in her stomach, so she can afford to ruminate—in fact, she must do so in order to digest her food. Human beings are not equipped to ruminate, and doing so is counterproductive to our physical and mental health.

No life is so damaged, no soul so stained, that God would disdain to die for it.

How do you know if you ruminate? A few questions will help clarify this point. Do you often feel insecure after spending time with a friend? Do you rehearse every aspect of the conversation in your mind? "I said this—did she think I meant that? Did I reveal too much about—whatever...? I disagreed about this ... does she still like me? Was I misunderstood?"

I used to follow up just about every social encounter with an apology or at least a thinly veiled effort to test my approval rating with significant others—even "negatively" significant ones—people who got on my nerves with their open disapproval or patronizing attitudes. Or at least what I perceived to be such. See what I mean? Ruminating did me little good, for I'm still uncertain, many years later, about whether I was socially inadequate or if the other person was just being a jerk.

Part of our insecurity comes from not being sure of what is acceptable to others. Everyone gossips. How much gossip is too much? When does talking become gossiping? We want to be godly women—and we want to be respected as such. Oh, the pressure this puts on us. Someone has said that we should "Perform for an audience of One." Good advice, but easier said than done for most of us. So we ruminate. *What is this person going to think about what I revealed about myself today?*

When you're tempted to keep mulling over past conversations, just don't do it. Refuse to ruminate. Accept that you're acting out of what's in your heart and leave the outcome up to God. When we constantly need to be affirmed in our relationships, we can wear out even the most devoted friend. And we give our power away to others. That power throws the relationship out of balance—we have made our friend feel superior to us. Then we resent it. Instead, do your best—and let God do the rest. If your friend is truly a friend, you don't have to get every word right. Your friend will evaluate your words by what he already believes is in your heart—not the other way around.

No life is so damaged, no soul so stained, that God would disdain to die for it.

We Can Learn to Laugh at Ourselves

Someone once said, "If you learn to laugh at yourself the whole world laughs with you." Laughter is the medicine of the soul and the Elmer's Glue of relationships. I know people like me if they laugh at my jokes, because I know my jokes aren't funny. One of my daughters once said, "Mom, I am not laughing with you, I am laughing at you." But she said it with such obvious affection that I took it as a compliment.

We can laugh—or we can get offended—when others notice our mistakes. It's hard to do both at once. Everyone loves a person who makes them feel comfortable. If we want to be enjoyed, we need to lighten up and refuse to take ourselves seriously.

Jesus said He came so that we might have life—and have it more abundantly. Abundant life sounds like fun to me. It's okay to have fun. It's better than okay, it is a necessary part of life.

We Can Choose to Spend Time with People Who Are Spiritually and Emotionally Healthy

We become like those we hang around with. Their attitudes rub off on us. I read somewhere about a man who lived in Sodom. He carried a sign that said, "Repent! The end is at hand!" An angel informed him that it was too late. Judgment had been decreed against that wicked land. But he continued to carry the sign. The angel asked, "Why do you continue to carry the sign when you know that no one is going to repent?" The man answered, "At first I carried the sign to warn others. Now I carry it to warn myself."

If you live with a negative, depressed, or controlling person, you will be affected by that person's attitudes. Only by spending time away from that person, involving yourself in activities with others who have positive attitudes, will you be able to resist the negative forces around you.

No life is so damaged, no soul so stained, that God would disdain to die for it.

We Can Learn to Forgive

I saved this principle for last because, for most of us, it's the most difficult to accomplish. Before we can do it, we'll need to understand what forgiveness is and what it is not.

Before I processed the abuse, I would have told you early on that I had forgiven my father. I forgave my mother for failing to protect me. I forgave myself for allowing twenty-eight years to pass before I got out of my father's house. And then I began to remember the past as it really happened, and I realized that forgiveness would be a process, and it would take a long time.

Before we can forgive, we have to take a good hard look at how wounded we really are. We have to grieve our losses, or at least begin the grieving process. Forgiveness without grief is not forgiveness at all—but denial.

In *Christ-Centered Therapy*, Neil Anderson says that it is hard to forgive because forgiveness requires that we pay the price of another's sin. Just as Jesus paid the price of our sin in order to forgive us, we must suffer the injustice of letting the offender go free in order to be free ourselves. Anderson reminds us that the offender is not off the hook with God because we choose to forgive—he is just off the hook with us. God will deal with the offender and we are free to move on with our lives.

Isn't that so much better than staying in an emotional battle that we can't win and expending all our energy on something that we can't change? Unforgiveness becomes bitterness in time.

Have you ever been around a person who was bitter about something? It's like driving down the road after a skunk has sprayed his scent, unpleasant at best. We can't help but be affected by the offenses of others, but we can choose to become better—not bitter.

No life is so damaged, no soul so stained, that God would disdain to die for it.

Chapter Thirty-three
Lessons Learned

MIKE AND I have moved frequently during our married life. Mike's dad calls us gypsies. Most of our moves have been across town. We bought a house, remodeled it, sold at a profit, and then reinvested in another "project." Some lessons I learned from our frequent moves: 1) It's easier to discard outdated or undesired possessions when we are moving; 2) the change is worth the effort; and 3) those things I value most travel well.

Keep Moving

I can generalize these principles to my life. I must not become static, slipping into unintentional living, for change and progress are not optional for me. As soon as I settle into complacency, relax my boundaries, begin to "take life as it comes," I lose my edge. Old habits and rituals, outdated defense mechanisms, begin to show up, uninvited, and take over my spiritual and emotional house. When I'm not on the move, the guard is asleep, and my city is unguarded.

Lest you think I'm advocating a lifestyle of hyper-vigilance, beset by stress and fatigue, let me explain. Thoughts run rampant through our mind during every waking hour. When we aren't consciously thinking, we're subconsciously at work on our environment, past, present, and future. Our subconscious thoughts will surface in dreams. So we don't have the luxury of a "thoughtless" life. It is imperative that we proactively take control over our thoughts, consciously guiding them into a positive, healthy direction.

Taking control requires work—steady, determined effort. It requires that we study, reflect, and take time for ourselves when we need it. Like Jesus, who drew apart, even from His closest friends, to spend time alone and in fellowship with his Divine Parent, we must not allow the busy "things" of life to rob us of the important things.

Change is Worth the Effort

The second lesson I've learned from my "gypsy lifestyle" is that *the change is worth the effort*. Each move has profited us in so many ways. We've gained new friends, met unexpected challenges, and learned to detach in healthier ways.

When we made our first move, we met the resistance of spiritual leaders who were reluctant to release us from their fellowship. Mike and I were wearing multiple "hats" and expending so much time and energy in the "busyness" of the church, that we were failing to take time to replenish our own spiritual and emotional reserves. The manner in which we detached was more like fleeing than healthy leaving. We left not only the church, but also the denomination, and slipped into a less religious lifestyle, sleeping in on Sunday mornings and confining our spiritual journey to tidbits of conversation with the Savior, primarily in times of crisis.

That didn't last long, because we were soon reminded of our need for intimacy

No life is so damaged, no soul so stained, that God would disdain to die for it.

with Christ—that need being the tether that binds us to something bigger and better than ourselves. We were soon back in church, back on track in our relationship with the Father, and ready to grow forward.

Those Things that Travel Well

Finally, the third lesson I learned was that *those things I value most travel well.* This principle has proved itself true over time. The relationships that were authentic have stood the test of time. We're still friends, and those who were truly our friends before, though few in number, are precious to us.

Mike and I have also learned to depend on each other and on God as we've adapted to our environment with all its changes and challenges.

I admit that there have been bumps along the road that upset the balance of our relationship. We have on more than one occasion needed the help of professional counselors to navigate the troubled waters of our souls. We have recognized the "dance" that occurs between his challenges and mine, and we've learned that most of the time when we "go around the same mountain" over and over, it's because we're relating out of our woundedness and not out of our health.

When we're wise, we stop, look, and listen. But sometimes we're foolish, and then we hit, run, and hide, striking out with emotional blows against an enemy that we cannot see and hurting one another in the process

Mike and I are committed—one hundred percent—to our marriage, our God, and each other. We are committed to the principles found in Malachi 2:15–16: that God hates divorce, and that the purpose of marriage is to raise up "godly offspring." We are committed to health, healing, and change, not only for our sakes but also for the sake of the children God has given us. We want to see them grow up loving God, taking care of themselves, and respecting us for our efforts to love them the way our

---

No life is so damaged, no soul so stained, that God would disdain to die for it.

Divine Parent does—with honor, consistency, and wisdom. Do we fail at this? Yes. Probably more often than we know. But we are committed to the task and it is our hope and belief that God, who loves our children more than we possibly can, will make up the difference, fill in the gaps between his ideal parenting and our muddled efforts to do it right.

No life is so damaged, no soul so stained, that God would disdain to die for it.

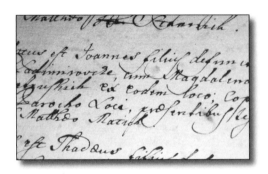

Chapter Thirty-four
Letters to Live By

A. ANALYZE EVERYTHING. This is not the overwhelming chore that it may seem at first glance. Every thought, every feeling, and every event that comes into our life will affect us in some way. If we consciously analyze everything, it will wear us out, leaving us confused, fatigued, and immobilized. Some things require conscious, deliberate scrutiny. Major decisions, lifestyle changes, a move across town… All the rest of it needs to be analyzed in the same way a bank teller analyzes currency that comes through her window. She has been taught by exposure to authentic currency to recognize what's counterfeit. She analyzes almost effortlessly, because she has been trained by the truth to recognize all that is false.

If we spend ample time in the Presence of Truth, allow our mind to be trained by Him, saturated in authenticity, we will analyze almost effortlessly and respond appropriately.

B. BEAUTIFY YOUR ENVIRONMENT. Confusion thrives in chaos. Clean the house, buy inexpensive ornaments if you need to, and create beauty in your home. Make it look good, smell good, and sound good through relaxing music that invites the soul to rest.

C. Clean it up. Our home, ourselves, and our environment.

D. Dare to do right. Dare to do what is right and leave the outcome up to God.

E. Edify yourself. Do those things that build up your spirit and your faith.

F. Forgive. Learn how to let go of blame.

G. Go. Get out of the house. Go do something that is good for you and others.

H. Help. Get help for yourself, and then help others who need your wisdom and comfort.

I. Invest. Invest your time, energy, and wisdom in the lives of others. Your investment will come back to you many times over.

J. Just do it. Don't wait until you feel like it. Don't wait until you feel qualified. You have a lot to offer at all stages of your recovery. You will never be more aware of the pain in others than when you're hurting, too.

K. Keep moving. Keep moving onward. Keep moving upward.

L. Let go. Let go of destructive ways of thinking and relating. Let go of destructive relationships. Let go of everything that hinders your health and healing.

M. Meditate on the truth. Apply God's truth to your experience. Do it every day.

N. No. Learn to say no. Learn to say no when you need to. It's okay to say no to good things if those things are not good for you—or if they're not good for you right now.

No life is so damaged, no soul so stained, that God would disdain to die for it.

O. OPPOSE WHEN NECESSARY. Oppose people, thoughts, and actions that bring you down. Jesus said that he came to bring a sword between even those of the same household. If someone in your family is behaving in destructive ways toward you—oppose that person with the truth. Learning how to oppose others in healthy, godly ways is one of the most important tasks of recovery. Opposition can be good!

P. PROCESS EVERYTHING. You wouldn't leave a splinter in your foot and say, *"Oh, it's nothing. Just a little splinter."* That splinter will fester. It will infect your entire body if you don't get it out.

Q. QUESTION EVERYTHING. Any "truth" that will not stand up to scrutiny is no truth at all, but a lie. God's truth is absolute. Our "truths" are relative; they're influenced by our experiences, our misconceptions, and our peers.

R. REPENT. "There is none righteous, not even one," the psalmist laments. (Psalm 14:3.) We know that we are not righteous. Christ alone is righteous, and he offers his righteousness to us.

Think of a child who has been targeted by an enemy. The enemy points his weapon in the child's direction. "You are guilty," he says. "You deserve to die."

The Father leaps in front of the child. He spreads his cloak over the child—and the child is saved. The cloak of the Father's righteousness covers us and will protect us from death and destruction.

What must we do to be saved, to be covered? We must repent. We must confess our sins to Him—our Divine Parent who will never—ever—use our confession against us. He will, as the scripture promises, *"Forgive our sins and purify us from all unrighteousness."* (1 John 1:9.) Isn't that what we crave? Isn't that purity what we all long for? To be absolutely pure, free of all the contamination of everything that has ever happened to us and everything that we ourselves have done that has muddied

No life is so damaged, no soul so stained, that God would disdain to die for it.

the waters of our soul. He promises to "purify us from all unrighteousness"—past, present, and future. All he asks is that we repent. Turn away from our sins and walk in a different direction.

"What sins?" we ask. Was the abuse our sin? Was our compliance sin? No! We are not responsible for the abuse or for our response to it. But we are responsible for our selfishness, our pride, our controlling ways, and our hatred of God. These and all other forms of unrighteousness are sins that we may have embraced, and healing will come only as we are able to repent and accept the righteousness of God as a covering for our past, present, and future sins. It is our responsibility to repent; and it is God's privilege and purpose to restore us. Every day.

S. Surrender to God's plan and purpose for your life. This is the hardest thing for us to do when we have surrendered to an abuser in the past and suffered for it. Surrender did not damage us—the abuser did. It is not our surrender that violates us, but the one to whom we surrender.

Surrendering to God, the perfect parent, the perfect lover, the absolute perfection, is our only hope, for it is by surrendering to God that we are saved from our propensity to surrender to fallen beings who will violate our trust and use us for their unholy purposes.

T. Trust appropriate others. This is another difficult task, for our trust has been violated in the past. Our heart once trusted and was torn because of it. The enemy of our soul targeted *our trust* for annihilation, for he knows that it is through trust that we attain intimacy with God. If he can keep us from trusting God, he will continue to victimize us all the way to the grave, for then we will place our trust in others who will fail us, violate us, or abandon us.

Trust in God will teach us to extend appropriate trust to others and withdraw it from those who are not worthy of it. Unlike love, which should be given uncondi-

No life is so damaged, no soul so stained, that God would disdain to die for it.

tionally, trust must be earned.

U. Understand. Develop an understanding heart. Learn to live the prayer of St. Francis of Assissi—that we seek not so much to be understood, as to understand others and become a person of compassion.

V. Vault beyond victimization! When we are victims no longer, we will think like a victor and behave like a victor—even when we don't feel like a victor.

W. Withdraw appropriately. I will withdraw from people who don't have my best interest at heart. I will take a step back—or two or three—whatever it takes to "guard my heart," for it is "the wellspring of life."

X. eXpress my truths. Learn to communicate honestly. Resolve not to hide, hint, or manipulate, but to be honest and direct about your feelings, your needs, and your expectations.

Y. Yell. Do not keep secrets at the expense of your own integrity.

Z. be Zealous in your quest for wholeness. Say to yourself: "I hereby declare that I, like James and John, the "sons of thunder" among the disciples of Christ, will ever be a zealot for righteousness.

No life is so damaged, no soul so stained, that God would disdain to die for it.

Come Away

"Come away my love!"
The Shepherd calls His frightened sheep.
But in her despair the creature runs
Headlong toward the precipice.
Hindered by her heavy wool
She hurries as quickly as she is able
Toward her impending doom.

Now, with gentle urgency
The Shepherd cries,
"Come away my love.
I will take you far away
From the one you fear.
Carried gently near my breast
You will be safe and I myself
Will care for you.

Slowly, stumbling feet cease
Their flight. She turns and looks
Into the eyes of the One who paid
Her price.

Finally, she rests
Her shepherd gathers her
Into his strong arms.
He faces her attacker—who
Runs pell-mell into the darkness
And is gone.

She rests her weary head
Upon her Shepherd's breast
And He carries her
Gently home.

SECTION 3
Reflections of Another Sort

~

Chapter Thirty-five
Loving Beyond Ourselves

SELF. How often we act, believing our actions to be loving, when, at the core, they're just another effort to accommodate ourselves. Giving in order to get. Sacrificing myself in the expectation that you, in turn, will sacrifice yourself for me. It's hard for the human heart to give without entitlement—the expectation that if I give, I will also get something from you, something I want. Something I need.

God alone is capable of providing totally selfless love. He is our example to be emulated, our Guiding Light who shines through our addictions, our worn-out defense mechanisms, and our unhealthy dependencies on others. It is by submitting to His will and His ways that we will rise above our self and become more godly, better at loving, able to forgive, and ultimately better persons.

When we spend time with someone, that person begins to "rub off on us." Love is more "caught" than "taught." By spending time with the Perfect Lover, we can begin to become more loving. Our love will become more other-oriented, like the love of the Savior who gave up a throne in the Celestial City to meander among the diseased remains of fallen humanity.

I doubt that I would give up a throne. I might go to India and visit the Untouchables, might even reach out to them, but I won't stay there. I can give only so much. The eternal Maker of all the worlds came, He gave, and He stayed. He spent his earthly life among us and then, when we killed him, he departed for a season, so that he could send us a different part of Himself—his Holy Spirit. Himself, unconfined by the robes of flesh, unhindered by physical boundaries, a divine Self so miraculous, so magical, so wonderful that He can condense Himself—the Creator of the Universe—into "something" that by its very nature can inhabit the space offered to Him by every heart that seeks to know Him.

Only by seeing—not just *knowing*, but *realizing*—who Jesus is and what He has done for me can I ever hope to become unselfish. If the opposite of selfishness is love, then he offers hope that I may, as I become more like Him, grow more loving and less selfish, centered less on pleasing myself and more on pleasing Him. I can become like the One who repeatedly commanded us, "love one another."

Nowhere does my insufficiency in love show itself more than in my relationship with the man I adore. Yes, I said that. I adore my husband—and that is not admirable. God alone is to be adored. I am learning to separate Mike from God, but it has taken some hard knocks along the road in order to teach me that my husband is not the one who fulfills of all my dreams or the designer of my destiny.

When I met Mike, I was coming out of a horror show in which I had played a minor character. I hardly saw myself back then, for I was focused on meeting the needs of my family—even the needs that sprang from such evil depravity as that of my father, who convinced me that I should become his defender against the wagging tongues that maligned him. "Cover for me. Let no one see… You don't want Daddy to go to jail."

I also felt responsible for meeting the needs of my mother, whom I believed

No life is so damaged, no soul so stained, that God would disdain to die for it.

could not protect herself. Her survival seemed to depend on my stepping up to the plate: "I'll go with you, Dad. I'll make you feel better. Stop shoving Mother around, and please put the gun away. Come on. Let's go."

And above all, my primary purpose in life was to meet the needs of my siblings, most of whom didn't know then, and don't know now, the violence, humiliations, and deprivations they escaped because I stood between them and our father.

The annihilation of myself did not make me a hero; it's not noble to lay down your virtue for another. Your life, perhaps. Your virtue, never. It wasn't noble, but it was the only thing I knew to do. It was the thing I understood that I must do, just as I must eat to live. Not to do it seemed selfish, and cruel to my siblings and my mother, those who needed me.

If I failed to understand need, I also failed to understand love. During my pilgrimage through victimization, need and love became so intertwined that I failed to recognize the difference. If I love you, then I will meet your needs. And you, of course, must do the same for me. If you fail to meet my needs, then you must not love me. This is toxic thinking, and it will surely lead to mental, emotional, and spiritual illness.

Heaven help us! As a dear friend is prone to saying, "We're all sick puppies." And we are—but we're not without a healer. The problem is that most of us, myself most of all, hate the scalpel. The Divine Surgeon wants to operate on our souls, and we resist. We run away. We beg to be relieved. We whine. We bargain. We find a way of escape.

Submit. Wave the white flag! Surrender to the Healer and He will cut away the cancer that consumes you. Submit to the scalpel of suffering and the sutures of forgiveness. Recovery is painful, but purifying. Once we submit, we will be changed. Some of us fear it. All of us dread it. Most of us avoid it. We must embrace the healing process if we would be transformed into the Image of Pure Love, centered on others

No life is so damaged, no soul so stained, that God would disdain to die for it.

and wholesomely engaged with the world around us.

We want that! I do—and I know that you do, too, or you wouldn't be reading this book. You could be swallowed up in your favorite novel, vicariously living
the lives of fictitious characters who dare to do the things you only dream of. Keep
dreaming, but start doing! There's life out there, and it has been purchased by the
one who gave His life for you. The wages of sin is death, but the gift of God is eternal
life, life on earth that overflows into life eternal. It is ours! But we will not possess it
until we submit to the Healer who is also the Provider of our treasures.

How do we do that? How do we submit? We put aside our foolish pride, our
wounded dignity, and our self-serving ways and enter the halls of the unholy—the
places where hurt people go to recover from their "hurts, habits, and hang-ups," as
they say at Celebrate Recovery. Maybe we even go outside the sanctified walls of the
local church and mingle with other sinners who linger at the tables in AA or Al-anon,
and listen, for a change, to those who don't always wear the badge of their sanctity
on their bosom. I'm not demeaning Christian recovery groups; I'm saying that I, in
my Christian pride, have often disdained what the "other," more secular group had to
offer.

I can tell you now that my habits are not holy and my hang-ups are not Christ-
like. I want to be like Him. Oh, how I want to be, but I need help. And I'll get that
help, when I take off my Christian mask and learn to get real.

I have worked in recovery groups within the church. Some of them are highly
effective, compassionate, and educated. But how easily many of us are offended. Let's
not say, "Higher Power," for that term does not adequately identify the source of our
healing.

What if God, as He has been represented to you in the past, is the source of
your pain? When I worked as a lay counselor in a Christian drug and alcohol recovery program, I lived and worked among the women who came into recovery—

No life is so damaged, no soul so stained, that God would disdain to die for it.

broken women, who had been violated in every possible way. As I listened to their stories, I realized that most of them had turned to drugs and alcohol as a way to anesthetize the pain they had suffered in childhood and in their youth. Nearly all of them had experienced sexual abuse, and many had been the victims of abandonment, neglect, and other forms of abuse as well. They didn't drink and take drugs because it was fun, they did it in an effort to survive. Many of these women came from religious backgrounds, yet their misconceptions about God were hindering them from receiving the grace and help they needed. Most of them had begged for His help at one time, but experienced His response as harsh, condemning, and condescending, a response often relayed to their tormented souls by Christian "helpers" whose own understanding of God was at best dysfunctional and often destructive.

If this has been your experience, you may need to distance yourself from the "god" of your youth, with the deliberate purpose of seeing who God really is, clearing your vision, discarding the destructive lenses with which the "child-you" viewed the Father of life, the Giver of Love, the Creator of the Universe. Maybe God looks just like your father, and your father, like mine, seemed like evil incarnate. Yet you need to trust a Power greater than yourself in order to begin to rise from the pit of your despair.

Then you are right to trust your "Higher Power," the One who is bigger and better and braver than yourself. According to the Holy Scriptures, those who seek will find Him. We who are confident in our knowledge of *who* He is may need to back off a bit and allow the wounded to come to him in their own way, their own time, and in their own brokenness.

Once I understood the purpose for believing in a "Higher Power" without giving him traditional names, I ceased to be offended. Our Higher Power is a big God and well able to take care of Himself. He doesn't need us to defend Him against the "sinners" who may be missing the mark in their quest of Him. He asks only that we

---

No life is so damaged, no soul so stained, that God would disdain to die for it.

"Love the Lord your God with all your heart, soul, mind, and strength" and "Love your neighbor as yourself." (Luke 10:27.) He, the Holy Spirit of God, the One who counsels, convicts, and converts, will do His work tunhindered by our feeble efforts to convince, control, and coerce others into His kingdom.

No life is so damaged, no soul so stained, that God would disdain to die for it.

Chapter Thirty-six:
SECRECY – The Bane of Abuse

Jesus said, "What you have said in the dark and what you have whispered in the ear in the inner rooms will be proclaimed from the roofs" (Luke 12:3), and "There is nothing hidden that will not be disclosed, and nothing concealed that will not be known or brought out into the open." (Luke 8:17.)

David performed his acts of adultery in secret. He murdered in secret. But when his sin was exposed—when the prophet thundered, "Thou art the man!" (2 Samuel 12:7)—then David repented publicly, in a way that would make his guilt known to all the land.

The Apostle Paul wrote in a public letter, "Alexander the metalworker did me a great deal of harm. The Lord will repay him for what he has done." (2 Timothy 4:14.)

The early church was told to bring the fornicators before the congregation so that their sin might be acknowledged—and then forgiven. (1 Corinthians 5.)

What is there about secrecy that we think is Christian? Why does holding back the knowledge of another's wrongdoing seem so friendly, so kind, when in fact the opposite is true? Known sin is sad. It hurts the transgressor and all who believe in him. But secret sin is insidious, twisting the insides of the sinner and bringing unjust suffering on those called upon to bear the secret knowledge of his sin

When sin remains secret, the innocent continue to suffer, and the guilty one has the freedom to go on sinning without coming face to face with the appropriate shame of his transgression, a shame that will lead to repentance if he is willing to submit to the awful discipline of disgrace. Only by acknowledging his sin and submitting to the natural consequences of it can he put it behind him and soar on wings of grace above the due penalty of sin—death and destruction.

Some of our greatest heroes have slid down the slope of disgrace before they ascended the heights of glory. Their failures became fruitful. Their shame became the shroud of glory that illuminates their passion and God's grace.

Would the story of John Newton evoke such wonder when we sing Amazing Grace if he had not been a slaver, a man of questionable morals and prone to drunkenness, before he became a man of God whose penitent heart produced the words of that great song? Paul was a persecutor of the church of Jesus Christ before he was the passionate Apostle and martyr who gave us thirteen books of the New Testament. Would his history sing as sweetly through the halls of glory if he had found some means of hiding his sin against the Lord Jesus Christ and His church?

Only by confessing our sin and turning our back on secret pacts are we free to live life unencumbered by the demands of our deceit. It requires great energy to keep dark deeds out of the light, energy that would be better expended living a life of freedom from the past, freedom that can be apprehended only by coming out of hiding, refusing subterfuge, and trusting our Redeemer God to restore His glory to us.

We often confuse secrecy with confidentiality. Secrecy is an unholy pact to conceal the truth from others. It is deceitful, addictive, and contagious. Confidentiality, on the other hand, refuses to disclose what has been willingly entrusted to the

No life is so damaged, no soul so stained, that God would disdain to die for it.

confidant's care. To ask for secrecy is to incorporate another into one's sin. To offer confidentiality is to provide a safe place for the process of repentance to occur, bringing the sinner to the place of exposing his own sin to God and others who have been offended by the sin.

The home where abuse abounds is a home accustomed to keeping secrets. The child reared in that environment will understand that keeping secrets is an act of love. They confuse secrecy with confidentiality, and will smolder in resentment when their secrets are exposed, especially by someone they trust. "You have betrayed me," their heart cries, for they don't know that it is the secrecy of their childhood home that has devoured them.

These children often don't know why they did not tell. Many times they have no recollection of being told to keep the family secrets, but they don't need precise memories to know what is expected of them. They have absorbed the rules like a small sponge soaked in the polluted water of dysfunction before they were old enough to make a choice about the matter. It became a part of their worldview that secrecy was synonymous with loyalty. They learned not to talk about the proverbial "elephant in the living room," and to faithfully maintain the family secrets, and their own, all the way to the grave.

James, the brother of Christ, advised, *"Confess your sins to each other and pray for each other so that you may be healed."* (James 5:16.) No more hiding. It's better to confess our sins and be made whole than to hide them and live in the fear of disgrace and the contagious disease of deceit that keeps us cowering in the dark.

A secret revealed has no more energy to grow, and is therefore dead. Once the storm of consequences has passed, the collateral damage evoked by our actions, we will be free to live transparent lives—lives of victory and purpose.

No life is so damaged, no soul so stained, that God would disdain to die for it.

Chapter Thirty-seven
Our "Besetting Sins"

M Y HUSBAND TELLS ME that he believes each of us has a "besetting sin," some particular, irritating, persistent "thing" that tempts us, tests us, and chronically "besets" us. The Apostle Paul tells us what to do with these challenges in his letter to the Hebrews (12:1): "…let us lay aside every weight and the sin which does so easily beset us." Lay it aside. Good advice, but easier said than done. I know the sin that "so easily besets" me, and it is fear. The scriptures tell us "fear has torment." Fear is no benign emotion that affects us from day to day, leaving us virtually unchanged by its assault, fear is evil! It torments us, taunts us, and will destroy us if we allow it to. Fear is so insidious in its effect on us that we're told in the final book of the New Testament that the "fearful and unbelieving" will "have their part in the lake which burns with fire and brimstone, which is the second death." (Rev. 21:8.)

Dear God! You would not banish me forever from your presence for what I can't control. In this thought alone there is hope—for if fear has the power to keep me from heaven, then I have the power, through Jesus Christ, to keep myself from fear. No more torment! I can wage war against my 'besetting sin,' and win!

> *For the weapons of our warfare are not carnal, but mighty*
> *through God to the pulling down of strongholds; casting*
> *down imaginations, and every high thing that exalts itself*
> *against the knowledge of God, and bringing into captivity*
> *every thought to the obedience of Christ.*
>
> —2 Corinthians 10:4–5

What in the world is a stronghold? Is it an addiction? An emotion? Our strong-holds may be replete with addictions and unhealthy emotions, but those things are merely the evidence of the strongholds in our lives. The Word is clear about what we are to "cast down." Imaginations, thoughts, and every "high thing" (pride, arrogance, self-sufficiency) that exalts itself against the knowledge of God. Humanistic thinking. Human striving. Let go, as the old song says, and let God! Let God have it. Let God be it. Let God fill it. Let God do it. For He alone can manage our lives in a position of power over all the enemies that occupy the strongholds that our genealogy, our experiences, and our choices have established in our souls.

When we admit that we are powerless over our fears and our faults, then we are free to look to Jesus, the author and finisher of our faith, to free us from them—one day at a time, one choice at a time, and one battle at a time.

No life is so damaged, no soul so stained, that God would disdain to die for it.

Chapter Thirty-eight
Hurts, Habits, and Hang-ups

THE APOSTLE PAUL had a thorn in the flesh. We are not told the nature of the thorn, only that it was "in his flesh," and that the thorn was sent by God to keep him from becoming conceited, to keep him humble. The same apostle writes in his letter to the church at Rome:

> *I am carnal, sold under sin. For what I am doing, I do not understand. What I will to do, that I do not practice; but what I hate, that I do... But now, it is no longer I that do it, but sin that dwells in me.*
> —Romans 7:16–17, NASB

How could the Apostle Paul understand me so well? Because he was human, like me. The truly spiritual person is not the one who rises above his humanity to look down upon those still groveling in the muck of their depravity, but the one who is in touch with his own "flesh," his own weaknesses, and his own battles; the one who dares to be honest enough to look into his heart and see his own depravity.

Could it be that our hurts, habits, and hang-ups are the tether that bind us to God? The link between deity and flesh that remind us that we dare not stand alone, that there truly is "something out there," and it's bigger than we are, and stronger? Our hurts, habits, and hang-ups then have purpose after all. They keep us dependent on our God rather than our self. They humble us and free us at the same time.

We know our limits, and we're confined by them and afraid to move out of them. If, as the wise king (Solomon) said, the *"fear of God is the beginning of wisdom,"* then we do well to appreciate the tether that binds us to the One who is the source of all wisdom, all goodness, and all love.

> *He who has no thorn has no need to be delivered of conceit. If he has no need to be delivered of conceit, then he is devoid of anything to be conceited about, or else his pride is so consuming that he limps along in life saying, "What thorn? I don't have a thorn."*

Reflections

Once, in Arizona, I saw a riverbed. It had run dry, but it was still the obvious channel for the water that would flow when the rains came, as they occasionally did in the desert. The contours of the dry bed were unmistakable. And when the rains fell, the water would flow as it had for centuries, through the deep depression in the sand that was the river's bed.

So it is with those deep depressions in the soul that come about through genealogy, life experience, and destiny, making their imprint in the sand of our soul and providing a channel through which our life will flow.

The study of psychology teaches us that the "worldview" of a child is estab-

---

No life is so damaged, no soul so stained, that God would disdain to die for it.

lished before the age of six. There is, it seems, little doubt that by that young age the thoughts that flow through the human brain have found a channel through which to flow, a course that will not change throughout his life. Our tendency to do wrong is so deeply etched in every cell of our brain that it is only by the strength of a power greater than ourselves that we may, though tempted to do wrong, choose to do what's right. Our riverbed is set, and it will flow where it will.

Does the drug addict choose his craving for drugs, or the sex addict his attraction to pornography? Does the obese woman choose to be tempted by food? We don't choose to be tempted by these things; we don't get up one day and say, "I want my temptation to be food (or sex, or money)." *"Every man is tempted when he is drawn away by his own lust and enticed,"* James, the brother of Christ, writes. (James 1:14.) Drawn away by our lust—the thing that hides in our cellar and demands to be fed. The Apostle Paul says, *"It is no longer I that do it [what is wrong] but sin that dwells in me."* (Romans 7:17.) This, my friend, is the human condition. *"For all have sinned and come short of the glory of God."* (Romans 3:23.) The area of our tempting is determined by the flow of our river, a fact we don't choose and can't change. The course of our river was forged by our genealogy, our early experiences, and our destiny. Temptation happens, and we do not choose it. That is why we pray the prayer of serenity: *God help me to accept the things I cannot change.*

I am a survivor of sexual abuse. That fact affects the flow of my river, the thoughts that spring unbidden from the depths of my soul, the temptations common to those who share my particular pain. I can't change that and I must not deny it. What I can do is seize upon the strengths that recovery demands of me. I can rejoice in the ways that I've come to know God in my brokenness, ways I might have missed had I not suffered abuse. And I can keep my river clean.

The water in our river may be muddied by sin, sorrow, and disorder, or it may be crystal clear, purified daily by the *"washing of the Word"* and fellowship with the

No life is so damaged, no soul so stained, that God would disdain to die for it.

Holy Spirit who *"cleanses us from all unrighteousness."*

You know by now that I came from a highly dysfunctional family. My teachers in school knew it, my church family knew it, and even my neighbors who witnessed the symptoms of our family dysfunction knew it. That knowledge was the source of chronic disrespect directed at a child who didn't fit in, who had no idea of how "normal" people lived, and who intuitively understood that she was somehow untouchable. Rejection was intensely feared, yet experienced daily.

Can you imagine the impressions these experiences made on the soul of a young girl? Maybe you can. Maybe you're remembering your own struggle with rejection. If so, your riverbed, like mine, has been imprinted with rejection, and you'll be prone to interpret anything that remotely resembles the rejection you experienced in the past as rejection today.

Don't believe it. Don't allow the negative experiences of the past to infect your life with false assumptions. When you were a child, you thought rejection meant you were inferior, that you didn't deserve acceptance. Now you know better. If you're rejected, that's the problem of the one who does the rejecting. He or she needs to deal with their pride.

The problem for me is that I often misinterpret unintentional slights as rejection. I join a group of friends and no one says hello to me. Rejected! I say something in a group and no one responds to my statement. Rejected! Someone points out a fault or flaw that I may have, no matter how lovingly; and I feel rejected.

I now have a choice. I can accept the lying voice in my head that tells me I'm being rejected, or I can identify the lie and refuse it. I talk to myself. Weird, my daughter says, but I do. "You're not being rejected, Linda," I say. "She probably didn't hear you." Or, "Maybe I do have a character flaw here. I'll think about it."

Weird or not, I talk back to the voices of the past that play inside my head. Like a tape recorder programmed to repeat negative messages, they never miss an oppor-

---

No life is so damaged, no soul so stained, that God would disdain to die for it.

tunity. That's fine by me—I never miss one, either! I use those difficult moments to layer positive messages over the negatives ones, and someday, I believe, the positive messages will override the negative.

If we attend any AA or Celebrate Recovery meeting, we will be encouraged, every time, to "read the literature," to set aside a time for daily meditation and devotion, and take time to do a daily inventory of our actions. We are encouraged to rejoice in our success when we do what's right, and make our amends to God and others when we've done wrong. Keep our river pure, unpolluted by our tendency to do what's wrong. Promptly admit our wrongs and repent; turn away from them and begin to do what's right. One day at a time.

I remember going to the lake as a child of nine or ten. I couldn't swim yet, but I wandered out too deep. When my feet could not touch bottom, I panicked, thrashing the water and yelling when I managed to surface. There was so much excitement— kids laughing, playing, splashing—that I knew no one could hear me. I was going to drown.

And then my aunt, three years older than I and a good swimmer, saw me. "I'll save you, Linda." Finally! In a few strokes she was at my side. But I was beyond reason at that point, intent on saving myself at any price. I pushed my aunt under the water and stood on her back, leaping into the shallows. She came up spluttering and coughing. "That's the last time I'll ever save you!" she yelled. I don't blame her. My instinct to survive at any cost had consumed any love I may have had for my aunt, and I didn't care, at that moment, whether she died, as long as I made it out all right. I was incredibly selfish, I know. I was then and I often am today. I like to think that I've matured beyond the nine-year-old girl who tried to drown her rescuer. But if you were to listen in on my arguments with my husband, my desire to be "right" and my frequent lapses into "survival mode," then you'd know that though the water in my river is renewed day by day, the course it flows through creates conflict between what

No life is so damaged, no soul so stained, that God would disdain to die for it.

I should do and what I do by default—those things that often drain me dry when I have been designed to carry life-giving water to a thirsty world.

The Psalmist of Israel writes:

> *God is our refuge and strength, a very present help in time of trouble.*
> *Therefore, we will not fear, though the mountains be carried into the midst*
> *of the sea…. There is a river whose streams shall make glad the City of*
> *God, the holy place of the tabernacle of the Most High!* —Psalm 46

Rejoice in our river, O God. Take pleasure in our streams. For we want nothing more than to be the source of your delight. *Be still,* you say, *and know that I am God.* We will be still—and know.

> **The Victorious Life is not about what happens to us—**
> **but what happens through us. Let the healing stream of**
> **God's love flow through you today.**

No life is so damaged, no soul so stained, that God would disdain to die for it.

Chapter Thirty-nine
Beauty for Ashes

OVER 2000 YEARS AGO, Jesus Christ stood up in the synagogue, and read from the ancient text:

> *The Spirit of the Lord is upon Me, because the Lord has anointed Me to preach good tidings to the poor; He has sent Me to heal the broken hearted, to proclaim liberty to the captives, and the opening of the prison to those who are bound.* —Isaiah 61:1

Jesus came, he lived, and he died to set at liberty those who are "bound hand and foot with grave cloths," as Lazarus was, though he came forth from the grave. Jesus came to free us. And he came to comfort us. The text continues: *The Lord has anointed me "to comfort all who mourn, to console those who mourn in Zion, to give them beauty for ashes, the oil of joy for mourning, the garment of praise for the spirit of heaviness."* (Isaiah 61:2-3, NKJV.)

204

I want it, Lord. I reach out my hand to take it from you—comfort, consolation, and beauty.

"Forget thy father's house and the King will desire your beauty." You spoke that word to me when I first fled my father's house in 1985 … and you speak it still, today. Forget … forget. I must remember, so that I will know what I must forget. I have remembered. I've done the hard work of processing the pain in those memories, and now I am ready to be consoled.

Comfort me, Holy Spirit. Come and give me beauty for ashes. Those who grieved in Zion sprinkled ashes on their heads to demonstrate their sorrow. My head has been covered with ashes long enough! I'm ready for your beauty to shine through me! I can't say I've forgotten my father's house, but I'm forgetting! I've unearthed so many truths, and I now possess them. They are mine, and no one will ever take them from me. I see the child that I was and the woman that I am with new eyes. And I am ready to praise You.

Here! Here is my garment! A beautiful white dress, overlaid with lace. I slip it over my head and twirl around. It flows like liquid snow—pure, white, virgin snow. "I will greatly rejoice in the Lord," Isaiah says, "for He has clothed me with the garments of salvation. He has covered me with the robe of righteousness." (Isaiah 61:10, NKJV.)

> ***Do not fear, for you will not be ashamed, nor disgraced.***
> ***You will forget the shame of your youth ….*** —Isaiah 54:4

No life is so damaged, no soul so stained, that God would disdain to die for it.

SECTION 4
Mining for Treasures from the Past

~

Chapter Forty
Getting Prepared for the Valley of Shadows

TRUTH, GRACE, AND TIME, the three essential elements of recovery. And none of them is available to us by our own efforts. They are a gift. We are the recipients. All we have to do is ask. God, through the work of his Holy Spirit on earth, dispenses them. He gives to all people freely. He says, "You do not have because you do not ask." (James 4:2.)

Our Divine Parent will not refuse us any good gift. And a good gift is *that which is good for us*, in keeping with the partially unveiled plan of our Maker. He who does all things well—and He alone—knows the end from the beginning.

Picture a traveler in the valley, surrounded by vegetation and high mountains. He is cold, tired, and hungry. He comes upon a path that ascends the side of a mountain. It's not too steep, and it looks like a shortcut to the king's house. The traveler knows that he'll be safe and warm if he can just get to the king's house.

The problem is there's a huge boulder blocking the entrance to the path, and a steep ravine on either side of it. He can't go around the boulder and he can't cross over it. The traveler can see the king of the mountain standing on the pinnacle, watching, outside his house.

"Hey!" the traveler yells. "Can't you send some angels or something to get this boulder off the path? I need to get out of this valley."

The king does not respond.

"Don't you hear me?" the traveler calls. "Or don't you even care that I've been stuck in this valley a long time? I want out!"

The king just shakes his head, then speaks in a whisper, "Don't you see the signs, my son?"

But the traveler just keeps shouting. He's jumping up and down now, waving his arms. "Hey, you up there." He can't hear the king above the sound of his own voice.

"Why are you so blind?" the king whispers.

The traveler turns away from the king. "I don't care," he decides. "I'll make my own way up the mountain. I don't need him anyway."

If the traveler hadn't turned away, he would have seen a white bird perched on the king's right shoulder, a bird so pure and white, and beautiful in form that it would have taken his breath away.

The king says to the bird, "Fly down and rest beside the sign. Perhaps then he will see it."

The white bird swoops into the valley and alights on a boulder beside an ancient sign. The weathered board bears the inscription "All who would see the king must first pass this way."

Finally, the king has the attention of the traveler, who stops at the sign, becoming very still. He doesn't want to frighten the bird away. He's enthralled with its beauty, its unique form, and its purity.

"What's that I hear? A whisper on the wind? It sounds... almost as if someone is speaking." The traveler looks around. Seeing no one, he turns his attention back to

---

No life is so damaged, no soul so stained, that God would disdain to die for it.

the sign.

"Why," he asks, "must all travelers pass this way? This passage is lonely. Sometimes it grows dark. The path is often confusing, and there are wild beasts hiding in the foliage. Why must I travel here?" He doesn't realize that he, too, is speaking in a whisper.

The white bird says, "Do you really want to know why all travelers must pass this way?"

The traveler is astonished. "You can speak!" He states the obvious.

"I speak only what the king tells me."

For once the traveler is silent.

"All travelers who would see the king must go through the valley because it is in the valley that the traveler is prepared for the mountaintop. He who has never suffered pain cannot appreciate comfort. And he who has not traversed the valley could not begin to appreciate the joys of the mountain. Besides this, there is one other reason."

The traveler is speechless, afraid to move lest the bird fly away and leave him uninformed. He cocks his head slightly to the side and raises one eyebrow, waiting.

"There is a huge mountain lion halfway up the mountain. He has been given dominion over this valley, and he hates all who would ascend the mountain. That is why the king placed the boulders across the path you wanted to climb. You would surely have died before you reached the top."

Just then the sound of a low snarl startles the traveler. Peering into the foliage he sees the glow of amber eyes, sees movement in the brush. The enormous head of a mountain lion emerges from the entangled vegetation, and a mouth that appears to the traveler like the entrance to a cavern, ridged with razor-sharp teeth, opens to emit a deafening roar.

The traveler's wild eyes stare about him, and then upward. The king of the

---

No life is so damaged, no soul so stained, that God would disdain to die for it.

mountain stands still, where he has always been. He raises his mighty arm and the lion slinks back into the jungle.

"Just keep your eyes on the king," the white bird says. "And you'll make it through the valley."

The valley of shadows is that place where you deliberately open your heart and mind to allow the Holy Spirit to work on your memories, your life constructs, and your character. As you trust him to operate on your flaws, cutting away the defense mechanisms and faulty thought processes that bind you to your past, you may often find yourself in the valley. Never forget that you're only passing through. You are on the way to the King's House on the top of the mountain. And you'll make it—if you keep your eyes on the King.

No life is so damaged, no soul so stained, that God would disdain to die for it.

Chapter Forty-one
Redeeming the Treasure of a Lost Childhood

WHAT DO I MEAN by the treasure of childhood? Childhood is more than the progression of years that begins at birth and ends somewhere between the ages of eighteen and twenty-five. Everyone ages, but not everyone experiences childhood in the sense that I mean here.

Childhood should be a time of carefree growth, a period of years unfettered by worries about finances, adult relational conflict, provision, and protection. The child should expect that his needs will be provided for by others who care for him, and that he can trust them to do so in ways that nurture and protect him. When these expectations are consistently disappointed, the child experiences a great loss, one that will haunt him his entire life.

"How can a man be born when he is old?" Nicodemus asked. (John 3:4.)

Nicodemus was a ruler in Israel, a teacher of teachers, yet he struggled to understand a spiritual law that we must apprehend if we would recover the precious treasure of a lost childhood.

One thing we must understand is that in order for something to be redeemed, it must first be forfeited. And if it has been forfeited, the first step in recovery is to acknowledge and then to grieve it. Only then does redemption become a possibility.

"Surely," Nicodemus says, "a man cannot enter a second time into his mother's womb to be born."

You're absolutely right, Nicodemus. For a grown man to enter a second time into his mother's womb and be reborn is impossible. Yet Jesus said, "No one can enter the Kingdom of Heaven unless he is born again."

Herein lies a magnificent mystery, a dimension of life that Nicodemus had not considered. What is not seen is greater than what can be experienced with the eyes, with taste, touch, hearing, and smell. The spiritual dimension creates possibilities that cannot even be imagined with the physical senses. But it is easier to apprehend what we can experience with our physical body, because that's what we are, flesh and bone. We are created beings who are still closely attached to the earth from which we were formed.

Jesus said, "Flesh gives birth to flesh, but the Spirit gives birth to spirit." (John 3:6.)

The birth that precedes our childhood happened once. It won't happen again. Our parents were given the responsibility of protecting and providing for us. If they didn't, or couldn't, then we have suffered a tremendous loss, the loss of our childhood.

And what's so grievous about that? Why is there a gaping hole left in the middle of our soul when we've experienced that loss? Shouldn't we just move on now that we're grown? Can't we just get over it, let the past go, and live for today?

If only we could, most of us would leap at the chance to fill the hole without the tedious process of grief. We don't want to think about our losses. Most of the time, we pretend that they don't exist. But we are aware of them, so aware that the nag-

No life is so damaged, no soul so stained, that God would disdain to die for it.

ging sense of loss, the absence of something essential to who we are, to what we have become, undermines our joy, depletes our energy, and insists that there's something innately wrong with us, some fundamental inferiority inherent in our being. Quietly and insidiously, this misconception invalidates all our accomplishments, all our victories, insisting that we are less than others, that we're damaged merchandise, bargain-basement goods. It predicts that we'll be rejected, abandoned, and dishonored, a prediction that may become a self-fulfilling prophecy unless we recognize the source and take the necessary steps to redeem the stolen treasure of our lost childhood.

So, cautiously, we put one foot forward and test the ground. It is solid. It won't crumble beneath our feet and thrust us into the void we have just emerged from. And so we begin the process of redeeming our childhood.

Perhaps the best way to start is by examining the needs required for a child to develop properly. On the most basic level, every child needs to be touched, needs to be held, needs someone to look into his eyes with tenderness and bathe him in affection. He needs to be loved, physically and emotionally. He needs to read "love" in his parents' eyes on an intuitive level. As he grows, he needs the time and attention required for that love to be transmitted to his emotional and intellectual being.

A child needs to be provided for, physically and emotionally. Busy parents often take refuge in the comfort of "My child never goes hungry. He has a roof over his head and clothes on his back." As essential as these are, providing the basics of food, clothing, and shelter addresses only the physical part of the child, and won't compensate for the lack of tenderness, understanding, and admiration that every child craves from his parents.

When a child is deprived of these things, he is vulnerable to anyone, even the predators among us, who offer him a counterfeit version of loving parents, further exacerbating the damage done to his young soul.

No life is so damaged, no soul so stained, that God would disdain to die for it.

If you have experienced sexual abuse, neglect, physical or emotional abuse, or all of these, then, like me, you've experienced the loss of your childhood. As difficult as it is to acknowledge the truth—to see our life not as we wish it to be, but as it really is—this is the beginning of all recovery. The redemption of our treasures must start here.

Jesus concluded his discourse with Nicodemus by saying, "Whoever lives by the truth comes into the light so that it may be seen plainly that what he has done has been done through God." (John 3:21.) We begin with the truth and we build a testimony to the faithfulness, power, and integrity of God. We testify that what has been done, the redemption of our treasures, has been done through God.

Out of the womb of a woman we emerged into the light. We lived in the truth as we perceived it, and did our best to become people who would make our parents proud. Every child, whether he realizes it or not, longs to please his parents. Perhaps we couldn't please them, or we felt that we couldn't. Maybe things happened that hurt us and others, and we thought it must be our fault. We knew we weren't perfect.

No child is responsible for the neglect or abuse he has suffered. He was not the perfect child. There are no perfect children. But he was a child. And every child deserves to be nurtured, loved, and protected. If you were left to grow up without parental involvement in the day-to-day victories and injuries that life brought your way, left to deal with your emotions on your own without an empathetic parent to listen and guide you through it, you suffered a loss. And unless you deal with that loss, the damage it did won't simply go away. Not when you're twenty-five, not when you're forty, and not when you're sixty. Time doesn't heal the damage of neglect. Only the processing of the truth and recovery of our treasures will rectify the damage done by the loss of childhood.

Some have said that neglect—the absence of the essential elements necessary to make a child feel loved, safe, and protected—is more difficult to resolve than

---

No life is so damaged, no soul so stained, that God would disdain to die for it.

abuse, because it is sometimes easier to resolve an obvious injury of commission than the subtler one of omission. It may be similar to the contrast between a verbal insult and one by body language alone. One you can prove, at least to yourself, and the other makes you doubt yourself. Self-doubt has a torment of its own.

How do we "live by the truth," as Jesus said? The truth is often hard to come by. Distractions, misbelief, and twisted perceptions get in the way. This is why it can't be done by "flesh" alone. It is the Word of God that divides between bone and marrow, the thoughts and intents of the heart. (Hebrews 4:12.) It is by contrasting the content of our memories with the truths found in the Word of God that the lies yield to the truths that will set us free.

Take some time and reconstruct your childhood memories. I know this won't be easy. Maybe you don't have many memories. Yet you lived through the years of childhood and things happened. Ask yourself, "Why don't I remember more?" Embrace the memories you have, process the pain, and mine for clues to the truths that you've long denied.

It's very important that you don't try to force your memories to come out of the shadows of the past. I've known people who wasted a lot of precious time and energy "trying" to remember, only to wind up feeling defeated by their inability to do so. The secret to success, I believe, is in allowing memories to return in their own time as you process the bits and pieces that you have, leaving the door open for other memories to emerge. Why do you think you're spending so much energy and emotion repressing your memories if they're not trying to make themselves known to you? Decide to let them come. Pray for the courage to open the door to the "cellar" and invite them to come out into the light of a new day!

But how do we do this? How do we open the door?

We ask questions.

The only answers that are truly meaningful to us are those that respond to the

---

No life is so damaged, no soul so stained, that God would disdain to die for it.

questions we are asking. We don't want other people's answers. We want the answers to the questions that nag at our hearts and disrupt our peace. Questions such as: Why am I the way I am? Why do certain words, events, or people provoke a vague uneasiness in me that I don't understand? Why is such a big chunk of my childhood missing? These questions offer clues to the answers that evade our consciousness while disrupting our peace and sometimes throwing us into a storm of pain and confusion.

Take Time to Focus

Thank God for the memories that you do have, and make the most of them. When I first remember an event, I recall it as I saw it with the eyes of a child. Only after I apply the maturity of an adult perspective to the remembrance do I realize what my memory is trying to tell me. The story recounted in chapter 14 of section 1 is a good example. I never forgot the incident of my father loading his car with guns to "go after" my grandparents. I just never asked the question: why did he need so many guns to go after one old man and his wife? He couldn't have used more than one. The obvious answer is that he used the opportunity to prove a point: Dad is not to be messed with, he has an entire trunk load of guns! Like us, our grandparents were subject to his power. Once I realized this, the memory changed from that of an enraged man going off to kill my grandparents, to that of a depraved abuser using his rage to impress his victim, me, with his total control. And it did impress me. I couldn't admit even to myself that I was terrified of my father, but from that day forward I was convinced beyond a doubt that his promises of violence were not empty threats, and that he was indeed capable of killing my loved ones.

Line upon line you'll write your story. One memory at a time, the truths you process will erode away the layers of defenses that bury the memories you can't bear

No life is so damaged, no soul so stained, that God would disdain to die for it.

to face, memories that eat away at you from their hiding place in your subconscious, infecting your present with dis-ease from the past.

You can face your memories now, learn from the drama of your past, and forgive those who committed even the most insidious acts. Not all at once, but one memory at a time, one day at a time, one act at a time, you can be set free. Remember: the redemption of our treasures is a process, and processing takes time. Don't rush. Don't obsess. Let go and let God do the work. "It is God who works in you to will and to act according to his good purpose." (Philippians 2:13.)

Out of the womb of death—the death of our dreams, hopes, and dignity— we've emerged into the light, born anew. But the work isn't over. We've acknowledged the truth, and the process has brought us face to face with the reality of our losses.

What if we've remembered traumatic events? What if we have memories that leave us trembling in the dark? What if we're experiencing posttraumatic stress that robs us our ability to function normally? That's why we buried our memories to begin with. For a child to carry the emotional load inherent in his victimization would be like binding a burden of bricks on his young back. God, in His wisdom, provided a way for the child to survive. We survived by submerging our traumatic memories into our subconscious, a holding place, a place of waiting until the child acquires the mental and emotional faculties necessary to remove the burden from his back and properly dispose of it.

We are ready to do that, ready to dispose of the dis-ease that robs us of the joy of living, of the vitality promised to those who live the abundant life. Jesus said, "I have come that they might have life—and have it to the full." (John 10:10.)

But before freedom comes, we have to deal with the pain. A woman in the midst of giving birth has no use for joy, pleasure, or anything but the pains that compel her to finish the job. By the deliberate unearthing of our treasures, we also

No life is so damaged, no soul so stained, that God would disdain to die for it.

unearth the raw pain of our abuse.

The sorrow in that—acknowledging the overwhelming sense of loss and reliving the agony of our shame—threatens to engulf us, as if death has reached out from the grave and wrapped its clawed hands around our heart.

In his book, *Finding God*, Larry Crabb says that we must come back to the fire. He paints a verbal picture of the abused person, rummaging in the attic of his mind, seeking the memories he must recover in order to understand his life. It is cold there, and dark. Dr. Crabb wants us to come back down out of the attic for a while, to see Jesus sitting at the fire, waiting to talk with us, to soothe and comfort us.

I want to climb into the lap of my Savior, to feel His arms around me, holding me close, sheltering me from the dark and the cold. I want to experience his love filling up the gaping hole in my soul. I want to feel His support and hear Him encouraging me, as a good parent does: "You can do this. I'm here for you. I won't leave you or forsake you. Nothing is too difficult for you, for I'll always be here, waiting for you to return from the attic and examine what you found there—in the light of the fire, in the warmth of the love shining from my eyes. You are my treasure. I have redeemed you, and I'm glad that you're here."

I have been in the attic. And I'll tell you that you can't go through this alone. Remember: that's what you did when you were a child. You were afraid to cry out, ashamed to ask for help. You're beyond that now. You can take care of yourself. Please find someone who understands, perhaps an experienced lay counselor or a professional therapist, to help you with the next step. To help you grieve your losses.

No life is so damaged, no soul so stained, that God would disdain to die for it.

Chapter Forty-two
Redeeming the Treasure of Freedom to Grieve

WHEN I WAS A CHILD, I wasn't allowed to grieve openly. Any negative or un–happy feeling had to be suppressed or at least concealed. How often did I go to my room, or to my eight-by-eight refuge, the bathroom, to shake with silent sobs. After a while, the tears no longer flowed. It was as if the fountain of my soul had dried up, leaving me to waste away, frightened and alone, in the desert of my pain.

The first time I cried, after more than a decade of grieving without tears, it was as if a dam had burst inside me and a flood of tears washed through the desert of my suffering, bringing with it new life. I'm quick now to acknowledge when I sense grief, and I process through it with confidence and grace—unmerited favor, from God, to me, and toward others. I don't always do it right, but more and more I pass through the stages of grief without getting stalled along the way.

What many people fail to realize is that every loss, every kind of loss, requires a grieving process if one would heal properly. Some losses inflict less pain than others do, but every loss brings with it a degree of pain that will never go away unless it's properly laid to rest.

What are some of the losses we may experience? We have just discussed the loss of our childhood. Perhaps we have suffered the loss of our innocence, loss of valued relationships, loss of a marriage, loss of love, loss of intimacy, loss of a job, loss of confidence, loss of opportunity. All of us experience loss, and that can debilitate us or mature us. We can come out of the experience better—or bitter. Or we may get stuck in grief and never come out of it, a tragic choice that can lead to depression or even death.

Frank Minirth and Paul Meier co-authored a book entitled *Happiness Is a Choice*. Actually, happiness is the outcome of many, many choices.

As Renee Rowe explains, "Choosing to grieve our losses is to embrace a process. The stages of grief are not straightforward. As Renee observes,

> *Research has proven that the stages of grief are different for each person, in order and length. One person may start with anger and then slip into denial, etc. The hallmark to HEALTHY grief is MOVEMENT, movement from one stage to the next—without any prediction of its direction. The only predictability to it is that if there is not movement, up and down, back and around… the grieving person will get stuck and experience dysfunction. They will become stuck in denial, stuck in depression… therein lies the fertile ground for bitterness.*

In Elizabeth Kubler-Ross' book, *On Death and Dying*, she identified five stages of grief:

The first stage of grief is denial. We attempt to dismiss the cause of our anguish. Did he really say that? Did she really just threaten me? Oh, he wouldn't. She couldn't. I must have misunderstood. Or, my childhood wasn't really so bad. So-and-so had it a lot worse. If we deny our pain, it might just go away. No. It won't. We have set our foot on the healing path. We dare not turn back now.

In this stage, we may doubt our own perceptions, especially if we've often experienced invalidation, the dismissal of our "reality" by significant others.

"You don't really mean that," or "You're not sad, you just want your way." As a powerful stream erodes a channel through which the muddy waters of a flood can pass, invalidation causes us to doubt our own perceptions, nudging us toward denial as a way of coping with pain and loss.

The second stage of grief is anger, that inner feeling of pressure that makes us want to get back at those who have hurt us, to see them suffer. We want to come up with a smart retort to "put them in their place." When the one who has hurt us is not accessible, the most available target for our anger is God. The second most available is our self. Anger with a history is depression. Anger turned inward can also become depression. Anger toward God may lead to apostasy. Anger toward others may turn to bitterness. We need to experience our anger, to allow it to motivate us toward positive change. Anger is a God-given response to pain, but we must not get stuck in it. The Bible says not to let the sun go down on our wrath—our intense anger. (Ephesians. 4:26.) That may seem difficult, but God never tells us to do something unless He has provided the way to do it.

The third stage of grief is bargaining. Bargaining is often a form of prayer, for it is frequently addressed to God. "I'll do anything you say if you will just get me out of this." Another bargain may be "I will give up (whatever) if you just stop the pain." Sadly, we often believe that if God doesn't bargain, then He must not love us, or maybe He doesn't even exist. If He does exist, we reason, He has no power to intervene.

We want Him to rescue us from our pain, but that is not His way. He usually takes us through our pain, not out of it. The writer of Proverbs said, "Hope deferred

---

No life is so damaged, no soul so stained, that God would disdain to die for it.

makes the heart sick." (Proverbs 13:12.) Heartsick describes the next stage in the process of grieving.

The fourth stage of grief is depression. Oswald Chambers, author of *My Utmost for His Highest,* said that the person who is never depressed—is dead.

Everyone gets depressed sometimes. If we are grieving a slight or minor injustice, we may pass quickly through this stage. But if we're grieving a loss that has affected us over a long period of time, or a sudden loss of severe intensity, depression may consume us awhile. Like a dark cloud, it may spread itself over our emotional horizon blotting out the warmth and brightness of the sunshine, depriving us of the joy of living. We may lose our appetite. We may gain or lose excessive amounts of weight. Our sexual appetite may diminish or forsake us completely. We may want to withdraw from society, nurse our wounds, and isolate for a while. If we are grieving well, taking care of our self in the process, and connecting with other people who can help us get through it, the sun will shine again.

Depression may open the door to guilt. Some of us feel guilty for feeling angry toward the person who had offended us. We feel responsible for the consequences that person experiences. "If I had just ignored the offense, shrugged it off, the person who hurt me would not have suffered. I brought this on him." *Someone once told me that I go on so many guilt trips that I should just leave my bags packed.*

Guilt has its place. When we do something wrong, we should feel guilty. We should feel badly about our misbehavior. This is not the same as shame. Shame is feeling badly, not about what we've done, but about who and what we are. Guilt may at times serve a godly purpose if it leads us to repentance. But shame is a consequence of the Fall of humankind in the Garden of Eden, and it should be rejected every time it shows up.

One of the most insidious lies couched in childhood animation is Thumper's

No life is so damaged, no soul so stained, that God would disdain to die for it.

quote to Bambi: "If you can't say somethin' good, then don't say nothin' at all." Sounds sweet, sounds right. But better advice would be "If you can't say something for the right reason, then don't say anything at all." Good words, angry words, harsh words—they all have their place in the process of pain. It's just as important to speak against what is evil as it is to speak well of what is good. One of the things I lost during the years of my victimization was my voice. I said, "Yes, sir" to my father at five years old, and I kept saying it for the next twenty-eight years. I finally got my voice back at thirty-three, and I have seldom shut up since—just ask my husband.

Another thing about guilt: The guilt we experience in the process of grieving abuse is often false guilt. I felt guilty for being abused. The abuser made me feel guilty for my own victimization. We call that kind of guilt "transferred guilt." Transfer that kind of guilt back to the abuser, where it belongs. It was not your fault. You're not to blame for your own victimization. No matter what you did, or how you may have responded to the seduction or violence or threats of the abuser—you are not to blame. The abuser bears the guilt alone.

What you are responsible for is dealing with the effects of the abuse. You're responsible for taking care of your self by immersing yourself in the truth. This is done by reading and meditating on the Word of God, through fellowship with other believers, and through proactive recovery work. If you're not taking care of yourself, you can start right now.

You might say, "But what about the things I have done in response to my pain, the hurts I have caused others? What about the people I have wounded by my anger, hostility, or bitterness?"

You may need to make amends to innocent people whom you have harmed by your response to the pain inflicted on you. Amends, or "making it right," is part of the recovery process. A qualified counselor can help you get through this process. There are recovery programs such as Celebrate Recovery and Open Hearts, an internation-

No life is so damaged, no soul so stained, that God would disdain to die for it.

al ministry that ministers to survivors of abuse. These ministries can help you work through this part of your recovery.

In the process of time you will be able to give your pain to God, and He has promised to forgive. What God has forgiven, He has forgotten. He has buried it in the sea of His forgetfulness, and he never goes diving. He has let it go—and so should you. When it comes back to haunt you, declare, "I have given that pain to God, I will no longer be victimized by it." Meditate on the promises you find in the Word of God.

Some of the promises that I have found encouraging are:

> *Fear not, for I have redeemed you. I have summoned you by name; you are mine. When you pass through the waters, I will be with you; and through the rivers, they will not overflow you. When you walk through the fire, you will not be burned, neither will the flames set you ablaze.*
> —Isaiah 43:1b–2

> *I will repay you for the years that the locust has eaten…You will have plenty to eat, until you are full, and you will praise the name of the LORD your God who has worked wonders for you; never again will my people be shamed.* —Joel 2:25–26

Did you notice that last phrase? You will never again be ashamed!

> *Surely he took up our infirmities and carried our sorrows; yet we considered him stricken by God, smitten by him, and afflicted. But he was pierced for our transgressions, he was crushed for our iniquities; the punishment that brought us peace was upon him, and by his wounds we*

No life is so damaged, no soul so stained, that God would disdain to die for it.

are healed. We all, like sheep, have gone astray; each of us has turned to
his own way; and the LORD has laid on him (Jesus) the iniquity of us
all. —Isaiah 53:4–6

No more guilt! Jesus has taken it all away! Let it go, God says, and be free.

Freedom comes with…

Acceptance, the fifth stage of grieving.

Any step program will have, as its first tenet of recovery, admitting that we were powerless. When we can't control something, when we don't have the power to change it, and we have no way to undo it—then we must accept it. A loss has occurred. When we reach the fifth stage of grieving, we are able to move into deeper dynamics of recovery, recycle the pain, and come out on the other side. I don't mean to imply that this is a one-time event. In my own experience, grief is a recurring experience triggered—set off like a fire alarm in the middle of the night—by unexpected words, deeds, sights, smells, or sounds. It is not that I have *finished* grieving, but that I've learned to grieve well, at least most of the time. I seldom get "stuck" in one of the stages anymore, and when I do, I know where to go for help.

Climbing out of the black hole of grief is somewhat like hiking up a steep hill. We may have to take a step back here and there, or go around some obstacle as we seek the summit, but we are still traveling upward and getting closer to the top.

> **He lifted me out of the slimy pit, out of the mud and mire;**
> **He set my feet on a rock and gave me a firm place to stand.**
>
> —Psalm 40:2

No life is so damaged, no soul so stained, that God would disdain to die for it.

Chapter Forty-three
Redeeming the Treasure of Sanity

W E ALL KNOW the definition of insanity: doing the same thing, in the same way, over and over, and expecting a different outcome. After dropping a brick from a ten-story building and watching it fall to the ground, only a mentally deranged person would keep climbing all 1,500 stairs, again and again, to drop the same brick, expecting it to fall up instead of down.

And yet we do it. All of us, at some time, slip over the edge of sane thinking and do crazy things. Think of the couple who have the same argument day after day, neither of them changing, believing that the problem will resolve itself if they keep fighting about it. They have allowed their passion to drive their behavior off the path of sane mental function.

During the first ten years of our marriage, Mike and I fought the same battle a thousand times before we both got sick of it, and I went to see a therapist, hoping she would straighten the man out. Instead, she helped me understand where my emotional baggage intersected with his and how both of us were being triggered emotionally to respond to pressures that came from unresolved conflicts in our past.

We've learned that when we find ourselves "doing the dance," shuffling back and forth between his issues and mine, it's in both our interests to focus in on the underlying issues. Is there a trust issue? Am I afraid? Is he distancing? Have we had this conflict before? Is there a pattern here?

Chronic conflict is guaranteed to deplete our mental and emotional resources. The Apostle Paul said, "As far as it depends on you, live at peace with everyone." (Romans 12:18.) Sometimes, we're battered and scarred by conflict that's not of our own doing. Let's face it: Some people are just contentious. They thrive on conflict. It feeds their flesh. Perhaps, for some, it's a distraction from a deeper pain. Whatever the reason, it hurts to live with chronic criticism, complaining, and contention.

For the sake of our sanity, we need to take steps to protect ourselves from chronic conflict. Communication, setting boundaries, and involving a wise counselor can help us do that. "Speaking the truth in love" and insisting that others do the same is a good start.

I hate the mind games that some people play. When someone says one thing while doing another, they are "messing with my mind." I'll protect my sanity like a jeweler protecting his fine crystal. I'll insist on keeping everything up front and clear, no hidden meanings, no double blinds. I won't stay in relationship with people who insist on a style of relating that forces me to guess their motives, second-guess their words, or play the game of pretend. If you're my friend, I'll fight and die for you, but don't say one thing when you mean another. Don't ask me to pretend to be happy when I'm sad. Don't expect me to feign appreciation for something if I don't like it.

Jesus said, "Let your 'Yes' be 'Yes' and your 'No' be 'No.'" (Matthew 5:37.) I like Jesus. I like the way He thinks. I want to be like Him, to say to the religious hypocrite, "Be gone, you whited sepulcher!" (see Matthew 23:27), to braid a whip of reeds and chase out the evildoers.

No life is so damaged, no soul so stained, that God would disdain to die for it.

Unfortunately, my assessment of the situation isn't always as astute as His, so I'm not often that bold. It is hard to eat humble pie from the hand of a righteously angry person. Jesus was always right and His heart was always pure—unlike mine.

Process everything. That's my motto. If a perceived offense is significant enough to nettle me, it requires my attention. Most of the time, when I work it through, I realize that whatever irritant I'm dealing with is nothing more than a misunderstanding or a difference of opinion.

When I say "process everything," I'm not talking about a two-hour process or two days or two weeks. Most of the time, if the irritant is minor, so is the processing. It may take a few minutes. If you obsess, ruminate, and distress about every irritant that comes your way, you're probably driving your family crazy.

We can change the way we process thoughts, and spend a lot less time being upset. Just because we are hurt doesn't mean that someone has injured us. Maybe someone has, or maybe we're reacting out of our own dysfunction. Perhaps we have (God forbid) even adapted some of the unhealthy attitudes and misbelief perpetrated by our family of origin.

Maybe we're reacting with worn-out defense mechanisms, the ways of relating that we learned in the sepulcher. If a soldier brings his weapon home from battle and carries it with him everywhere he goes, the instrument that once saved him will now alienate him from society.

So it is with the survivor of abuse. As children, we needed our defensive "weapons" in order to survive abuse, but continuing to use them as adults will backfire, and destroy the very things we're trying to protect—our dignity and our relationships.

Let's take the high road. Let's open our hearts and minds to change. Oh, Lord, please change me. That's a prayer He will always answer. He asks only that we cooperate.

The best way to regain sanity after the craziness of abuse, and to maintain sanity

No life is so damaged, no soul so stained, that God would disdain to die for it.

in the after-life, is to learn to process our thoughts well and to mature into a person of integrity.

> **Test everything. Hold on to the good.** —I Thessalonians 5:21

Chapter Forty-four

Redeeming the Treasure of Integrity

MERRIAM-WEBSTER GIVES three definitions for integrity. The first is *incorruptibility or firm adherence to a code of... moral or artistic values.*

When we're deprived of our will and forced into compliance with someone who is stronger and more powerful than ourselves, one of our greatest sorrows is the loss of our innocence, the corruption of our soul—our mind, will, and emotions. The result is that once we've escaped the abusive environment, we find that the abuse is still at work, corrupting us in the very core of our being, infiltrating our mind with thoughts and images that we abhor, compelling us to comfort ourselves in unhealthy or immoral ways.

Some survivors turn to pornography to anesthetize their pain. They, the victims, become the powerful masters over someone who is subject to them, at least vicariously through the Web, magazines, or videos.

I've seen women reading "verbal porn"—romantic novels that describe in explicit detail the sexual activities between men and women, tantalizing and arousing their readers. What am I saying? I've done it myself, not by procuring books from sleazy bookstores that offer "adult entertainment," but by reading passages in some otherwise very good books that provide too much graphic detail about the intimate lives of their characters.

Other survivors become promiscuous themselves. A missionary once told of rescuing women and young girls from the sex-slave trade in a third-world country. She said that after the rescue, a secondary problem that often surfaces in the victim is sexual addition.

Renee Rowe explains it this way:

> *They go back to illicit sex because they are reenacting the trauma. Maybe they were sold into sex trafficking and had no choice. They were powerless. When they go back to it—it is a choice they make. It is about power and control, not pleasure. It is a similar dynamic to that of sexual abuse victims who become sex abuse perpetrators: victim-powerless/ perpetrator-powerful. This same dynamic is played out in prostitution. Most prostitutes are sex abuse survivors.*

According to Dr. Pamela Pine, founder of Stop the Silence, "Approximately 73% of prostitutes overall and 95% of teen prostitutes were sexually abused before the age of sixteen." (www.stopcsaorg/RACE/Media.org)

Another survivor told me: "After being abused I went into a sex addiction myself—and it was only through the grace of God that He brought me out of that. I confused intimacy and love with sexuality. Now I have to untangle the two—and it is extremely difficult and painful. For me, it wasn't about power, but about the need for love."

Promiscuity, the drug of choice for many abuse victims, adds insult to injury,

---

No life is so damaged, no soul so stained, that God would disdain to die for it.

piling hurt upon hurt, as unconcerned partners offer their bodies, their diseases, and their own neediness to the unhealed survivor of sexual abuse.

Merriam-Webster's second definition of integrity is soundness, or *an unimpaired condition*. How does the survivor of sexual abuse hope to become unimpaired or sound? There are so many wounds to heal, so many developmental deprivations, so many losses to grieve. How do we do it? How can we possibly be unimpaired or sound again?

We can't change the past. We'll never be able to undo the misery we experienced during abuse. We can't go back and reconstruct Eric Erickson's eight psychosocial stages, becoming the adored infant whose parents hold and love him into *soundness*. We can't become the developing child who gets his needs met and moves gracefully into the next stage, and the next, with confidence and completeness.

The good news is that we don't have to. Erickson, author of the well-accepted concept of social development through eight psychosocial stages, is in agreement with the teaching of the Word of God, that "there is a future and a hope" for all of us because we can accomplish those stages in retrospect, according to Dr. Erickson and, more important, according to the Word of God. For in Christ, all things are made new, and we are being transformed into the image and nature of Christ. Jesus Christ is one hundred percent healthy, one hundred percent whole, despite the ridicule, abuse, and crucifixion that he suffered, and he will make us whole as well.

Finally, Merriam-Webster defines integrity as *being complete or undivided*. No more ambivalence. When we suffered abuse, our heart was divided between hatred of the abuse and dependence on or attraction to the abuser. He had something to hold over our heads, some leverage to use against us to keep us under his control. Sometimes we found ourselves wanting—against our will—the experience of pleasure to anesthetize the pain, and the two "wants" became so confused in our hearts and minds that we hated ourselves and felt responsible for our own victimization.

No life is so damaged, no soul so stained, that God would disdain to die for it.

Today is the day to recover your integrity. Forgive yourself for your response to the abuser. It wasn't your fault. Everything you felt was the normal response of a human being in your position. If the abuser hadn't known that it's the nature of a child to respond as you did, he wouldn't have dared touch you. He knew it and he used it—and you are not responsible for that.

It's time to take back your integrity. You can be incorruptible. A child no longer, you are stronger, wiser, and braver because of your journey to wholeness.

"God has not given us a spirit of fear, but of power, and of love and of a sound mind." (2 Timothy 1:7, KJV.) God's gifts often come in stages. He offers them to us, but only as we are able to receive them. Our Divine Parent offers us a sound mind. Integrity. And through the application of truth, grace, and time, we will redeem the treasure of our integrity.

No life is so damaged, no soul so stained, that God would disdain to die for it.

Chapter Forty-five
Redeeming the Treasure of Trust

I N THE SEPULCHER, we learned that trust is dangerous. We trusted those who should have protected us, and they violated not only our trust but also our innocence. Trust became illusive. Like a child who has wandered too near a hot stove, we sought warmth and got burned. The injury has left us scarred.

I don't despise my scars, for each is the mark of a wound that has been healed. The scars we bear are signs of life at work in us—for only those who are dead or dying will not heal of their wounds.

It's the open wound that we must address, as those are the wounds that often become infected with unforgiveness, bitterness, and despair. These infections hinder our healing and bind our wounded hearts to a broken past. As we let down our defenses and allow the power of love, friendship, and fellowship to touch our wounded hearts, we will experience healing. The antiseptic of truth will cleanse our wounds. Only then will scars begin to form over our brokenness, providing a protective covering that will keep out infection, while remaining tender when it is bumped—a reminder that we are indeed alive and the object of the Healer's touch. As our wounds are cleansed and our hurts are healed, we find that trust, like homing birds in the spring, will return to take its rest in our hearts.

A trusting heart is a peaceful one, for trust and fear cannot abide in the same home. When fear comes in, trust goes out the door. When trust comes in, fear takes flight!

Trust restored is one of the many benefits of recovery, but recovery doesn't happen instantly. It happens one day at a time, one battle at a time. Every recovering soul has had its share of battles—with denial, fear, and shame.

I believe you're ready to do battle, or you wouldn't be reading this. The bitter chill of frozen emotions has thawed just a bit, or you'd throw the book in the trash. The survivor who remains apathetic, convinced of his own helplessness, can't accept the truths in this book. You've put your toe to the mark, you'll run the race, and you will win.

Perhaps Dr. Seligman's dogs didn't jump out of the box after having learned helplessness, but God didn't make dogs in his image, He did that for us. We have vast potential for healing and growth. That potential resides inside every person made in the image of God. Hope, faith, joy, a tremendous capacity for love, generosity, forgiveness—it's all there. Wake up, my soul! It's time for you to open your eyes and see the glory of your God. This is recovery!

Trust in God

Where were you, God? I was in you. Why did you allow me to suffer so? *I gave mankind free will and I won't violate it.* How can I learn to trust you now? *Get to know me. If you really know me you'll trust me, you'll understand that I love you with an everlasting love. When you walk through the flood, it won't inundate you. When you pass through the*

No life is so damaged, no soul so stained, that God would disdain to die for it.

fire, it won't burn you.

Flood and fire are devastating forces when they rage out of control. They were overwhelming back then, but we no longer walk alone. We've come out of the sepulcher, and He was waiting. He called. He waited and He wanted us. We are His treasure. God gave His only begotten son to redeem us. That is why we can trust Him.

My destiny and yours are woven into a tapestry, a work of redemption provided by our Divine Father for those who share the fellowship of suffering. Not just suffering, in a generalized way. For as Job said, "Man is born to sorrow as the sparks fly upward." (Job 5:7.) Everyone suffers, but survivors of abuse have suffered a particular pain, an insidious injury that assaulted the very core of who we are. It's an injury that goes deep into the soul, like a splinter, and it will give us no rest until we get it out, cleanse the wound, and allow it to heal.

Removing the splinter involves stripping away denial, submitting ourselves to the excruciating process of extracting the lies from our belief systems, and applying the antiseptic of reality to the wound so that we see it as it really is, not as it appeared to the child that we were. It requires revisiting our memories bearing the banner of truth, questioning why. Why did I feel the way I did? Why do I react with such an emotional load to particular events or challenges that occur in my life today, events that seem unrelated to my traumatic past? Why am I in so much turmoil? What is my "inner self" telling me? What really happened back there? It requires reexamining the past with an attitude of grace and truth. It requires the hard work of digging up the foundation of our spiritual and emotional "house" and repairing the flaws, for a house built on the shifting sands of deceit and distorted realities will crumble in the storms of life.

We can do it. We can go back and rebuild our foundation upon the Rock that is Jesus Christ, the Rock that is truth, the Rock that will not be moved though the floods come and the fires rage, the Rock that is eternally committed to making our

---

No life is so damaged, no soul so stained, that God would disdain to die for it.

foundation sure.

Recovery begins with redemption of our trust in God. Jesus said that if we have faith as a grain of mustard seed—the smallest of its kind—we can remove mountains. If you read that passage in the King James Version, you'll find it doesn't just say, "move mountains." It says we can remove them and cast them into the depths of the sea! So it is with recovery. A tiny baby-step taken with a trembling heart and weak knees will initiate a tsunami of change that will rock our world.

Trust in Our Intuition

Another facet of trust that we desperately need in order to outgrow our vulnerability to re-victimization is trusting our own intuitions. Remember the story of the child who told her grandmother about what her mother's boyfriend was doing to her? When her mother convinced the child that she should not have told her grandmother about the abuse, and made her doubt that it had even happened, the mother damaged the child's trust in her own intuitions.

Something inside the child said, *this is wrong. He shouldn't be touching me this way, or on this part of my body. I don't like it. I need to tell someone.* But that "something" was invalidated when the mother confused the child by denying her pain. She set the child up for future abuse. The child is not only unlikely to tell, but is less likely to *know* that she's being violated. She has learned a terrible and very dangerous lesson: "What I feel caused a lot of trouble, and it couldn't be as bad as it felt to me, or surely my mother would have wanted me to tell."

While the child is still in pain, and while the abuse has radically changed her life, she doubts her own reality. She has learned that she can't trust her intuitions. What she intuitively knows, in that inner sanctum of God's image within her heart, is subject to suspicion, and she dares not trust it.

No life is so damaged, no soul so stained, that God would disdain to die for it.

This is called the victim mentality. I've been told that rape victims often report having had a "feeling" that someone was following them, but dismissed the feeling because they didn't see anyone who looked suspicious. One reason that women often don't get the help they need when approached by a rapist is that they wait too long to scream for help. What is it that makes us so afraid of creating a scene that we risk our lives by waiting until our assailant is close enough to get his hand over our mouth? It is that we don't trust our intuition?

I've found that when I'm feeling threatened, it's due to one of two reasons: either there really is a threat, or something about the situation triggers the emotions in me that have been aroused by previous dangers. I've learned that when I feel threatened, it's imperative that I put aside all distractions and attend to the situation at hand. Like a German shepherd that's always on guard, I raise my nose to the wind and use all my energy to discern the reality inherent in the threat I'm intuiting.

Being on guard doesn't mean that we live in fear. Once we learn to protect ourselves appropriately, guarding is no different from breathing. Every few seconds, we inhale and exhale, and we don't spend a lot of time thinking about it. The good King Solomon must have learned this lesson because we so often quote his words "Above all else guard your heart, for it is the wellspring of life." (Proverbs 4:23.)

The word "guard" conveys the idea of a person in authority who stands at an entrance and decides whom to let in or out. A guard doesn't stand at attention twenty-four/seven. He exerts that energy only when a potential threat is present. And what is he guarding? He's guarding our heart, the core of our being, deliberately selecting the good for entry and turning away the bad. And why? Because out of our heart flow the issues of our life!

"Wellspring," or in the older KJV, "issues," is an interesting word. *Strong's Concordance* defines the Hebrew word used here to mean deliverance or boundary. Wow! The boundaries that we enforce will be determined by what we take into our

---

No life is so damaged, no soul so stained, that God would disdain to die for it.

hearts. Deliverance itself depends on what the guard decides to admit, for every element that we internalize will have its effect on our mind, will, and emotions.

If we feel threatened, we need to be alert. The guard needs to come to attention. And we need to trust what he tells us. If he tells us that a certain person is unsafe, we need to try to determine why that may be true. Not all that's real is intellectually discerned. If a person is not safe for us to be around, we need to be very careful about how we interact with that person, and we need to establish strong, well-defined boundaries to protect our hearts.

Learning to Trust Others

We are learning to trust God and learning to trust our intuition, and now we need to learn to trust other people. I'm not speaking of blind trust, which is what we had as children. Blind trust failed us in the past and it will lead to our re-victimization as adults. A normal part of growing up is learning to trust wisely. It's in the nature of a child to trust everyone. That's why we must warn our children not to go with strangers. A smiling face, a tender voice, or a puppy on a leash will instantly earn the trust of a small child. The tragic statistics of child abuse and violence against children are evidence of that.

There are at least three essentials to appropriate trust: Discernment, boundaries, and time. It takes time to get to know someone well enough to trust that person with our treasures. If we learn to discern and to establish healthy boundaries, we can take our time in the development of friendships, and establish relationships that will stand the test of time.

I want to reiterate one final facet of trust: trust the process. Recovery is a process, and that means each aspect of recovery is a process as well. You won't leap from mistrust to mature, confident trusting in a single bound. Recovery of trust will take

No life is so damaged, no soul so stained, that God would disdain to die for it.

time, effort, and courage. One day at a time, one battle at a time, we will redeem the treasure of trust.

> *Trust in the Lord with all your heart and lean not on your own understanding. In all your ways acknowledge Him and He will make your paths straight.* —Proverbs 3:5–6

No life is so damaged, no soul so stained, that God would disdain to die for it.

Chapter Forty-six

Redeeming the Treasure of Appropriate Boundaries

WHEN, AT THE AGE OF FIVE, I said no to my father, I was asserting a boundary. The first boundary a child learns is to say no. If you've been around a two-year-old very long, you've heard the word well used. "Honey, pick up your toys." No. "Honey, do you need to go to the bathroom?" No.

When appropriate no's are disallowed, the child learns at an early stage of development that his boundaries will not be respected. Obviously, this doesn't mean that we give small children everything they want, but we can respond to their no in ways that make them feel safe and accepted, even when we can't allow them to have their way. And we can examine our own motives to be certain that we're saying no because it's best for our child, and not just because a yes is an inconvenience to us or because we're too wrapped up in our own affairs to give our child something that's important to him.

When I said no at five years old, I was speaking out of a strong sense of justice.

My brother had provoked me. If I should apologize, then he should do so as well. But the word "no" was forbidden in our house. If you were told to do something, you had better do it or the belt came out. If you were told not to do something, and you did it anyway, you paid a high price. The salvation of our souls was synonymous with obedience to my father, for the disobedient child was certainly an offense to the god my father served. There was no allowance for the normal process of growing up, developing mature character, and becoming a person of integrity. Break the will—that was his method of parenting. And if you break the spirit in the process, then you have indeed accomplished the ultimate goal—total submission.

Parenting from hell. I wonder how they learn it. Perhaps by experience. Maybe by being led by the spirit that is in them, a spirit of control, selfishness, and, in my father's case, lust. Some will say that I am bitter or unforgiving because I'm honest in assessing my father's behavior. I don't believe that I am—but I ask for my reader's patience if I'm mistaken. Maybe if I rewrite my story a fourth time I'll have accomplished another level of healing, and I can address my father's behavior with less abrasion.

Appropriate boundaries will protect us from the evil man or woman. They will allow us to say no when we need to and to say yes when it's in our heart to do so. We will not be ruled by the actions and attitudes of others. If we trust our God-given boundaries, they will protect our treasures from predators. Doctors Cloud and Townsend use the illustration of a sheepfold to help us understand what boundaries are and how they work. Just as a fold keeps the sheep in and the wolves out, our boundaries will provide safety and security while allowing the shepherd (the guard) to rest, knowing that the sheep are safe.

A sheepfold has high walls and a door. The sheep are safe inside its walls, but they do not live there; they graze in green meadows beneath blue skies. A good shepherd never leaves them alone, but travels with them, keeping a watchful eye out for

---

No life is so damaged, no soul so stained, that God would disdain to die for it.

danger. When nightfall approaches, he takes them into the fold, closes the door, and sleeps there so that predators can't enter.

Some people construct their sheepfold, their boundaries, and neglect to install the door. They withdraw with their sheep, their treasures, into the shadowy confines of four walls, and live out their lives in the darkness of the fold. That which was created to protect them becomes their prison. Most of us know at least one recluse who has few or no friends, who lives alone or with an unhappy companion, who cohabits with the fold, and spends the days isolated from the world. Recluses don't graze in verdant pastures. They miss the grandeur of resting beside still waters. They live in the muck and mire of a penned-up fortress and call it home.

Others live in the pasture but can't enjoy the abundance of nature's joys because they're constantly on guard, tired, tormented and afraid. They've seen the wolves; perhaps they've been torn by a wolf's treacherous fangs in the past, and spend their days in fear of his return. Maybe this time he'll come in sheep's clothing, so they fear the other sheep as well.

I was like that. My father had clearly communicated to me that no man could be trusted. I used to tell my husband, "I know that if any man can be trusted to be faithful to his wife, that man is you. But can any man be trusted? How do I know you won't abandon me for another woman?"

I know my doubts hurt my husband. He showered me with love and demonstrated his faithfulness every day. I felt like a tiny ant holding up a huge boulder. If I gave in to the aching tiredness in my bones and dropped the stone, it would fall on me and on my husband, and we and our marriage would be crushed.

Time for another trip to the counselor. After perhaps fifteen years of fighting the same battle, living out the insanity of expecting a different outcome every time Mike and I had a conflict, I was ready to be free of the emotional distress my doubt and confusion created. I decided in my heart that, like Esther, "If I perish—I perish."

No life is so damaged, no soul so stained, that God would disdain to die for it.

(Esther 4:16.) I wouldn't live with distrust any longer.

Ironically, through counseling I learned that Mike and I were "doing the dance." I was failing to trust, and he had never learned how to establish appropriate boundaries with the women who found him attractive. Mike's a charming guy—so there were lots of women who cast more than one glance in his direction. As in so many other areas of conflict, Mike and I discovered that the two really are one flesh—my emotional baggage exacerbated his baggage, and his emotional "stuff" did the same to me. We got on the same team, and broke the bondage of distrust through learning how to establish appropriate boundaries and hold each other accountable to them.

Establishing Appropriate Boundaries

It is easier to understand boundaries, what they are and how they work, if we first establish what they are not. They are not a way to manipulate others, to force them to behave so that all will be right with our world. They are not weapons of manipulation, malice, or selfishness. They do not allow us to withdraw from the world or annihilate our feelings. Instead, they help us to protect ourselves by establishing up front—before the pressure is on—how we will live our lives. They establish what we will accept from others and how we will respond to them. They provide a way for us to distance ourselves from unsafe people in a kind and loving way, and they protect our heart from those who maliciously, or through ignorance, would do it damage.

I know someone who bounces from one conflict to another. She is always the wounded one, and it is always someone else's fault. She really believes that others, who do not give in to her inappropriate demands, are damaging her.

King Solomon wrote: *"A perverse person stirs up dissension, and a gossip separates close friends."* (Proverbs 16:28.) Merriam-Webster defines perverse as *corrupt, incorrect, or wrongheaded, cranky or perverted, marked by peevishness or petulance, obstinate in*

No life is so damaged, no soul so stained, that God would disdain to die for it.

opposing what is right.

What do we do when we find ourselves in relationship with such a person, and that person refuses to change? The Apostle Paul said in his second letter to Timothy: "The Lord's servant must not quarrel; instead, he must be kind to everyone, able to teach, not resentful." (2 Timothy 2:24.)

This is a blueprint for appropriate boundaries. If your relationship with someone produces constant quarrels, you must still be kind to them, teach them a better way by your words and your example, and determine not to be resentful.

The first two requirements of Second Timothy 2:24 are not that difficult for me. I am a pleaser by nature, and find it difficult to deal with harsh truths, especially with someone I love. It is the third requirement that drives a nail into my heart.

How do we keep from resenting someone who diminishes us, criticizes us, and seems set on turning others whom we love against us?

We can't do it—not in our own strength. At least, I know that I can't. But there is good news! The battle to conquer resentment forces us to grow in ways that we never thought possible when we choose to allow our Heavenly Father to purge us of the toxins that so easily infect our human heart.

I don't always want to allow it—it hurts to be purged. I have a right to my pain. However, it is only by giving up that right that I am free to heal, and to grow!

Like an oak tree on steroids, the soul that resists resentments will reach for the Heavens and spread her branches wide. She provides shade to all who linger in her presence, becoming a source of comfort and life. The development of healthy boundaries has enabled her to put an end to strife.

Recommended Reading

Doctors Cloud and Townsend have made available to us so many wonderful materials about boundaries, that we have no excuse to not avail ourselves of them and establish good boundaries. Their books should be required reading for every individual, couple, Christian leader, and counselor.

Thank God for the counselors among us, for the wisdom of Solomon dictates, "In the multitude of counselors there is safety." (Proverbs 11:14.) These men counsel many in their offices, but they offer their wisdom, through the printed word, to the thousands of us who desperately need the guidance they have provided through their books and other counseling materials.

Thank you, Doctors Cloud and Townsend, for providing direction for me—a survivor of sexual abuse who had to start from scratch in my thirties—to redefine where other people end and I begin.

Boundaries are about controlling our self and allowing others to do the same.

> *Whoever has no rule over his own spirit is like a city broken down, without walls.* —Proverbs 25:28

No life is so damaged, no soul so stained, that God would disdain to die for it.

Chapter Forty-seven

Redeeming the Treasure of Autonomy

AUTONOMY REQUIRES THAT we separate ourselves from others so that we can stand alone, like a tall oak tree, providing shade to those who come to linger beneath its branches. But disentangling from the carnivorous vines that wrap themselves around the young sapling and leach the strength from it can be excruciatingly difficult, especially if the vines spring from your family tree.

Family. We can't survive without it, but some of us have found that the very organ provided by God to give us life, can become the instrument of death, to deprive us of it as well.

In his book, *The Way of the Wild Heart*, John Eldredge writes:

> *Now for a truth that is both difficult and dangerous, wonderful and freeing. Because we have come home to Father and to true sonship, every other relationship has been fundamentally changed. Forever. Including—no, especially—family ties.*

Jesus said, "Anyone who loves his father or mother more than me is not worthy of me." (Matthew 10:37.) If love is not a feeling, but an action, then how do we love our fathers or mothers more than we love Jesus? I believe it's by placing them first, making them into idols that we serve with our primary loyalty. It's by sacrificially bending our will to theirs, allowing their character flaws to entwine with our own, and prevent us from carrying out the divine mission that we're entrusted with. It's by allowing them to "write our book" rather than allowing God to do so. Our mother carried us in her womb, but it was our God who knit us together and gave us breath, and it is God alone who is entitled to our allegiance.

I used to read the scripture, *"A man shall leave his father and his mother and be united to his wife,"* as a command, a responsibility. Now I understand that it's a proclamation of emancipation, a divine order to switch allegiance from the family we were born in, to the family that God intends us to create—first by marriage to a spouse who will become one with us, and then by producing children.

Here, more than in any other environment, we must guard our hearts, for the darts aimed at tender flesh will more often find their mark when hurled by family members than by any other person. More often than not, the aim is not to injure, but to get some selfish need met at the expense of the child who has always been ready to meet such needs in the past. The abuser can always count on the small pleaser who learned early on that his needs were less important than that of his parent, or weren't important at all.

Merriam-Webster defines autonomy as *the quality or state of being self-governing*. The person who has redeemed the treasure of his autonomy is no longer governed by the dictates of another person's will, but of his own. How will we ever submit our will to God if it has already been commandeered by someone stronger than ourselves, someone with a history of manipulating it according to the dictates of his heart and not our own? We will never be fully adult until we have fought and won this battle.

No life is so damaged, no soul so stained, that God would disdain to die for it.

Regaining our autonomy will require rejecting the tears of the parent who controls from behind her shield of neediness, the anger of the parent who manipulates through his skill at intimidation, and the guilt that any others would try to assign to us. Regaining our autonomy means becoming the fully mature adults that God designed us to be.

> *...if you do not stand firm in your faith, you will not stand at all.* —Isaiah 7:9

No life is so damaged, no soul so stained, that God would disdain to die for it.

Chapter Forty-eight
Redeeming the Treasure of Dignity

IT IS DARK, and the house is silent. I am alone except for the one who has broken down my defenses and is in the act of molesting me. I participate—but not I. It's the woman who walked out of the bathroom who participates; the woman who has beaten herself senseless lies here, not only submitting to the abuser but also responding physically while hating herself for it.

What if my mother returns early and walks in on this? What if one of my siblings comes into the room? I visualize it. I see my mother standing there, her eyes accusing. She doesn't have to say it. I know what I am: Dirty! Whore! Her anger turns to tears. Betrayed, she turns away. How could you? Now it's my sister who stands, staring, in the doorway. She gasps, she doubles over, vomiting. It hasn't happened, but I feel it anyway—the humiliation, the disgrace.

Are you sure no one is home? Dear God, I hate myself. I hate him. I'm sick to my stomach, sick in my head. I want to tell him to stop, but the person who is lying here, responding to his sexual touch, is not who I am. That person is lying on the

252

bathroom floor, curled into a tight ball like a fetus in the womb.

I die a thousands deaths in this room. A thousand humiliations. I wear my shredded dignity as a shroud, a funeral garment. It's dirty and pitch-black, and it weighs heavily on my shoulders. Even when this incident is over, I will continue to wear it, for I know what I am. If only I could die, maybe I could forget.

～

You just read about the death of my dignity. Shame became my constant companion in the sepulcher, and it walked right out with me into the light. Attaching itself to me like a bloody leech, it sucked the life out of me long after the physical act of abuse was past.

How does one recover dignity after experiencing the shame of sexual abuse? How does one survive the humiliation of incest? Only by the grace of God, by God's unmerited favor. But how does one survive anything? All of us have sinned and fallen short of God's glory. And the heart of every one of us is deceitfully wicked according to holy writ. Our righteousness—even the best of us—is as filthy rags. So how should we live?

> **Sin lives in us, but God, our Redeemer, lives through us!**

We live by the knowledge that "Where sin abounds—grace abounds even more." (Romans 5:20.)

Saved by Grace

That's the only way to make it, the only way to continue to climb out of the Valley of Suffering and ascend the mountain to the King's house. God's unmerited favor is His gift to us. It is His hand extended to the weary traveler who has had one run-in too many with the lion who prowls the valley, one encounter too many with the one who

---

No life is so damaged, no soul so stained, that God would disdain to die for it.

comes to kill, steal, and destroy.

Listen to the words of Paul to the church at Corinth: "If anyone is in Christ he is a new creation; the old has gone, the new has come! All this is from God who reconciled us to himself through Christ and gave us the ministry of reconciliation…." (2 Corinthians 5:17–18.)

If you have emerged from the sepulcher of abuse and have been redeemed by the blood of the Lamb of God, who gave His life for you, then you are a new creation!

If you knew Christ before or during your abusive experience, you may feel, as I did, that you failed the Lord because of your submission to the abuser. I grieve my lack of faith, I sorrow over my confusion and my years ravaged by physical, mental, and emotional chaos. But I have finally come to understand that I didn't have a choice. My choice was stolen from me when I was too young to do anything about it, leaving me to wander in a chronic state of shock through the wilderness of pain and fear. I settled early on that I couldn't walk away; the cost was too great.

It's a miracle that a loving God patiently stayed at my side and worked through the maze of conflicting emotions to set me free. I'm not worthy of His love, but I'm a grateful recipient of it. I'll never cease to sing the song he gave me as I flew, on the wings of grace, away from the violent man. It is Mary's *Magnificat*—and mine as well.

> *My soul doth magnify the Lord and my spirit has rejoiced in God my Savior.* —Luke 1:46–47

No life is so damaged, no soul so stained, that God would disdain to die for it.

Chapter Forty-nine
Redeeming the Treasure of Love

To some of us, love looks a lot like its cousins: Pity; dependency; neediness; obligation; lust. All of these and many other pretenders masquerade as love. But they aren't love. In fact, they're often the enemies of love.

So what, then, is love? That question is equal in complexity to the one posed by Pilate, "What is truth?" (John 18:38.) We could answer, "Jesus" to both, and we would be absolutely right. Jesus is the pure embodiment of truth and love.

God is love. We all know that. But what does that look like to us? How do we act like Jesus in living out the truth? How do we love as He does?

Love Gives

God so loved the world that he gave… Love is giving. It has been said that the opposite of love is not hate, it's selfishness. We need, we want, we get—any way that we can. We work for it, we plan for it, we manipulate others, and we tell ourselves that we're doing it "for them." Not all the time, not in everything, but in those arenas where we've convinced ourselves that our desires must come first.

Giving is love when it focuses on what's best for others rather than what's best for ourselves—and what's best for others always moves them toward God. We can give our children everything they want, and ruin them in the process. Perhaps our giving is just our attempt to compensate for working too many hours or hiding behind busyness to make ourselves emotionally unavailable. Time is our most precious commodity, and it will make love blossom if we invest it in others with a heart that seeks their good and not our own.

Love Has Self-control

The writer of Proverbs says: "Like a city whose walls are broken down is a man who lacks self-control." (Proverbs 25:28.) If we can't, or don't, control ourselves, then our enemies, those spiritual forces that come to destroy, will invade our "city." They will take over our mind, our will, and our emotions, pillaging our witness, our family, and our future.

I grieve for the politician who recently resigned—caught in a sex-sting while getting his "needs" met in a public restroom. The disgrace of that, the awful shame, will erode what's left of his "city" as acid eats away at a battery, leaving him wandering in the wasteland of despair. Sadly, his actions cast their pall over the family that was once proud to bear his name. He is a city broken down, without walls.

My teenage daughter tells me about friends who are living the lie that "if it doesn't hurt anyone else, then what I'm doing is okay." My heart breaks. Don't they know that everything we do perpetuates the sin our ancestors introduced into the Garden of Eden hurts the heart of God?

"I can't help it," they say, or "I was born this way." If we accept sin, embrace it, and have no conviction of it, I doubt the Spirit of the Holy God is at work within us.

No life is so damaged, no soul so stained, that God would disdain to die for it.

For "God disciplines those He loves… "that we may share in his holiness." (Hebrews 12:6,10.)

Love Is Holy

Holiness is defined as being pure. Therefore it's evident that true love will be pure, clothed in righteousness. If "love" demands that we shed our purity in order to give it—then it's not love, but an impostor, a wolf in sheep's clothing. A deceiver. A fraud.

All those years that I spent in the sepulcher, convinced that I was protecting my loved ones by sacrificing myself on the altar of my father's depravity, I believed I did what I did because I loved them. I was essentially laying down my life for them.

Now I know I was motivated by fear, mind-numbing, paralyzing, all-consuming fear. I stumbled through life in a state of trauma-induced shock, tormented by a false obligation. I was bound by lies projected on me by the abuser, lies that made me accept responsibility for the consequences of his actions.

If you are caught in the web of an abuser's deceit, paralyzed, as I was, by his verbal or implied threats of violence against you or your loved ones, I'm going to make a statement that may set you free if you dare to believe it. I hope and pray with all my heart that you do: The immeasurable pain and the unbelievable sorrow that we face as victims is often prompted by the *false belief that we don't love others if we allow them to suffer by refusing to yield our flesh, our virtue, our life, hopes, and dreams, to the demands of an abuser.* If you say no to the perpetrator and he retaliates by committing a crime against someone you love, you are **not** responsible for his crime. In my situation, the sad truth is that I wasn't protecting my loved ones from my father's depravity, as I believed—and you may not be, either.

Satan, the master deceiver, has gained control of the heart and mind of the perpetrator of abuse who would rob you of what God has provided for all his children:

No life is so damaged, no soul so stained, that God would disdain to die for it.

life, faith, hope, joy, purity, autonomy, and a path of your own choosing. Do not let the abuser hold you hostage by your love for your siblings, another family member, or anyone else he threatens to harm if you break free from him. Those you love are harmed already if they're under the power of an abuser, and the best thing you can do for them is to show them the way out.

No life is so damaged, no soul so stained, that God would disdain to die for it.

Chapter Fifty
Redeeming the Treasure of Romantic Love

SHE IS A PRINCESS. Head held high, she rides a proud steed along a dappled path beneath towering oaks. Her dress is glorious. Her hair shines like the beams of a golden sun.

A rider approaches. By his bearing and royal garments, she knows he is a prince. She looks away, refusing even to glance in his direction. He turns in the saddle, and the stallion that he rides paws the air as the prince pulls back on the reins.

But he will not turn around. He will not pursue the princess. Something about her rigid posture repels him. Her icy stare into the distance warns him that there is no comfort here. There will be no welcome embrace should he manage to pierce her protective shield, invisible to his yearning eyes, yet daunting.

He can't know the chaos inside the princess, the longing for love. He can't read the journal of her life or he would know her demeanor is just a façade, one that won't crumble until the warmth of tenderness has thawed its icy shell. He won't know, for he rides on, and the princess is left to wander alone among the predators of the forest, who watch and wait in the shadows.

In his book, *Hiding from Love*, Doctor John Townsend takes us through "the withdrawal patterns that isolate and imprison us." With amazing clarity, Dr. Townsend identifies the problem of hiding from love, and the solutions that would set us free if we could only grasp them. Books like these have counseled me through the tenuous process of recovery from violent abuse and helped me to heal.

Longing for love but withdrawing, longing for love but distancing ourselves from those who would give it, this is a pattern well known to those of us who have suffered abuse. How can we respond to the prince? If he only knew, if he knew what we've done…. Shame washes over us and we turn away from love.

What *we* have done? No! If he knew *what was done to us*….

If he's truly your prince, the person designed to complete you, to love and comfort you, his heart will melt when he knows the pain of your past. His love will blossom as he does what all good princes do—come to the aid of the damsel in distress.

John Eldredge says that every man has "a battle to fight, an adventure to live, and a beauty to rescue." In the book *Captivating*, co-authored by John and Staci Eldredge, it is said that every woman desires a prince to rescue her, hence all the fairy tales we loved as children. The Eldredges encourage us to use those God-given desires to help us become women of beauty, "captivating," as the title says.

Those of us whose wounded hearts withdraw from love may find ourselves at war with our desires. We want romantic love and we reject it with equal and opposite force—a force that will escalate with time until the pressure of our ambivalence explodes within us and sabotages the relationship.

If you've experienced the pain of failed relationships in the past and are afraid to try again, don't lose hope. And don't go down the same path you've traveled before and expect to end up at a different destination. We can learn to love well. We can bring our deepest fears and darkest secrets out of the cellar, and dispose of the

No life is so damaged, no soul so stained, that God would disdain to die for it.

myths that cause us to withdraw from love.

Many of Our Myths Are Based in Fear

We Fear Abandonment

What if I give my heart to you and you abandon me? Loneliness is better than abandonment. Loneliness is sad, but abandonment is worse. Loneliness is a clean sadness, but abandonment is love betrayed, and is therefore sadder by far than mere loneliness.

We Fear Disappointment

What if you change, or worse yet, what if you're not what you appear to be? What if I don't want you after a while? What if you don't want me?

We Fear We Won't Measure Up

What if I'm less than you expect of me? What if I fail to please you? What if I'm too needy?

We Fear Losing Control

If I give my heart to you, will you take away my freedom? I've been controlled before, manipulated by an abuser's control over my body, my choices, and sometimes even my mind. How do I know that you won't deprive me of my "self" after I give my heart to you?

We Fear Losing Our Identity

I'm afraid you will consume me.

No life is so damaged, no soul so stained, that God would disdain to die for it.

Enemies of Love

Mistrust

Seeds of mistrust were planted early in my life, not only by my personal experiences but also by the stories my father told me. He never missed an opportunity to point out to me that there's no faithfulness among men. Perhaps he tried to justify his own depravity by convincing me of its commonality. I don't know, but the words went deep and were reinforced by the abuse I experienced. They produced a harvest of mistrust that wreaked havoc in my life and marriage. I begged my husband to convince me that he would never abandon me for another woman. He tried to, but couldn't find the words to offer the "one hundred percent guarantee" that I craved. I now realize that God alone could settle the uneasiness in my frightened heart, and God alone could be trusted on the level that I was demanding of my husband.

We know our intentions, and we may believe that we'll never fail at love, but only God can guarantee He will never do so. Promises to be faithful are good and right between a man and his wife, but they are only that, promises, and promises can be broken. Nothing can change that fact. So it's not in the reassurances of a human lover that we must take our rest, but in the knowledge that God loves us with an everlasting love—an unchanging love. In trusting in the truth that His Love never fails and His grace is sufficient for us, we defeat the lies that distrust has sown into our hearts.

Hyper-vigilance

Those of us who've experienced abuse, and especially sexual abuse, often become hyper-vigilant. We've been injured—and we're determined never again to allow a predator to sneak up on us. We sleep with our eyes open and look before we leap—multiple times. We will not be hurt again!

No life is so damaged, no soul so stained, that God would disdain to die for it.

Most of us have at times sensed "vibes" radiating from some needy person who was, as my therapist says, "throwing sexual energy." And yet we doubt our intuition. We second-guess ourselves and feel confused and angry because we experience an awareness of an energy that's undetected by our spouse or others around us.

It's not the presence of heightened awareness that damages our relationships and robs us of peace, it's what we do with it. As long as the internal response to our heightened awareness is one of fear and distrust, we'll try to control how our spouse responds to it, and marital conflict is bound to result.

The good news is this: We can learn to replace our fear with love. Remember the words of John the beloved Apostle: "There is no fear in love, but perfect love casts out fear. For fear has to do with punishment, and he who fears is not perfected in love." (1 John 4:18.) The last thing we want to do is punish the man we love for the pain inflicted upon us by the abuser, and yet distrust causes us to do just that.

We must give up our right to protect ourselves at any cost, and give our husband freedom to demonstrate his integrity by responding appropriately to the situation. If he does, then our trust grows. If he doesn't, our feeble efforts to protect our marriage are an exercise in futility. The writer of Proverbs said, "A wise woman builds her house but a foolish one tears it down with her hands." (Proverbs 14:1.) Fear blinds us to the pain we inflict on others, and panics us into reactions that destroy our relationships.

A therapist once told me, "It's your job to make your husband aware when you sense a threat, but it's his job to deal with it. When you try to take control, you dishonor your husband and damage your marriage."

I was ready to receive those words, because I was tired of fighting, exhausted by my efforts to "protect my marriage," and ready for a change at any price. So I went home and told my husband what the therapist had said. I told him I was committed to changing my ways and honoring him in the process.

No life is so damaged, no soul so stained, that God would disdain to die for it.

As soon as I told him, I felt an incredible relief, and I saw a picture in my mind that has never left me.

The Mental Picture

I was standing beneath a huge boulder—the size of a house—trying to hold it up by my own strength. Underneath the boulder was a platform, which I understood to be our marriage. I was sweating profusely and trembling with fatigue. My husband was standing at a distance from me, looking defeated. I was shouting at him, "Why don't you come and help me? Can't you see this rock is going to fall and destroy our marriage?"

Then I heard a voice. I knew it was the voice of God. He said, "Let go of the rock." At first I was afraid to do it. Then I let go. But the rock didn't fall. It stayed exactly where it was when I let go. Then I realized that I've borne the weight of the rock, but I haven't been the one who held it up. It was ridiculous to believe that my small strength could have held up such a boulder. Then I saw the hand of God holding it up, and I knew it was God who held up the rock all along and kept my marriage from being destroyed.

From that moment, our marriage was delivered from distrust. Mike and I grew closer and gained a unity that had never existed before. Another interesting thing happened: Mike began to discern for himself when boundaries were being crossed and respond in a firm but kind way in such situations, often without my saying a word to him.

We have learned that hyper-vigilance does not have to be damaging. It can, if exercised with love, become a source of protection and understanding. If we can learn to "cast out" our fears by confidently sharing our cautions with each other, then we can respond in love to the hurting people among us who may sometimes seek to soothe their troubled souls in inappropriate ways or without proper boundaries.

No life is so damaged, no soul so stained, that God would disdain to die for it.

Codependency

Those of us who've suffered abuse often develop codependency. The term "codependent" may sound like a label to you, but I rarely go shopping without reading the labels at the grocery store. Labels won't tell me what the product tastes like, but they'll help me identify the ingredients that make it what it is. So it is with codependency. Every individual is unique, and we act out our disorders differently, but all codependents struggle with trying to fix their world by "fixing" other people in it. All of us think we'll be destroyed if the other person doesn't get his or her act together. Books such as Melody Beattie's *Codependent No More* are gold mines of wisdom for helping us find our way through the maze that is codependency.

> *Codependency often looks like love, kindness, and compassion, but beneath the sweetness is a bitter aftertaste that's deadly to the beauty and glory of a woman and toxic to health of our relationships.*

We Carry Our Emotional Baggage from Past Hurts Into the Relationship

When We Harbor Lack of Forgiveness from Past Hurts

Unlike the newborn baby whose slate is clean, we come into relationships with wounds from past experiences. Often those wounds are open and bleeding, or quietly festering with our inability to forgive. It's easy to project the pain from the past onto the new object of our love. Resentment travels with us, and, if left unchecked, will breed bitter offspring in our wounded souls.

When We Model the Axiom "Hurt People Hurt People"

I don't know who first published that statement, but I've lived long enough

---

No life is so damaged, no soul so stained, that God would disdain to die for it.

to recognize the pattern. People who are stuck in their hurt become self-focused and fail to see the pain they inflict on others. Only by stepping out of their place of woundedness and into the light of recovery will they begin to see the ways they hurt other people.

When We Harden Our Heart to Protect It from Further Hurt

The problem with this defense mechanism is that it not only keeps out hurt, but also keeps out love. And the death of love will hurt, no matter how hard we try to protect ourselves. Hardening our hearts is therefore self-defeating.

How Do We Then Love?

Confess Our Faults to One Another and Pray for One Another that We May be Healed

Our first instinct is to confess *our loved one's fault*. But that's not God's way. If we would love perfectly, we confess our faults, thereby making ourselves accountable to change, accountable to grow!

Practice the Principles of I Corinthians 13 (The Love Chapter)

Love is patient, love is kind. It does not envy, it does not boast, it is not proud. It is not rude, it is not self-seeking, it is not easily angered, it keeps no record of wrongs. Love does not delight in evil but rejoices with the truth. It always protects, always trusts, always hopes, always perseveres. Love never fails. (1 Corinthians 13:4–8a.)

People are human. People fail. But love never fails. Perfect love will overcome our fears, our selfishness, and our pride if we allow it to work in our hearts.

No life is so damaged, no soul so stained, that God would disdain to die for it.

Get Into Recovery

If you've suffered abuse of any kind, or neglect, or abandonment, you need recovery. The human soul needs the fellowship of others who've shared their suffering to best recover from their pain. That's why there are grief support groups, divorce and separation support groups, AA, Alanon, Celebrate Recovery, etc. Recovery, someone said, is another word for sanctification. I agree. Recovery focuses on allowing God to remove our character defects and help us live the best life possible. The best thing I ever did for our marriage was to discover that I'm codependent and begin working toward positive change.

Take an Inventory of Your Relationships

Are your relationships inundated in conflict? Do you often seethe in anger or withdraw in misery? Does every day, or most days, look bleak and uninviting? You may be dying for lack of knowledge.

Today, as never before, knowledge is available to us. Christian men and women who've been called by God to heal a hurting world have poured themselves into countless books of wisdom. They've studied, applied education to their own experience and others', and labored over volumes of life-changing text. They offer their wisdom to us in the form of counseling offices around the country, books displayed in countless bookstores, and through radio and television programs. Knowledge is available. Most of it is free, but like Salvation, it comes with an obligation—for the acquisition of knowledge demands change. And change is costly.

The treasure of romantic love is priceless. It's a treasure that every human heart is created to crave, and to possess. The predators wait in the shadows for the prince to pass by so that they—the beasts of the night who prefer pillage to purity—can pounce upon our lonely souls and devour us. Offering us the shallow promise of

---

No life is so damaged, no soul so stained, that God would disdain to die for it.

fulfilling our needs without intimacy, they maintain the pretense of love by providing pleasure to anesthetize our pain.

Rise up, my soul! Your prince comes with healing wings. Perhaps, when you've broken through the dark clouds of despair, like a tiny Cessna against the sky, then you will dance. Put on your purest white dress, light the candles, pour the wine, and meet your beloved at the door. Draw him into a warm embrace and waltz the night away, redeeming the treasure of your romantic love.

No life is so damaged, no soul so stained, that God would disdain to die for it.

Chapter Fifty-one

Redeeming the Treasure of Intimacy with God

CHUCK SWINDOLL, author of *Intimacy with the Almighty*, packs an amazing amount of wisdom into seventy-nine pages. He says there are at least three components of intimacy with the Almighty: silence, solitude, and simplicity.

Those three elements were certainly available to each of us in the womb—post-conception, pre-birth—the time during which the hand of the Almighty moved upon us, forming us in His image. The Psalmist says: *"You created my inmost being; you knit me together in my mother's womb...."* (Psalm 139:13.) The Almighty was there. And he knew us. David continues: *"My frame was not hidden from you when I was made in the secret place. All the days ordained for me were written in your book before one of them came to be."* Not only did he know us, he knew our future. And he committed himself, no matter what the cost would be; regardless of the pain he would suffer with us, in us, or through us, to be our constant companion.

David, who was "a man after God's own heart," was not always exemplary in his behavior. His record includes adultery, murder, and so much violence that God

269

denied him the privilege of building His house, yet the Almighty did not depart from him.

God, whose ways are above our ways as the stars are above the earth, and whose mercy is generous beyond our comprehension, knew David's heart. He had, after all, knit him together in his mother's womb and foreordained his days; He had "written his book," and He knew that David despised sin in his heart, even though he was often guilty of it. He knew that David had a tender heart, though it often went astray. He knew that repentance was ever at the door of the Psalmist's heart—and that when he understood his sin, he would not allow it to separate him from the Almighty. He would rather die.

So David says, "*If I go to the heavens, you are there; if I make my bed in the depths, you are there. If I rise on the wings of the dawn, if I settle on the far side of the sea, even there your hand will guide me, your right hand will hold me fast.*" (Psalm 139:8–10.) David experienced intimacy with the Almighty.

Every human soul was created to crave that intimacy, but we are often ignorant of how to attain it. I suspect that, like every other good thing, it is more of a journey than a destination, at least this side of heaven. Intimacy with the Almighty is assured in our eternal home, just as it was in the womb. But here on earth, that's another matter. Silence, solitude, and simplicity—these essentials are difficult to come by in the world we live in.

It's rarely silent in our home. My husband and I have two teenage daughters and a nephew who live with us. Throw in a multitude of friends for good measure, and noise is the order of the day. In addition to voices, music, and loud, obnoxious games that splay across our big-screen television, phones ring and answering machines go off.

There's only one way I can escape the noise of everyday life: by rising early in the morning, while the night owls sleep, and creeping into my prayer room, as Mike

---

No life is so damaged, no soul so stained, that God would disdain to die for it.

does the same in another part of the house. Together, but separately, we seek the face of God.

In the solitude provided by my prayer room, I sit quietly. Sometimes I pace. Sometimes I interrupt the silence that I've so carefully constructed by singing. Not that my voice is so melodic, it's just that the overflow of God's love and His manifest presence in the solitude of my quiet place rises to the surface and I can't contain my song. Remember when my I lost my song and couldn't get it back? It has returned, like nesting birds in the spring.

In other moments, I wait quietly and sense His healing hands at work. It's as if I rest in the arms of the Almighty and His peace permeates my being. I'm refreshed, strengthened, and secured as I spend quality time with my Creator.

And then there's simplicity. Oh, if only Chuck Swindoll had left off the third requirement, everything would've been fine. But he's right. It's impossible to develop intimacy with the Almighty if we've overcomplicated our lives.

Two businesses, a writing career, raising children, maintaining a marriage, sustaining friendships—simplicity? Dear Lord, how can I manage that?

As he was taking us through the disciplines of life, the leader of our small group announced he was going to teach on the discipline of simplicity. A convenient necessity came up that prevented me from being there, and I was secretly glad. I didn't want to hear about the discipline of simplicity, and I certainly didn't want to discuss it with our group, who can be painfully discerning and prone to speak the truth—albeit with a whole lot of love.

And then something happened, as it always does, to get my attention and open my heart to hear the voice of God. Simplicity. I may not know how to achieve it—at least not right now—but I can't deny my need for it, either. I need to simplify my life.

I'm working on it. My husband has taken over many of my responsibilities in our businesses, and I've hired an assistant who takes a tremendous load off my

No life is so damaged, no soul so stained, that God would disdain to die for it.

shoulders. If I need to hire others, I will, because I'm determined to return to the simplicity of a life lived in intimate fellowship with the one who has redeemed me and restored my life from the power of the grave.

Our God is gracious. He knows my feeble efforts and He rewards them according to His mercy. I thank God that he is a God of Mercy and that He takes us as we are, not as we ought to be.

When I recognize the good He has bestowed upon my life, then I'm free to approach Him. When I understand that He doesn't hold me accountable for what I had no power to control, I come to Him unashamed. When I fall at His feet and experience His forgiveness for what I've done—my frequent failure to forgive, to extend grace, to trust—I come away pardoned, justified, "just as if it had never been," and I can't help but love Him.

Understanding may come as a flash of insight, and it occasionally does, but most of the time it comes to me through the difficult work of taking out my treasures, scrubbing away the dirt and the grime of their burial, and assimilating them into my life, one day at a time, one treasure at a time.

Redeeming the treasure of intimacy with God is the foundation for building a spiritual house that will not be shaken in the storms of life. Intimacy—"into-me-see"—requires a vulnerability produced by stripping away the grave cloths of abuse and standing face to face with Jehovah El Roi, whose name in Hebrew means the God who opens our eyes to see.

> ### *Blessed are the pure in heart, for they will see God.*
> —Matthew 5:8

Purify our heart today, O God, we for we want to see you.

No life is so damaged, no soul so stained, that God would disdain to die for it.

Three Crosses on a Hill

There were three crosses on the hill
One bore a suffering Savior.
Impaled beside Him was a thief
The guilty! He found favor.
Yet one more employed the hill
But he shared not the Savior.
We have heard no more of him.

Chapter Fifty-two
Forgiveness Is Not a Synonym for Reconciliation

THROUGHOUT THIS BOOK we have discussed the need to forgive and the nature of forgiveness. We understand by now that forgiveness is a process and it must not be rushed. It can't be hurried, but is inherently linked to our understanding of the actual nature of the wrongs committed against us, the willingness of the offender to take responsibility for the offense, and the work of grace within our hearts that moves us to give something that costs us so much.

Forgiveness is often confused with reconciliation. A major difference is that forgiveness is an action that occurs within the heart and soul of the offended. It's not dependent upon the response of the offender, and, though it greatly benefits the offender, it is for the sake of the offended one that forgiveness must be offered.

Reconciliation, on the other hand, is an interaction that takes place between the offended and the offender. Both may choose whether or not to reconcile. An example would be the death of Christ on the cross. He forgave the world of its sins, but we must confess our sins and repent—turn away from repeating them—in order to be reconciled with Christ. Reconciliation allows the offender to live in harmony with the offended. It demands appropriate boundaries, boundaries that protect the offended from re-victimization while simultaneously allowing the offender to prove himself over time by honoring the boundaries of the one he has wounded.

In *Door of Hope: Recognizing and Resolving the Pains of Your Past*, Jan Frank writes:

> *Reconciliation does not condone, applaud or rubberstamp what the offender has done. It seeks harmony or peace between those who have offended and those who have been offended. Yet reconciliation does not deny what has happened or the pain that has resulted.*

As related in her book, Jan's personal experience is a journey of pain, processing, and restoration. I applaud her for her selfless quest for healing, not only for her own pain, but also for the healing and restoration of the stepfather who abused her and the mother who failed to protect her. I believe I'd be missing an essential element of healing if I didn't address the possibility of reconciliation with the abuser and others who colluded, or as Jan said, "co-participated," in his crime.

Some have asked if I ever reconciled with my father. The answer is no. There are several reasons; the predominant one may be that I hadn't reached a place of healing and confidence that I would have needed to confront my father with his sins. I still lived in fear that he'd make good on his threat to harm those I loved if he should ever locate me. I had nightmares about him abducting my daughters. Twenty-eight years of violence and threats will do that to you.

Another reason reconciliation wasn't an option for me was because I believe, in my personal situation, that God Himself had closed that door. When I went to the Old Mill and grieved the loss of my father, the father I'd never had, the abusive

No life is so damaged, no soul so stained, that God would disdain to die for it.

father that I did have, and the father I would never have, God—who is a Father to the fatherless—became a father to me in a way I'd never experienced. I entered a father-daughter relationship with my Father God that gave me strength to walk away, even though I was convinced at the time that my earthly father would make good on his threat to kill himself because I did so. In my heart and mind, I buried him then.

When my father died a few years ago. I didn't go to the funeral. I couldn't bring myself to join the ranks of those who chose to ignore his crimes and stand up at his wake to proclaim that my father was a good man who was most likely in heaven. I hoped he was, but I couldn't pretend that I believed it. I would have wanted to stand up and shout, "You don't even believe that yourself. Why not speak the truth so the other predators in the crowd will be warned of the consequences of their sins and stop molesting little girls?" I stayed home and grieved that the truth was still less important to many of my loved ones than making everything look good. Others could do as they must; my grieving wasn't for the dead but for the living. It was for those who carry their denial, their guilt, and their shame around with them and try to pretend that all is well with their world when, in fact, the dysfunction that pervades my family has wreaked havoc on its children.

I went to work the day my father died. I worked part-time with my husband in our family business. There was a strange awkwardness among our staff, most of them long-time employees who'd once attended church with us and knew a little of my past. After a while I realized the reason for the tension: No one knew what to say. Do you say, "I'm sorry your father died," when you know the history of his crimes against his daughter? So no one said anything, except Terry, our general manager. When he said he was sorry my father had died, I found a quiet place to weep, not because my father was dead, but because he had died and I had no grief to spare. My grieving was over. It was as if a stranger had died, I knew, intellectually, that the stranger was my father, but I didn't know him as such. I wept because I knew the man who died as my

---

No life is so damaged, no soul so stained, that God would disdain to die for it.

abuser. I was sorry the abuser died without repentance, as far as I know, but glad I no longer had to wonder if he would somehow find me and harm me or my family.

One thing that comforted me was something that happened a year or so before he died. I felt God was telling my heart to write my father a letter. Though terrified by the idea of opening communication with him, even anonymously, I wrote the letter and sent it by the hand of my sister who still lives in Arkansas. I didn't keep a copy, but I know that it went something like this:

> *To my father:*
>
> *I have prayed for God to give me the grace to forgive you. You molested me from the age of five years old. You have expressed no sorrow for your actions nor have you accepted any responsibility for what you have done. For this, I want you to know that you will not see me again on this earth. For it is not my wish, nor that of my husband, that I should ever have to look again upon the face of the one who has so abused and used me.*
>
> *However, it is important to me that you know this—I and my husband have chosen to forgive you. While I cannot pardon you, for that is up to God, I will not hold your sins against you. We have prayed for you, that you may come to a place of repentance. By this letter, I hope to set you free to seek forgiveness from the only One who can save you, Jesus Christ.*
>
> *I and my husband hope that you will choose to do this, so that we may see you restored someday in heaven, as a child of God.*
>
> *—Linda*

No life is so damaged, no soul so stained, that God would disdain to die for it.

I don't know if my father made his peace with God. Some say he did, others doubt it. That's between himself and his Maker. I'm glad I submitted to the gentle persuasion of my Father God to write the letter, for I know my father didn't go to the grave hindered by a lack of forgiveness on my part.

∽

For me, the process of forgiveness continues. I forgive as God gives me grace to do so. I refuse to ruminate on evil, and commit each remembrance to God for cleansing and healing. That's my part of the process.

And healing happens—slowly. I've read that some survivors experience healing as a distancing, almost as if it had happened to someone else. This, I believe, is healthy detachment. While denial will keep the pain alive forever, the healthy detachment that comes from processing our memories will wring much of the pain out of them and allow us to experience them in a position of power over them, not as the victim that we were "back then," but as a mature adult who has embraced her pain, faced her most dreaded fears, and lived to triumph over them.

Each of the memories I've shared in this book is a healed memory. I can tell you about it without being re-victimized by it, without ever again experiencing the debilitating pain it caused me in the past. My memories have been processed through the filter of God's grace, His truth, and time. I examine them in the same way a pathologist performs an autopsy, searching for the mysteries they contain, clues to the development of the person I have become, indicators of why I do the things I do and why some things provoke reactions that seem wildly out of proportion to their present cause.

Our experiences have changed us in ways that will follow us to the grave. But they have changed us for the better because we have found God among them—and

---

No life is so damaged, no soul so stained, that God would disdain to die for it.

that has made all the difference.

I end this book with a treasure that I recovered only days ago, as I wrapped up the writing, a treasure that required over twenty years of healing, thousands of hours of processing, and many, many tears, to recover. It suggests a step over the threshold of forgiveness that I thought I'd never be able to take.

I wrote my father's story. Its less than three pages, but it's all that I know of him, other than what you've read between the covers of this book. More than history, it's evidence of forgiveness at work, of a miracle in progress.

I close by telling you what little I know of my father's story, the part you haven't heard, the part that allows the child who once adored her father to remember the man that was before the monster, and to grieve his loss as well as her own.

～

The History of a Lost Soul: My Father the Abuser

I can see him now, from the scant information that I've heard. He is the only child of a sixteen-year-old girl. The man who impregnated her is twenty-seven. Some say he loved her; I don't know, but I do know that he left her and the child. The child heard stories about his father—a man who drank and fought a lot, a man who made money during the Depression by making ties for the railroad, a man who came around occasionally and paid his penance by dropping a wad of money into his child-wife's hand.

Sadly, the money did little good, for the child bride would spend the money on clothes, but when her estranged husband heard that she had male admirers, he'd go into a jealous rage and burn the clothes she'd bought with his money.

The sixteen-year-old girl was dependent on her mother, a woman who married frequently, or at least had a succession of men who lived in the house. Those men

---

No life is so damaged, no soul so stained, that God would disdain to die for it.

produced children, and there was a houseful of extended family trying to grow up during the Depression with little guidance or supervision.

The child had red hair and blue eyes. He was mischievous. I know this because of the family stories I've heard. He was abused. This I also heard from family members. He started drinking at a young age and traveled around the country with his friends for a while. When he was twenty-seven, he met my mother at a blueberry camp in Michigan. They were married a few months later.

I don't remember much about my father. I knew the abuser far better, but I do remember that he struggled. I believe there was a time when his crimes crushed him. I remember days—no, weeks, or maybe it was years—that he spent a lot of time on his knees, crying out to God for something that I didn't understand. He sometimes spent the entire day kneeling by his bed, tears flowing, praying in words I couldn't comprehend.

He was pitiful then. My tender heart was overwhelmed for the man who suffered so much. I thought he was grieved by his arguments with my mother, by his struggle to give up smoking, which we believed was a terrible sin, and the pain of chronic back problems. Looking back, I believe he struggled with something far more sinister. If I had known, I would have prayed, too.

He was a man without an education. He knew how to read, but most of his learning was done outside the classroom. He became a mechanic and was proud of his reputation. Then he decided to go into real estate. He and my mother would work together. They got their license, and things were better for a while, but jealousy reared its ugly head. My mother was better at selling real estate than he was, and he couldn't tolerate that. He began to abuse her, physically and emotionally. There were late nights of yelling and arguing, plates broken, tables crashing, mother crying.

That's when I believe he ceased to struggle. He didn't just abuse—he became an abuser. He justified it. He settled in his mind that he wasn't responsible for his

---

No life is so damaged, no soul so stained, that God would disdain to die for it.

actions and he accepted it. At that point, everything he did, everything he said, revolved around getting his "needs" met. Nothing was pure. It was all manipulation and denial.

Near the end he called my mother and asked her to come to the hospital. She believed he wanted to say, "I'm sorry." She went to his bedside. He told her, "I want you to know that I'm fine with God. I know I'm going to heaven."

No apology, no regrets, he just wanted to be sure she knew that he was going to win. Heaven was his, without repentance. I can't know where my father will spend eternity. If he's in heaven, that's good, because I know the abuser couldn't go there. Maybe I'll see my father again, the one that I adored when I was five years old. The one that I trusted.

~

Commentary by Dorothy Murry, wife of George Murry who served as Associate Pastor at the church Linda Settles and her family attended from the time she was about nine years old until she left Arkansas at age thirty-three.

My husband, George Murry, was a pastor at the church where Linda grew up. George and I both were so burdened for her family that we didn't know what to do. I reached out to Linda every way that I could. My heart broke for her because I knew she was in a great deal of pain. She went to the altar often, crying her heart out, those deep wracking sobs that you know come from somewhere so deep inside that the pain of it is inexpressible. I knew something terrible had to be happening to Linda to cause her so much anguish. How I wished she would open up and share with me. I wanted so much to help, and so did my dear husband, George, but there was nothing we could do except pray for Linda and her family, encourage them, and let them know we cared about them.

No life is so damaged, no soul so stained, that God would disdain to die for it.

One of the problems was that Linda's family seemed to be such an upstanding Christian family. Her father seemed to be a Christian businessman. I think I sensed that he could be violent, but there was nothing we could do to prove it, and I am not one to accuse someone based on my own personal feelings.

After Linda left, the Senior Pastor at the time came and talked to George and me. We were devastated. This had been going on through out the years that the family was in our church, and we had missed it. We didn't know how we could have intervened, but it flooded our hearts with sorrow that we had not been able to do so.

From the time Linda left Arkansas until the death of her father, it seemed that Ed was begging God for something. He never missed an opportunity to go to the altar and cry his heart out. Weeping and travailing. Was he seeking forgiveness? Did he make his peace with God? I can't say, but I know that he suffered. I hope that he repented, for I would like to see him in Heaven someday.

—Dorothy Murry

A Special Word to Survivors of Incest and Other Forms of Parental Child Abuse

I went to my father's gravesite a few weeks ago. It was my first—and final—visit to his grave. I noted, with some sadness, that his was one of the few unmarked graves among the interred remains housed at Willow Grove Cemetery. There was nothing to certify his final resting place, nothing except a tiny metal plate, placed there by the cemetery staff. The glaring absence of a stone marker seemed to announce:

> *Three of the most misunderstood commandments in the Bible are the commands to forgive, to honor, and to love.*

No life is so damaged, no soul so stained, that God would disdain to die for it.

"Here lies a man who died without honor."

Get Ready to be Challenged

I am going to talk about three of the most important choices you will make during your lifetime. Each of these choices will have a profound impact on the direction of your life flow. They will affect every relationship you have on this earth and every person within your personal sphere of influence. These choices will affect your physical and emotional health and your relationship with God.

I believe the reason so many people make poor choices in the areas we are about to discuss, is because they misunderstand what these three things really mean and what God has to say about them. Are you ready to dig in? Okay, then, here we go.

We have discussed the first choice throughout this book. We can choose to forgive—or not. I believe most of my readers already understand by now that forgiving the abuser does not always require the survivor to open the door to reconciliation—even to the most repentant abuser. If I kill a flower in my garden by poison or neglect, I may be sorry I killed it but my sorrow will not restore life to the flower. So it is with relationships. Some things kill relationships. We must forgive the offender but our forgiveness does not necessarily obligate us to return to a relationship that has violated our innocence and destroyed our trust.

It is not our place to convert the abuser or to bring him to repentance. That is the responsibility of the Holy Spirit. It is our duty to take our hands off, to "Let Go and Let God do it." If the abuser repents, reconciliation may be an option, but unlike God, who is perfectly whole, undamaged by the sins of others, and utterly beyond victimization, we must determine why, how, and if reconciliation will be in the best interest of our own recovery.

The second choice is honor. Before we decide to do, or not to do something, we should have a clear understanding of what that something is. My stomach has

---

No life is so damaged, no soul so stained, that God would disdain to die for it.

turned so many times when self-righteous teachers, or uninformed believers, have flung a demand to "honor your father," toward me. That usually means that I should say nothing that would diminish the man who planted his seed in my mother's womb. Some have taken it further to suggest that it is my duty to regard the man with respect. Say good things about him, or demonstrate some kind of positive emotion toward him. Such requirements feel like re-victimization, and yet, they are usually backed up by a blithe rendition of the fifth commandment or a New Testament quote to the same effect.

So I Ask, What is Honor?

The word "honor" used in Exodus 20:12 is the Hebrew (or Chaldean) word: *kâbad* (kaw-bad') from the primary root: to be heavy. Some of the words used to define honor (as used in this commandment) are as follows:

Honor (self), honor (man), glorify, very great, honorable, nobles, prevail, promote... Interestingly, this word also means: burdensome, severe, more grievously, afflict, lay heavily, harden, be sore, stop.

When reference is made to honoring our father and mother in the New Testament, it usually refers back to the fifth commandment. The New Testament seems to suggest the expectation of mutual honor between parents and children, just as it suggests mutual submission between husbands and wives. "Submit yourself one to another out of reverence for Christ." (Ephesians 5:21.) The Apostle Paul quoted the fifth commandment, "Honor your father and your mother—which is the first commandment with a promise—that it may go well with you on the earth." Then he added, "Fathers do not exasperate your children, instead bring them up in the training and instruction of the Lord." (Ephesians 6:2–4.)

The definition of the word honor as expressed in the New Testament is *timao* (tim-ah'-o) which is defined as: to prize, or to fix a valuation upon (ideally with rever-

No life is so damaged, no soul so stained, that God would disdain to die for it.

ence). This definition reinforces the idea of combining a God given responsibility to treat our parents with respect, with an equal responsibility to render that respect based upon the truth as it is, and not necessarily, as we would like it to be.

Therefore, the fifth commandment is simultaneously demanding and freeing: commanding us to accept the affliction, the grievous burden of working through our hurts, our suffering, and yes, even our violation, with integrity and perseverance, while freeing us to establish appropriate boundaries to protect our heart from further victimization.

How many of us have felt our stomach clench at the well-intended words of a pastor or leader who has insisted that in order to obey God we must honor our parent, while clearly assuming that honor demands that we respect the unrespect-able and open the doors of communication with someone who has raped us of our dignity and self-worth?

No wonder we find ourselves in so much anguish if we are forced to accept a truth that exposes the dreaded reality that our parent(s) are dishonorable, ignoble, and absolutely unworthy of respect while believing that we are obligated to treat them as if they were both honorable and respectable.

Perhaps, we have believed a simplistic distortion of the command to honor our parents and it is killing us. Many survivors would rather turn away from God than submit to re-victimization at his command. He never has—and never will—demand that we sacrifice our present and future well being in order to be in harmonious relationship with the perpetrator of abuse. The relationship God is most concerned about is our relationship with Him.

Jesus said:

> *Do not think that I came to bring peace on the earth; I did not come*
> *to bring peace, but a sword. For I came to set a man against his father*

No life is so damaged, no soul so stained, that God would disdain to die for it.

and a daughter against her mother, and a daughter-in-law against her mother-in-law; and a man's enemies will be the members of his household. He who loves father or mother more than Me is not worthy of me; and he who loves son or daughter more than Me is not worthy of me."
—Matthew 10:35–37.

Any relationship that robs us of our peace and keeps us focused on the past, must come under the sword of the Holy Spirit.

A huge part of recovery is accepting that truth and allowing our parent (s) to determine what they will make of themselves without the codependent need to "fix them so that we can go on with our life." Some adult children of abusive parents may be able to honor them by conferring respect and nobility upon them. But for many of us honoring our parents consists of bearing the grievous burden of forgiving without reconciliation. It means moving on with our lives in the absence of any positive contribution by parents who make it impossible for their children to promote them or herald their glory. We honor them by refusing to allow them to hold us back, by stepping out of their power and into the power of the Holy Spirit. One definition of honor is stop. Just stop. Stop the blaming. Stop the abuse. Stop the damage and degradation. Get away from the toxic parent and allow our selves to heal. Don't rush it, even if it takes a life time. Don't give away your power and don't let anyone judge you for taking care of yourself. It is your time—your time to heal.

Just as we must forgive if we would heal, we must honor our parents if we would live righteous lives. Living a life that pleases God is surely the greatest honor anyone could bestow upon a parent. If the purpose of marriage is to raise up Godly children, as the Bible tells us in Malachi chapter two, then our resistance to the abuse of power or any other unholy dynamics in our birth family honors even the one who dishonored us by his sin. What could be better than that?

No life is so damaged, no soul so stained, that God would disdain to die for it.

The third choice has to do with love, loving yourself as you love your neighbor. Most of us (abuse survivors) have been conditioned to love our self last, to take care of everyone else, and to lay down our life, not in healthy purposeful ways, but because somebody has to do it and we think less of our self than of anyone else. Our life is less significant. We are expendable. Lies! Lies, every one of them. We have to choose to turn back the tide of toxic thoughts and know we are precious in the sight of our Heavenly Father. We matter to him and we are worthy of his Love. We are worthy because He has chosen us. We are the Bride of Christ, "without spot or wrinkle." Brand new! Every day we are born anew like the Apostle Paul who said, "I die daily." (1 Corinthians 15:31, KJV.) We face new challenges and fresh opportunities. Everyday, we put to death the lies from the past that race through our heads, the coping skills that we are outgrowing—replacing them with new and better ways. Every day we are making choices.

> *Today I challenge you to choose well. Three choices. Three challenges. Three opportunities to grow and to heal!*

A Word to the Abuser

If you're reading this book, I hope it's because you're deeply and painfully sorry for the wrong you have done. I hope you're ready to take full responsibility for the damage done to your victims' souls.

If you're willing to repent and make restitution as much as you're able, with sorrow and honesty, if you're ready to pay for counseling and other medical necessities that are needed to help get the survivor back on track, then there's hope for you.

It will be a long road. It's a journey that requires humility—a virtue foreign to you—for you must acknowledge the depth of your depravity. You have violated certain boundaries in order to perpetrate your abuse. These were violations that are universally recognized as heinous acts against those who couldn't protect themselves.

No life is so damaged, no soul so stained, that God would disdain to die for it.

Some people insist that "one sin is no greater than another." Don't you believe it. Some sins can create sorrow and damage beyond that caused by any other behaviors. Abuse in all its many forms is among those—sins that rip the heart and soul out of the victim. Don't tell me that God, the Divine Parent, has no greater reaction to your sin than to the sin of someone who utters a swearword or steals from his neighbor.

Jesus said that it's better to have a millstone hung about one's neck and be cast into the depths of the sea than to "offend" one of these little ones, one of the children who have come to Him (Matthew 18:6).

The term "victim of abuse," as you should know by now, applies not only to children but also to adults whose protective armor has been penetrated by one whose power or authority doesn't allow them to take care of themselves. God makes it clear in His Word that there is unspeakable punishment stored up for those who harm widows and orphans. In other words, God has a special place in His heart for the weak, for those who cannot help themselves, and His punishment will be fierce on those whose unrepentant sin places them before His throne of judgment without the benefit of forgiveness.

I believe that you've descended a slippery slope from which it's almost impossible to return, for few of those who choose to abuse will ever repent. And even those who do so often "repent" on a superficial level calculated to manipulate, control, or even re-victimize the survivor. Most abusers who "repent" expect forgiveness, reconciliation, or even pardon in return for their cheap apologies.

That just won't cut it. Unless your sorrow descends into the abyss of suffering to allow your own heart, mind, and soul to comprehend, as much as you're able, the awful damage done to the victims of your crimes, and unless you repent of the unspeakable grief and sorrow you've caused by your sin, unless you do everything in your power to make amends, expecting nothing in return, you will face a Divine

No life is so damaged, no soul so stained, that God would disdain to die for it.

Parent whose wrath is perpetually against you.

Nothing short of total acceptance of blame, nothing short of full acknowledgment of your sin, with sorrow and absolute remorse, nothing short of unconditional acceptance of responsibility, without excuses or attempts at justification, will even begin to mend the hole in the soul of the person you abused. Anything short of that is re-victimization, and any discussion of a perpetrator's actions without authentic repentance is disgusting and inappropriate.

You can be forgiven, and I pray that you will be, but those are the rules. If you can't do all of this with a meek and contrite spirit, then you have no right to ask forgiveness, and you can look forward to your just reward from the One who suggested a millstone should be tied around your neck.

Nothing is hidden from the Divine Father, and He will not overlook your sin. He will forgive it, but His forgiveness isn't cheap, and He will not allocate the blood of His Son to cover a sin that bears no repentance. There is only one way—and if you're not ready to walk that way, then don't you dare go near your victim and act as if nothing has happened. And don't even think about discussing the abuse with your victim or offering up a cheap apology. It's all or nothing. Those are the conditions. There are no other choices.

It's the victim's turn to set the rules. I hope the victim you damaged has the courage to refuse any contact with you unless you can—and do—live by them. And even then, I hope that the one you violated will give herself permission to forgive in her own way, at her own pace, and when her judgment, not yours or that of any other person, gives her the confidence, healing, and freedom to do so. Anything less is re-victimization, and as such it grieves the heart of God.

∼

No life is so damaged, no soul so stained, that God would disdain to die for it.

My Prayer for Today

Oh, God of wonder, You have a plan for each of us, a plan for good and not for evil. Help us to understand it, to strive for it, to abandon all else to obtain it, for Your ways are above our ways, and Your thoughts above our thoughts. We take our hands off and surrender our need for justice to You. We forgive, not because the perpetrator deserves it, but because we deserve to be free of the abuser's involvement in our life—and only by forgiving do we release him to Your justice and *ourselves* to Your grace.

Amen.

No life is so damaged, no soul so stained, that God would disdain to die for it.

Chapter Fifty-three

Accepting an Invitation

WHAT IS THE HOLY SPIRIT of God saying to you? You can't answer this question if you don't know Him. The only thing you'll hear from Him is an invitation. *Open the door and I will come and enter into fellowship with you.* Open the door to your heart, your wounded, broken, bleeding heart, your guilty, deceitful, embittered heart. Regardless of its condition, your heart was created to be His abode, the dwelling place of the Holy Spirit of God.

The victim asks, always, "What will this invitation cost me? If I accept, will I be obligated to do things that are against my will?" No, for He will not violate your will—He will challenge it, for your good. Always, ultimately, for your good.

"What will I have to give up?" Everything that would draw you away from His presence and His plans to "prosper you and give you a future and a hope."

"Will it be easy?" No. It will require that you lay yourself and everything that you hold dear on the altar.

"Dear God, no," you say. "You ask too much."

That's because you don't understand the altar. It is a place of sacrifice, but also a place of resurrection, a place of new beginnings, for out of the ashes of sacrifice arises the aroma of a sweet perfume, the fragrance of a life redeemed.

The Israelites at times misunderstood God's purpose in demanding an altar. They forsook him and sacrificed instead to Baal and other deities who had no power to change them. And they suffered for it. Their dead gods didn't harm them, for they were inanimate objects, but the displacement of their adoration destroyed them.

Sound familiar? What did we adore back there? What did we protect? Whatever it was, we have to lay it on the altar if we would be set free. And still, there's more.

Bring your bitterness and your pain, your guilt and your fear, your resentment and your sin. Lay them on the altar, all of them, and watch them go up in flames.

Remember the castle maze? The progression of rooms? As you enter each room you'll find other idols there, along with your treasures. Bring them to the altar. Never stop coming, and don't be ashamed, no matter how long it takes.

I write with transparent words. You know me by now, you know my weaknesses and my struggles. Even as I've written, I've discovered traces of incomplete forgiveness that linger in the room where I dwell. It's a large room, replete with treasures. But there's still an attic, and I've rummaged long enough. I must get back to the fire, back to the comforting arms of Jesus. I need to bask in His presence and in the warmth of the fire.

I'm glad I have written, and glad you've read, my story. It isn't finished, and we may yet meet again.

> **He who has begun a good work in you will complete it....**
> —Philippians 1:6

No life is so damaged, no soul so stained, that God would disdain to die for it.

Chapter Fifty-four
Free at Last!

IT'S TIME TO SAY goodbye. You've traveled with me on a long and difficult journey in search of wholeness. Together we've explored the dynamics of an injury so insidious, a wound so horrendous, that many people die without ever daring to acknowledge it.

We are survivors. More than that, we're thrivers. We've come into the light, and nothing—nothing—will take that away from us. We're doing the hard work of recovery, and we know the work isn't yet finished. Indeed, the work is never done this side of eternity. But a day is coming when every tear will be wiped away and every heart made whole. In that day we'll stand together, side by side, and I will know you, I'll recognize your scars because they look just like mine.

When Jesus rose from the grave, he set an example we could follow, for we are redeemed by his blood and healed by the stripes that were lashed across his back. He took our infirmities upon himself—our mental, moral, and physical weaknesses. And that is why we are free. Free at last! Free to love, free to serve, and free to live a life of victory and purpose.

Epilogue

MINE IS THE PEN of a ready writer, but what does that mean? It means that I write when inspiration flows. Since I'm merely human, not divine, and not like the writers of old who proclaimed the mind of God with thunder and authority, I make no claim to have all the answers, or to write without a trace of my own misguided perception of the truth.

An Encounter

In a story recounted in John 4, Jesus was compelled to pass through Samaria. There he met the woman at a well. She had been often compromised by her choices, and bore the shame incurred by them. Coming, alone to the well when the other women wouldn't be present to condescend or condemn, she met a "prophet" who said to her, "Give me a drink."

"How is it that you, being a Jew, ask *me* for a drink?" *You must be patronizing me. A lofty Jew would never ask a lowly Samaritan for a drink—and a compromised woman at that!* "You Jews," she says, "have no dealings with the Samaritans."

Refusing to take the bait, Jesus replies, "If you knew the gift of God and who it is that says to you, 'Give me a drink,' you would have asked him and he would have given you living water."

I was raised with the understanding that to question authority was to rebel against it. I've learned, through life's difficult and often painful lessons, that what I was taught wasn't always in my best interest as a child of God, or a child, period.

I'm learning to question everything, responding to reality as it is, not as I want it to be.

The Samaritan woman asked three questions, and Jesus answered each, drawing her to himself by the powerful, persuasive presence of Truth.

Finally, she is convinced. He isn't patronizing her. He's not there to condemn. He's there to give her something, something wonderful! And so she asks.

"Give me this water that I may not thirst, or come here to draw." No more waiting in the shadows while other, "worthier" women share the well without her, no more condescension, no more patronizing glances in her direction. She would have it all—living water with its power to quench her thirst forever.

Jesus grants her request, and the Samaritan woman leaves her water pots. She doesn't need them anymore. She goes to the men in the city and says, "Come see a man who told me all the things that I ever did."

Scripture does not record the telling of "all the things" she ever did, but it seems to me Jesus, the Divine Counselor, must have laid his finger on the hurts behind the hang-ups, the pain beneath the problem. Perhaps he adjusted the Samaritan woman's perception of her past, freeing her to accept His truth. *I that you speak to am He, the Messiah, the One who is to come.*

Why does AA invoke a "Higher Power" while insisting on leaving Him nameless? Because too often a wolf in sheep's clothing has ravaged the flock. He is not who we think he is. At its core, all recovery is nothing more than stripping away the

No life is so damaged, no soul so stained, that God would disdain to die for it.

deceptions that would keep us from Christ, the source of our living water.

That's why I process, even in my sleep, often awakening early in the morning with a chapter in my head. "Come now," says the prophet Isaiah, "let us reason together. Though your sins be as scarlet they shall be white as snow." Purity is restored to the "bargain-basement" woman. At the well in Samaria. Wherever the Divine Counselor is compelled to go, He asks only that we give Him a cup of water from the well—and He will give us living water from a well that will never run dry. Compare a cup to an artesian well! Never-ending cleansing for the compromised among us. For all have sinned and come short of the glory of God. (Romans 3:23.) There is none righteous, no not one. (Romans 3:10.)

It is quiet now. The teens are sleeping. I creep out of bed and stumble to the kitchen where I fumble for the coffee filters and fire up the old machine that will give me "strength for the morning." I need my caffeine.

But more than caffeine, I need to be quiet in the presence of the Almighty. He is omnipresent—a big word for an unimaginable concept. He is everywhere, all the time. He is here, and He is speaking.

If He is everywhere, then He's also there with you, in the quiet places of your heart. He is speaking to you, too. Listen to Him, and He'll be your guide.

Trust in the Lord with all your heart and lean not on your own understanding. (Proverbs 3:5.) That scripture doesn't mean that our understanding—of life, of God, of our environment—is unimportant, for we must have understanding or we would have no opportunity to lean on it. Get to know the truth, understand it—naked reality, the truth, the real truth—but don't lean on it. Don't trust in your understanding of the truth to get you through it. Trust in the Lord whose understanding is perfect, His perception pure, and His deliverance certain.

Trust in the Lord with all your heart and lean not on your own understanding, in all

---

No life is so damaged, no soul so stained, that God would disdain to die for it.

your ways acknowledge Him and He will direct your paths. (Proverbs 3:5–6.) One translation says, "He will make your paths straight." No dangerous curves to derail your train, no hidden transitions where the lion lurks, waiting to pounce when you come around the bend. No hidden traps. no setup. For your Divine Director, the one who knows the end from the beginning, dictates directions to you from his vantage point in the universe, omnipresent, omnipotent, and omniscient. He is everywhere, He knows all, and He is all-powerful.

No wonder, then, that suffering suggests that we should doubt God. If He is all these things, then how can He possibly allow the horrendous sorrows and injustice that saturate the human condition, the who, what, when, where, and how of life. If we understood all these realities, then we would be Sublime Truth, a position that belongs only to our Creator.

But we want to! We long to know all things. That longing is the wonder of humanity—and its curse. For knowledge of **what** is, without submission to Jesus Christ, the One **who** is, will lead to pride, the first sin, and one that's perpetuated throughout all time by the genetic flaw passed through the seed of the first man and borne from the womb of the first woman, continuing through the outcasts of the Garden, whose children live in the tangled mantle of the earth without the benefit of Paradise.

But don't lose heart, for we will return to the Garden, and better than the Garden, we will occupy the mansions that our Lord, Jesus Christ, has gone before us to build for us in our eternal home.

"Come, Lord Jesus, come," cries the Beloved Apostle, in the final chapter of the apocalypse. "The grace of our Lord Jesus Christ be with you all," he writes in his final letter to the suffering church. "Amen." The end.

His words echo through the chambers of our hearts: "Come, Lord Jesus!" Come and show us a better way, make the crooked paths straight.

No life is so damaged, no soul so stained, that God would disdain to die for it.

Glossary and Word Study

Section 1

Glossary and a brief study of words used in Scripture, including the Merriam Webster definitions and references from *Strong's Concordance* of Hebrew/Chaldean and Greek words.

Word Study and Glossary

Merriam Webster defines boundary as: *something that indicates or fixes a limit or extent.*
Scriptural reference: Guard your heart with all diligence for out of it are the issues of life. (Proverbs 4:23 KJV.)

The Hebrew or Chaldean word for *issues* is (*to tsa ah*), which means: *boundary, issues, outgoings, going forth, or border.*

A boundary proceeds from the heart and will fix a limit on something, or a border around it. It will define how we "go forth."

Have you ever experienced an emotional "boundary moment"? One of those times when someone has demanded that you do something, or go somewhere, and you felt a "no" rise up from somewhere deep inside? Did you respond to the need to take care of yourself, or did you force yourself to go along and justify your compliance by assuring yourself that you were doing something good for someone else? When I have done that, I have been aware of my peace flowing out like water from an unplugged drain.

When our boundaries (our right to say yes or no according to what is in our heart) are violated at a young age, it is difficult to build them as an adult. But that is what we must do if we would guard our heart from re-victimization.

Our boundaries set limits on what we will allow, enabling us to reject sin and limit wounding by irresponsible or unhealthy behaviors (our own or others') that would distract us from our true purpose—to live a life worthy of the calling of Jesus Christ.

Merriam Webster defines *forgive* as: (1) a: *to give up resentment of or claim to requital for* <forgive an insult> b: *to grant relief from payment of* <forgive a debt> 2): *to cease to feel resentment against (an offender); Pardon* <forgive one's enemies>.

The definitions in Merriam Webster fall short of the scriptural meaning of forgiveness, a fact that may, unfortunately, account for much of the misunderstanding and distortion that surrounds the use of this word. Many survivors struggle with the concept of forgiveness, not

No life is so damaged, no soul so stained, that God would disdain to die for it.

because they are unwilling to forgive, but because of the way the words have been twisted and the meaning distorted to minimize the damage that has been done to them.

Let's look at the word "forgive" as defined by *Strong's Concordance*.

There are at least three different Greek words that are all translated as "forgive." Each word has a different meaning, in much the same way that there are several Greek words for love, all of which are translated into the English word "love." Before we exhort others to forgive or to love, we should know which word best fits the reality of the situation; otherwise we may encourage a married woman to love (*dod*) her coworker—a highly inappropriate behavior unless the coworker is her husband—when we should have encouraged her to love (agapao) him.

- agapao: (ag-ap-ah'-o) to love in a social or moral sense
- dod: (pronounced dode) eros, or romantic love

The word that I hear most often applied to the victim/abuser situation is forgive (*charizomai*). This Greek word was used only once. The Apostle Paul used it in his letter to the Corinthians, in the following context:

> *So forgive and comfort him, (the offender) or else he will drown in his excessive grief.* (II Corinthians 2:7.)

If the person who abused you is drowning in his excessive grief, then the following is a description of the way in which the body of Christ should respond to him.

Forgive (*charizomai*) him, means: grant as a favor, gratuitously, in kindness, pardon or rescue.

What if that person is not "drowning in excessive grief"? What if he, in fact, denies any wrongdoing, or worse yet, admits it but demands that you and others gloss over the pain and sorrow his crime has inflicted on you and others? How then should you forgive? Maybe it will help to look at some other Greek words that have been translated "forgive."

The Greek word most frequently interpreted as "forgive" in English translations of the word is *aphiemi*. It is this word that often accompanies the warning that God will not forgive those who refuse to forgive (*aphiemi*).

What exactly does this word mean? It is closely aligned with the first definition given by Merriam Webster, but not with the second, *cease to feel resentment*, which is not included in any of the Greek definitions that express the meaning of the word "forgive."

No life is so damaged, no soul so stained, that God would disdain to die for it.

While relief from resentment would be wonderful, and may with time come to those who seek it, it is inaccurate and extremely detrimental to the survivor to command her to forgive while warning her that God will abandoned her (her greatest fear) if she does not somehow make her wounded heart cease to resent the one who has broken her soul.

When we understand the biblical meaning of the word "forgive" (*aphiemi*), survivors may experience great relief. The word means: to cry, forgive, forsake, lay aside, leave, let go, omit, send away, remit, suffer, yield up.

Though forgiving (*aphiemi*) is not easy, it is possible. It will take time, honesty, and a work of Grace in our heart to enable us to forgive, yet *aphiemi* is the very thing that most of us are dying to do—to let it go, to send the offense away, to yield it up, especially when we realize that by doing so we are not invalidating our pain or justifying the offender; we are freeing ourselves of the burden of the abuser's crime, we are yielding him, with all his choices, up to the One who is entirely righteous and able to hold him accountable for all that he has done.

There is yet one other Greek word translated "forgive." It is used in Luke 6:37: "…forgive and you will be forgiven." This scripture does not take into account the attitude of the offender. It simply says, forgive. The word (*apoluo*) means to fully free, relieve, release, dismiss, pardon, divorce, forgive, let go, loose, set at liberty.

How do you pardon and at the same time divorce? Does this mean that you dissolve the relationship with the perpetrator and go your separate ways without hostility or continued animosity? Sometimes, I believe it means just that. At other times, I believe (as in the case in II Corinthians 2:7) reconciliation is possible. The most important component of this truth is that we should not allow others to dictate which of the many possible meanings of *forgive* is right for us. That is the work of recovery, and it is as individual as each person's own particular history—as different as each thumbprint, and entirely a matter of the heart— which is known and understood by God alone.

When you look at it like that, forgiveness is a God-given gift offered to the survivors of abuse, a gift that frees us from an unhealthy bond with the abuser and allows us to move on with our life.

Merriam Webster defines the verb "honor" as: (1) a: to regard or treat with honor b: to confer honor on.

The fifth commandment demands that we honor our father and mother. Applying the Merriam Webster definition of the word, the command to honor parents who may have abused, neglected, or abandoned us is at best confusing. The word has been used far too

No life is so damaged, no soul so stained, that God would disdain to die for it.

often by uninformed advisors who have managed to re-victimize the survivor by binding upon her a burden too heavy to be borne—a burden imposed not by the authors of Holy Writ, but by those whose interpretation of it is casually rendered and just as casually studied.

What does the fifth commandment actually demand?

It commands that we honor our parents. But what does "honor" mean, as Moses penned the word? The Hebrew or Chaldean word that was translated as *honor* in Exodus 20:12 is *kabed* (pronounced kaw-bade') which means: to be heavy, burdensome (in a bad sense), severe, or dull, and in a good sense, numerous, rich, or honorable. It means to make weighty, abounding with, more grievously afflict, boast, be chargeable, to be dim, to glorify, to make glorious, very great, be grievous, hard, make heavy, be heavier, lay heavily, bring to or had in honor, promote, be rich, be sore, stop.

Jesus quoted from Exodus 20:12 in Matthew 15:4—"Honor your father and your mother," which is the first commandment with promise.

The Greek word used in the New Testament for honor is *timao* (pronounced tim-ah-o), to prize, i.e., to fix a value upon (by implication to revere or value). If we are to fix a value upon our parents, the indication is that we are to take very seriously the valuation that we place upon our parents. It does not say that we are to pretend that our parents are honorable if they are not or to deny the harm that may have been done to us by abusive or neglectful parents.

Section 2

Glossary of Words Often Used in Clinical Analysis

denial. Refusing to acknowledge that an event has occurred.

dissociation. Separating oneself from parts of your life.

fantasy. Escaping reality into a world of possibility.

intellectualization. Avoiding emotion by focusing on facts and logic.

projection. Seeing your own unwanted feelings in other people.

rationalization. Creating logical reasons for bad behavior.

repression. Subconsciously hiding uncomfortable thoughts or memories.

somatization. Psychological problems turned into physical symptoms.

suppression. Consciously holding back unwanted urges.

triggers. External cues that bring up feelings from the past.

trivializing. Making small what is really something big.

No life is so damaged, no soul so stained, that God would disdain to die for it.

Post-traumatic Stress Disorder (PTSD) Signs and Symptoms
(Updated April 12, 2007; content provided by MayoClinic.com)

Signs and symptoms of post-traumatic stress disorder typically begin within three months of a traumatic event. In a small number of cases, though, PTSD symptoms may not occur until years after the event.

Post-traumatic stress disorder symptoms may include:

Flashbacks, or reliving the traumatic event for minutes or even days at a time;

Shame or guilt;

Upsetting dreams about the traumatic event;

Trying to avoid thinking or talking about the traumatic event;

Feeling emotionally numb;

Irritability or anger;

Poor relationships;

Self-destructive behavior, such as drinking too much;

Hopelessness about the future;

Trouble sleeping;

Memory problems;

Trouble concentrating;

Being easily startled or frightened;

Not enjoying activities you once enjoyed;

Hearing or seeing things that aren't there.

Recommended Reading

Allender, Dan B. *The Wounded Heart: Hope for Adult Victims of Sexual Abuse.* New York: NavPress Group, 1996.

Cloud, Henry, and John Townsend. *Boundaries: When to Say Yes, How to Say No to Take Control of Your Life.* Grand Rapids: Zondervan, 2002.

Crabb, Larry. *Finding God.* Grand Rapids: Zondervan, 1995.

Eldredge, John, and Stasi Eldredge. *Captivating: Unveiling the Mystery of a Woman's Soul.* Danbury: Thomas Nelson Incorporated, 2007.

Townsend, John. *Hiding from Love.* New York: NavPress Group, 2007.

Recommended Organizations

Open Heart Ministries
161 East Michigan Ave. Suite 600
Kalamazoo, MI 49007
Through Grace Groups offered in churches around the country, people find hope and strength in the midst of struggling with the wounds of living in a fallen world. Open Heart Ministries offers the abused a healing path through the love of Christ: www.ohmin.org.

Celebrate Recovery
Celebrate Recovery groups offer a safe place for people with any kind of hurt, hang-up, or habit to find freedom. Over 10,000 people at Saddleback church have completed the program and have found victory through Christ's power. Find a group by visiting their website: www.celebraterecovery.com.

American Association of Christian Counselors
Offers a national referral network of state licensed and/or certified professional Christian counselors. Use the Christian Care Network to find a counselor near you: www.aacc.net.

No life is so damaged, no soul so stained, that God would disdain to die for it.

American Association of Christian Counselors
Post Office Box 739
Forest, VA 24551

Cloud-Townsend Solutions for Life
Cloud-Townsend
18092 Sky Park South, Suite A
Irvine, CA 92614
The authors of the Boundaries books also offer many other resources including relationship books, online videos, community playlists, and information about finding a good Christian counselor: www.cloudtownsend.com.

Meier Clinics
2100 Manchester Road, Suite 1510
Wheaton, IL 60187-4561
Offers a wide variety of Christian counseling service options to meet the needs of individuals, couples, and families, including outpatient counseling, day treatment, intensive outpatient, and life coaching. Their mental healthcare programs are unique as they treat the whole person—emotionally, physically, and spiritually. Locations are nationwide: www.meierclinics.org.

National Coalition for the Protection of Children & Families
800 Compton Road, Suite 9224
Cincinnati, Ohio 45231
513 521-6227
The coalition offers a free online counseling service. It is a secure individual forum where you can share your struggles with one of our trained pastoral counselors: www.nationalcoalition.org.

No life is so damaged, no soul so stained, that God would disdain to die for it.

Scripture and Quote Index

The Agony of Christ

CHAPTER FIFTEEN, pg. 93

Whatever has been done to the least of those who love me (Jesus) has been done to me. —Matthew 25:40

Authenticity

CHAPTER SIX, pg. 40

The Apostle Paul said, "I am what I am." —1 Corinthians 15:10

The voice of God in the burning bush on Mt. Sinai (speaking to Moses) "I Am that I Am."

If we will be all that we can be—authentic in our day to day experience—and approach the burning bush as Moses did, expecting to be changed, then our suffering has purpose and our life is worth living. —*Redeeming Our Treasures*

Boundaries

CHAPTER FORTY-FIVE, pg. 240

Above all else guard your heart for it is the wellspring of life. —Proverbs 4:23

CHAPTER FORTY-SIX, pg. 248

Like a city whose walls are broken down is a man who lacks self-control. —Proverbs 25:28

CHAPTER FORTY-NINE, pg. 256

If we can't, or don't, control ourselves, then our enemies, those spiritual forces that come to kill, to steal, and to destroy, will invade our city. They will take over our mind, our will, and our emotions, pillaging our witness, our family, and our future. —*Redeeming Our Treasures*

CHAPTER FIFTY, pg. 263

A wise woman builds her house but a foolish one tears it down with her hands. —Proverbs 14:1

Fear blinds us to the pain we inflict on others, and panics us into reactions that destroy relationships. —*Redeeming Our Treasures*

Conflict

CHAPTER FORTY-THREE, pg. 229

As far as it depends on you, live at peace with everyone. —Romans 12:18

No life is so damaged, no soul so stained, that God would disdain to die for it.

Counselors

In the multitude of counselors there is safety. —Proverbs 11:14

A wise counselor will not tell us what to do, but will teach us to evaluate our reality and make healthy decisions for ourselves. —*Redeeming Our Treasures*

Secrecy is a tool forged by Satan to keep the confused soul in bondage. —*Redeeming Our Treasures*

Fear

The Lord is my light and my salvation; whom shall I fear? The Lord is the strength of my life, of whom shall I be afraid? —Psalm 27:1-2

Perfect love drives out fear. —1 John 4:18

God has not given us a spirit of fear, but of love, of power, and of a sound mind. —2 Timothy 1:7, NKJV

It is by facing our fears that we conquer them. —*Redeeming Our Treasures*

Fear not for I have redeemed you. I have summoned you by name; you are mine. —Isaiah 43:1b–2

Forgetting

This one thing I do, forgetting those things which are behind ... I press toward the mark ... of the high calling of God in Christ Jesus. —Philippians 3:13–14, KJV

... what the enemy of our soul would like to negate is that remembering is an integral part of forgetting. —*Redeeming Our Treasures*

Forgiveness

True forgiveness isn't found in pretending that the offense never occurred, but in fully embracing the extent of the wrong and deciding to "let the offender off the hook with you and on the hook with God." —Neil T. Anderson, *Christ-Centered Therapy*

Only by forgiving could I be free of the awful despair of remembering. —*Redeeming Our Treasures*

No life is so damaged, no soul so stained, that God would disdain to die for it.

Glossary, pg. 299

…forgive and you will be forgiven. —Luke 6:37

A Foundation That Stands

Chapter Thirty, pg. 165–166

When the foundations are being destroyed, what can the righteous do? —Psalm 11:3

If we submit to the storm and seek God in it, we will always find Him there. He destroys the old foundation, the faulty foundation that will not support the righteous life, and builds in its place a firm foundation, one that will not be shaken. —*Redeeming Our Treasures*

As you come to Him, the Living Stone, rejected by men but chosen by God and precious to Him, you also, like living stones are being built into a spiritual house. —1 Peter 2: 4–5

Freedom

Chapter Two, pg. 4–5

"Take off the grave clothes," He commanded, *"and let him go!"* —John 11:44

How eager are we today to grasp the soiled cloths of our brother's wounding and begin the tedious process of setting him free? —*Redeeming Our Treasures*

Grace

Chapter Forty-eight, pg. 253

Where sin abounds—grace abounds even more. —Romans 5:20

Sin lives in us but God, our Redeemer, lives through us! —*Redeeming Our Treasures*

Happiness

Chapter two, pg. 5

Happiness is a fleeting illusion at best, here one moment and gone the next. —*Redeeming Our Treasures*

Honor

Chapter fifty-two, pg. 283–284

Honor your father and your mother. —Exodus 20:12

…the fifth commandment is simultaneously demanding and freeing: commanding us to accept the affliction, the grievous burden of working through our hurts, our suffering, and yes, even our violation, with integrity and perseverance, while freeing us to establish appropriate boundaries to protect our heart from further victimization. —*Redeeming Our Treasures*

No life is so damaged, no soul so stained, that God would disdain to die for it.

Chapter Fifty-two, pg. 283

Definition of Hebrew or Chaldean word used in this scripture:

Honor (self) Honor (man) glorify, very great, honorable, nobles, prevail promote, also, burdensome, severe, more grievously, afflict, lay heavily, harden, be sore, stop.

Hope

Chapter Eighteen, pg. 110

Being confident of this, that He who began a good work in you will carry it on to completion. —Philippians 1:6

Chapter Thirty, pg. 164–165

I (God) know the plans I have for you. Plans to prosper you and not to harm you, plans to give you a future and a hope. —Jeremiah 29:11

As our mind is transformed by the truth … we can be freed from the fetters of false beliefs that would undermine our joy and damage our future. —*Redeeming Our Treasures*

When the storm has swept by, the wicked are gone but the righteous stand firm forever. —Proverbs 10:25

Joy

Chapter Twenty-two, pg. 135

… my head shall be lifted up above my enemies all around me. Therefore I will offer sacrifices of joy. —Psalm 27:6 (NKJV)

Knowing God

Preface, pg. xxii

I know that my Redeemer lives … and in my flesh I shall see God. —Job 19:25a–26b

Our hurts, habits, and hang-ups … get in the way of our view of God and blur His perfect image, blinding us to the wonder of His life in us. —*Redeeming Our Treasures*

Chapter Two, pg. 5

I have come to this place in my life where I need to know God better, or I won't make it. —Larry Crabb, author, *Finding God*

Letting Go

Chapter Twenty-nine, pg. 159

Parable of the child and the rope

The child is me and the Father is God. I could not let go the rope because another father had convinced me that it was not safe to drop into Father's arms. —*Redeeming Our Treasures*

No life is so damaged, no soul so stained, that God would disdain to die for it.

Pg. 161
God's response to our cry for help. —Psalm 18

Living

Preface, pg. xxi–xxii
Whoever wants to save his life will lose it, but whoever loses his life for me will save it...."
—Matthew 16:25, John 6:51

To live forever, not just exist until our earthly frame dies—but live! —*Redeeming Our Treasures*

Love

Chapter Fifty, pg. 263
There is no fear in love, but perfect love casts out fear. For fear has to do with punishment, and he who fears is not perfected in love. —1 John 4:18

Chapter Fifty, pg. 266
Love is patient. Love is kind. It does not envy, it does not boast, it is not proud. It is not rude, it is not self-seeking, it is not easily angered, it keeps no record of wrongs. Love does not delight in evil but rejoices with the truth. It always protects, always trusts, always hopes, always perseveres. Love never fails. —1 Corinthians 13

Maturity

Chapter Four, pg. 23
When I was a child I thought as a child, I spoke as a child, but when I became a man I put away childish things. —1 Corinthians 13:11

We can mature into responders who process our feelings and then act on them. A child is a reactor. She acts on her feelings and has no means to process them. That is why she believes what others tell her. —*Redeeming Our Treasures*

Memories (Remembering)

Chapter Four, pg. 25
Renee Rowe (therapist): The blessed reality of recovery is that we need to know the depth of our pain, not all the memories. —*Redeeming Our Treasures*

The Presence of God in Our Lives

Chapter Fifty-one, pg. 269
You created my inmost being; you knit me together in my mother's womb... My frame was not hidden from you when I was made in the secret place. All the days ordained for me were written in your book before one of them came to be. —Psalm 139:13

No life is so damaged, no soul so stained, that God would disdain to die for it.

Pg. 270

If I go to the heavens, you are there; if I make my bed in the depths, you are there. If I rise on the wings of the dawn, if I settle on the far side o the sea, even there your hand will guide me, your right hand will hold me fast. —Psalm 139:8–10

Purity

Chapter Thirty-four, pg. 181

He is faithful and just to forgive our sins and purify us from all unrighteousness. —1 John 1:9

Chapter Thirty-seven, pg. 196

Let us lay aside every weight and the sin which does so easily beset us. —Hebrews 12:1

Chapter Forty-eight, pg. 254

If anyone is in Christ he is a new creation, the old has gone, the new has come! All this is from God who reconciled us to himself through Christ and gave us the ministry of reconciliation. —2 Corinthians 5:17–18

Chapter Fifty-one, pg. 272

Blessed are the pure in heart, for they will see God. —Matthew 5:8

Recovery

Chapter Five, pg. 33

The victorious life is not about what happens to us—but what happens through us. —*Redeeming Our Treasures*

Chapter Thirty-nine, pg. 205

Forget thy father's house and the king will desire your beauty. —Psalm 45:10

I will greatly rejoice in the Lord for He has clothed me with the garments of salvation. He has covered me with the robe of righteousness. —Isaiah 61:10, NKJV

Chapter Forty-one, pg. 216

Whoever lives by the truth comes into the light so that it may be seen plainly that what he has done, has been done through God. —John 3:21

We begin with the truth and we build a testimony to the faithfulness, power, and integrity of God. We testify that what has been done, the redemption of our treasures, has been done through God.—*Redeeming Our Treasures*

No life is so damaged, no soul so stained, that God would disdain to die for it.

Pg. 217

For the word of God is living and active, sharper than any double-edged sword, piercing until it divides soul and spirit, joints and marrow, as it judges the thoughts and purposes of the heart. —Hebrews 4:12

It is by contrasting the content of our memories with the truths found in the Word of God that the lies yield to the truths that will set us free. —*Redeeming Our Treasures*

Chapter Forty-three, pg. 231

Test everything. Hold on to the good. —1 Thessalonians 5:21

Shame

Chapter Thirteen, pg. 82

Surely he (Jesus) took up our infirmities and carried our sorrows; yet we considered him stricken by God, smitten by him, and afflicted. But he was pierced for our transgressions, he was crushed for our iniquities; the punishment that brought us peace was upon him, and by his wounds we are healed. We all, like sheep, have gone astray; each of us has turned to his own way; and the LORD has laid on him (Jesus) the iniquity of us all. —Isaiah 53:4–6

Intentionally, deliberately, He did that for us, and we have no right to continue to carry what He died to purchase. (Our sin and our shame.) —*Redeeming Our Treasures*

Chapter Sixteen, pg. 98

The shame belongs to the abuser—and recovery demands that shame—like misdirected mail, be returned to the sender. —*Redeeming Our Treasures*

Chapter Thirty-nine, pg. 205

Do not fear for you will not be ashamed, nor disgraced. You will forget the shame of your youth. —Isaiah 54:4

Chapter Forty-two, pg. 226

I will repay you for the years that the locust has eaten …. You will have plenty to eat, until you are full, and you will praise the name of the LORD your God who has worked wonders for you; never again will my people be ashamed. —Joel 2:25-26

Finding Purpose in Suffering

Preface, pg. xxii

After intense suffering, Job proclaims:

"I know that my Redeemer lives … and in my flesh I shall see God." —Job 19:25a, 26b

---

No life is so damaged, no soul so stained, that God would disdain to die for it.

If we will be all that we can be—authentic in our day to day experience—and approach the burning bush as Moses did, expecting to be changed, then our suffering has purpose and our life is worth living. —*Redeeming Our Treasures*

Man is born to sorrow as the sparks fly upward. —Job 5:7

Everyone suffers, but survivors of abuse have suffered a particular pain, an insidious injury that assaulted the very core of who we are. It is an injury that goes deep into our soul like a splinter, it will give us no rest until we get it out, cleanse the wound, and allow it to heal. —*Redeeming Our Treasures*

Temptation
Every man is tempted when he is drawn away by his own lust and enticed. —James 1:14, ASV

Does the drug addict choose his craving for drugs or the sex addict this attraction to pornography? Does the obese woman choose to be tempted by food? We don't choose to be tempted by these things—we don't get up one day and say, "I want my temptation to be food (or sex, or money)." —*Redeeming Our Treasures*

For all have sinned and come short of the glory of God. —Romans 3:23

Our tendency to do wrong is so deeply etched in every cell of our brain that it is only by the strength of a Power greater than ourselves that we may—though tempted to do wrong—choose to do what is right. —*Redeeming Our Treasures*

The Treasure of God's Word
I have hidden your word in my heart that I might not sin against you. —Psalm 119:11

Trust
In quietness and confidence shall be your strength. —Isaiah 30:15, NKJV

No life is so damaged, no soul so stained, that God would disdain to die for it.

Victory

CHAPTER THIRTY-SEVEN, pg. 197

For the weapons of our warfare are not carnal, but mighty through God to the pulling down of strongholds, casting down imaginations, and every high thing that exalts itself against the knowledge of God, and bringing into captivity every thought to the obedience of Christ. —2 Corinthians 10:4–5

Let go, as the old song says, and let God! Let God have it. Let God be it. Let God fill it. Let God do it. For He alone can manage our lives in a position of power over all the enemies that occupy the strongholds that our genealogy, our experiences, and our choices have established in our souls. —*Redeeming Our Treasures*

He knows the way that I take and when He
has tested me I shall come forth as gold.

—Job 23:10

No life is so damaged, no soul so stained, that God would disdain to die for it.

Speaker, Teacher, Counselor

Linda Settles delivers keynote addresses, and conducts workshops and women's retreats. She also facilitates women's groups and recovery and support groups in her church and community.

Linda shares a dynamic and powerful message about abuse, its aftereffects on survivors, and the role of the church in identifying abuse and healing its victims.

Topics include:

- Redeeming the Treasures of Innocence, Trust, Faith, Love, Integrity, and More
- How to Help the Survivor in Your Life
- Abuse Issues that Impact Marriage
- Abuse Issues that Impact Parenting
- Launching a Church or Parachurch Ministry to Heal the Wounded Heart
- The Unbounded Life: Breaking Free from the Lies that Imprison our Spirit
- Release from False Responsibility

Coming soon! Companion Workbook to *Redeeming Our Treasures!*

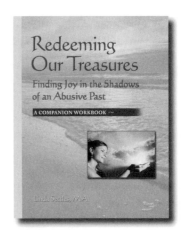

For more information, to receive a speaker packet, or to schedule Linda to speak to your group, visit www.RedeemingOurTreasures.com or e-mail Linda at speaker@RedeemingOurTreasures.com.

No life is so damaged, no soul so stained, that God would disdain to die for it.

About the Author

Linda Settles holds an MA in Christian Counseling and is currently working on her Ph.D. With her husband of more than twenty years, she is active in ministry and business. She has trained lay counselors in church ministry, spoken at women's retreats, and written materials for children's church curricula. She and her family reside in Virginia. They are active in their church and involved with local community and prison ministries.

Linda's background has had significant influence on her writing and the message she brings to women and men today. Born in Newport, Arkansas, Linda was the oldest daughter, and her brother, Eddie (eleven months older), was her best friend and protector. When Eddie died at the age of nine, Linda suddenly became the eldest in a family that grew until there were six children. Taking on the role of caregiver to the younger children, Linda lived a life of terror and deprivation, trying to balance her small influence with a violently abusive father against the potential damage he threatened to carry out against her loved ones. Afraid to tell anyone what was happening to her, Linda found an outlet for her pain in writing.

As a teenager Linda wrote poetry, which was often published in *Latchstrings*, a newspaper in North Little Rock. She wrote a poem that was featured in the first real estate section of the *Arkansas Democrat* and wrote poetry that was used by Dr. Wayne McFarland in his national campaign to help addicted smokers overcome the habit.

Linda wrote her own curriculum and worked in churches and low-income housing projects to help children and the poor. She became the "kids' church" teacher to thirty under-privileged children who came from the projects to the all-white Southern church she attended. She fought to keep the kids in the church when some

No life is so damaged, no soul so stained, that God would disdain to die for it.

would have shipped them across town to an all-black church.

A week after fleeing her father's home, Linda was on staff as a lay counselor at a recovery program for people suffering addictions, emotional problems, and spiritual bondage. Though she couldn't free herself at that time, Linda was always an activist against oppression. Turning that energy into her counseling studies, she earned a MA in Counseling while raising her children and helping her husband develop his business. Together they started Celebrate Recovery in their local church in 2004.

Today Linda delivers a powerful message to women through her speaking and writing, encouraging them to rise above all obstacles to become the women of God they were created to be.

No life is so damaged, no soul so stained, that God would disdain to die for it.

Photo Permissions

Page	Illustration ID	Copyright
Cover	4938973	©iStockphoto.com/skynesher
Cover	3232753	©iStockphoto.com/csourav
Cover	4015626	©iStockphoto.com/LordRunar
xvi	4678838	©iStockphoto.com/digitalskillet
xvii	7662714	©iStockphoto.com/AccesscodeHFM
xxiv	4339035	©iStockphoto.com/rdegrie
xxix	3395963	©iStockphoto.com/wakila
1	836494	©iStockphoto.com/llhoward
4	4699163	©iStockphoto.com/doulos
12	56236	©iStockphoto.com/zdog18
15	3629212	©iStockphoto.com/Nikada
20	4178817	©iStockphoto.com/KarenMassier
24	3287441	©iStockphoto.com/ranplett
27	1897989	©iStockphoto.com/AnitaPatterson
28	4078680	©iStockphoto.com/AlterYourReality
34	4132080	©iStockphoto.com/appletat
35	4506417	©iStockphoto.com/EricVega
36	3267777	©iStockphoto.com/PeteWill
38	2084832	©iStockphoto.com/MrPants
44	212907	©iStockphoto.com/Dizzy
45	6055567	©iStockphoto.com/PeteWill
53	3635440	©iStockphoto.com/vasiliki
54	4367693	©iStockphoto.com/FreezeFrame Studio
55	138277	©iStockphoto.com/duncan1890
55	3203645	©iStockphoto.com/HomeStudio
56	3507049	©iStockphoto.com/Soubrette
57	3571693	©iStockphoto.com/rasento
61	4676898	©iStockphoto.com/Cryssfotos
64	3045180	©iStockphoto.com/LOUOATES
68	35909	©iStockphoto.com/CallNeg151
74	4253677	©iStockphoto.com/LeggNet
80	3750706	©iStockphoto.com/IlexImage
83	4378634	©iStockphoto.com/LordRunar
86–88		"The Raising of Lazarus," from a painting by Karl Isakson
92	2211422	©iStockphoto.com/McIninch